White-Collar Government

Chicago Studies in American Politics

A SERIES EDITED BY BENJAMIN I. PAGE, SUSAN HERBST, LAWRENCE R. JACOBS, AND ADAM J. BERINSKY

White-Collar Government

The Hidden Role of Class in Economic Policy Making

NICHOLAS CARNES

The University of Chicago Press
Chicago and London

Nicholas Carnes is assistant professor of public policy in the Sanford School of Public Policy at Duke University.

The University of Chicago Press, Chicago 60637
The University of Chicago Press, Ltd., London
© 2013 by The University of Chicago
All rights reserved. Published 2013.
Printed in the United States of America

22 21 20 19 18 17 16 15 14 13   1 2 3 4 5

ISBN-13: 978-0-226-08700-9 (cloth)
ISBN-13: 978-0-226-08714-6 (paper)
ISBN-13: 978-0-226-08728-3 (e-book)
DOI: 10.7208/chicago/9780226087283.001.0001

Library of Congress Cataloging-in-Publication Data

Carnes, Nicholas, 1984–
    White-collar government : the hidden role of class in economic policy making /
    Nicholas Carnes.
        pages cm — (Chicago studies in American politics)
        ISBN 978-0-226-08700-9 (cloth : alk. paper) — ISBN 978-0-226-08714-6
    (pbk. : alk. paper)—ISBN 978-0-226-08728-3 (e-book) 1. Representative government
    and representation—United States. 2. Class consciousness—Political aspects—United
    States. 3. United States—Economic policy. 4. White collar workers—Political
    activity—United States.   I. Title. II. Series: Chicago studies in American politics.
    JK1021.C365 2013
    338.973—dc23

                                                                                    2013014446

♾ This paper meets the requirements of ANSI/NISO Z39.48-1992
(Permanence of Paper).

For my son, Joseph,
who has made me rich
beyond my wildest dreams

The real difference between democracy and oligarchy is poverty and wealth. Wherever men rule by reason of their wealth . . . , that is an oligarchy, and where the poor rule, that is democracy.

ARISTOTLE

CONTENTS

ACKNOWLEDGMENTS

Writing this book never really felt like work. On some level, it really wasn't. I've spent more of my life cutting two-by-fours, bussing tables, answering phones, ringing up groceries, and loading trucks than I have being a professor in a college. Compared to a day of hanging Sheetrock or a Saturday night washing dishes in a catfish restaurant, a day of research and writing is a piece of cake. But even as research goes, this book was an easy yoke to bear. And that was thanks in large part to the many wonderful friends and colleagues who helped me along the way.

I started working on this book while I was at Princeton University from 2006 to 2011. It's hard to overstate how much I owe my mentors, Chris Achen, Doug Arnold, and Larry Bartels. Each of them provided input on every aspect of my early research on this project—from the methodology to the writing. And each of them provided me with constant encouragement along the way. Between Larry writing me a supportive note in a signed copy of his book, Chris calling me "Professor Carnes" at the coffee machine, and Doug letting me ask "just one more question" five more times at the end of our meetings, I never doubted that the three of them believed in me. I couldn't have asked for better professional role models, and I'll always be grateful.

I also owe a lot to many of the other faculty, students, and staff I worked with while I was at Princeton. Fred Greenstein provided careful and generous feedback on drafts of everything I wrote. Paul Frymer shared valuable insights about research, teaching, and life as a college professor. Jessica Trounstine shared her data on city councils, helped me analyze them, and reviewed several of my early chapter drafts. Steve Rogers helped me access data on state legislators' occupations and provided me with encouragement throughout the process. Congressman Edward P. Beard generously spent an entire afternoon showing me around Providence, Rhode Island, and sharing his experiences, expertise, and wisdom with me. Phil Wallach was an excellent office-mate and offered many helpful suggestions on my work, including that I contact Congressman Beard. Jeff Tessin was a tremendous help and a wonderful friend throughout the entire process. Marty Gilens gave me advice and input every step of the way. Noam Lupu provided me with constant friendship, encouragement, and help with my work—and only asked for an occasional chai latte in return. Helene Wood was a constant source of warmth and support who made my days in Princeton much brighter. And Michele Epstein's friendship and advice were among the highlights of my time in New Jersey.

While I was at Princeton, I also had the good fortune of meeting many scholars who were willing to patiently listen to early (and sometimes half-baked) versions of my ideas and provide me with quick and helpful feedback. I'm especially grateful to David Mayhew, David Canon, Jeff Cohen, Cesar Zucco, Kate Baldwin, Rikhil Bhavnani, Adam Bonica, Fred Solt, Kathy Newman, Josh Bolten, Theda Skocpol, Karl Rove, Meredith Sadin, Ben Lauderdale, Matt Incantalupo, Mike Miller, Melody Crowder-Meyer, Alex Murphy, and Carol Ann MacGregor. I'm also grateful for the opportunities I had to present various parts of this project at the Princeton University American Politics Research Seminar, the Princeton Research Symposium, the Princeton Joint Degree Program research seminar, the Princeton Fellowship of Woodrow Wilson Scholars, and the annual meetings of the Midwest Political Science Association and the Southern Political Science Association (I'm especially thankful to two of my SPSA discussants, Michael Crespin and Scot Schraufnagel). At the Social Change: A Harvard-Manchester Initiative summer workshop, Bob Putnam gave me extremely helpful input on an early version of my analyses. I also benefitted from helpful feedback from the faculty and students at Allegheny College, Cornell University, Duke University's Sanford School of Public Policy, the Massachusetts Institute of Technology, the University of Maryland, and the University of Tennessee.

My work at Princeton wouldn't have been possible without the financial support I received from the National Science Foundation (under Grant SES-0921163, "Doctoral Dissertation Research in Political Science: Social Class and Congressional Decisionmaking") and the Dirksen Congressional Center. And my work would have been much slower without the Princeton Center for the Study of Democratic Politics, which generously provided me with office space and a five-year supply of free espresso.

I moved to Durham, NC, in 2011 to take a job as an assistant professor at the Sanford School of Public Policy at Duke University, and I've been racking up even more professional and personal debts ever since. The Sanford School gave me a teaching release during my first semester that allowed me to make significant progress on this project. During my second semester, my colleagues Jay Hamilton, Judith Kelley, and Kristin Goss organized a workshop for my book and invited Kay Lehman Schlozman, Rick Hall, John Aldrich, Dave Rohde, and David Brady to join them in commenting on the entire manuscript. The feedback I received that day fundamentally improved the book in more ways than I can possibly list here.

Many of my new colleagues and neighbors at Duke also gave me invaluable moral support as I finished writing this book. I'm deeply grateful for all of the lunches with Ken Rogerson, walks with Alma Blount, coffees with Laurie Bley, sci-fi movies with Hugh Macartney, chats with Ellen Gray, and conversations about heavy metal with Marc Bellemare.

I've been fortunate to work with some amazing people during the final stages of writing this book. Linda Benson edited most of the manuscript. One of my students, Sarah Selenich, read the book cover to cover and commented on every chapter. Jacob Hacker, Paul Pierson, Dorian Warren, Shamus Kahn, and Jeffrey Winters gave me advice and moral support as I was finishing up. Three anonymous reviewers provided me with some of the most helpful and constructive feedback I've ever received on my work. Larry Jacobs advised me on how to make sense of it all and how to further improve the book. And my amazingly supportive editor at the University of Chicago Press, John Tryneski, helped me navigate the whole process, encouraged me to write more clearly and thoughtfully, and pushed me to be the best author I can be.

I've accumulated a lot of debts while writing this book, but I have some that are even older that I need to mention here, too. If it hadn't been for some of my high school teachers, writing a book would be the last thing on my mind at this point in my life. Ms. Smith, Ms. Williams, Ms. Roth, Ms. Kohl, Ms. Cohagen, and Mr. McElroy kept me on the right path during a very difficult few years, and I'll always be grateful for it. Several of my professors at my alma mater, the University of Tulsa, picked up where they left off, especially Professor Joli Jensen, who encouraged me to get a PhD, and my advisor, Professor Jeffrey Hockett, whose teaching and mentoring profoundly changed my life for the better.

I also owe a tremendous debt to my wonderful extended family—Jack and Max; Grandma Frances; Kristie and Larry; Kim and Walter; Kerry, Jessie,

Kelsey, and Adalyn; Ka-Ka and Mark; Shelly and Darren; and Cor-Cor—for all of their love and encouragement over the years.

My greatest debt in writing this book is to my dear friend and ex-wife Grace Carnes. My book and my life are both much better because of her.

I'm truly grateful to everyone who has helped me with *White-Collar Government*—in the words of Kurt Cobain, I'm lucky to have met you. But this book is dedicated to someone who has influenced my life in an even more profound way, the person who gave me the single nicest complement I've ever received: "I love you, Daddy."

I love you, too, Joseph. You're my greatest accomplishment, and you make me happier and prouder than any of my scribbles ever will.

ONE

White-Collar Government

In 1971, a house painter from Providence named Edward Beard was elected to the Rhode Island state legislature. Beard's political prospects initially seemed uncertain: he had never held a public office before, and to make ends meet he had to continue working full time as a painter while serving in the state legislature. However, Beard was a determined politician, and his down-to-earth style quickly earned him a loyal following in his largely working-class district. In 1974, he stunned the state's political establishment by running for Congress and defeating an incumbent from his own party in a campaign that cost Beard just $900 and, in his words, "a hell of a lot of work" (Siddon 1977, 2). The following January, Edward Beard quit his house painting job and was sworn into the United States Congress.

Perhaps not surprisingly, Congressman Beard—who had "never earned more than $9,800 a year [the equivalent of roughly $35,000 today] before drawing his congressional salary" (Stuart 1977)—spent much of his time in Washington promoting causes that he saw as important to the interests of working-class Americans. He consistently voted in support of prolabor legislation; during his first term, the AFL-CIO gave him a perfect score in its annual ranking of legislators' voting records. By his second term, he had been appointed chair of the House Committee on Education and Labor's Subcommittee on Labor Standards. And in 1977, Beard founded the House's first Blue Collar Caucus "to let people know that blue collar workers can be in Congress . . . [, that] Congress is not just for lawyers and professional people" (Siddon 1977, 2).

The connection between Beard's humble background and his energetic populism was not lost on political observers, or on Beard himself. He kept a small paintbrush in his coat pocket and on the door of his congressional office as a "symbol of who I am and where I'm from—the working people"

(Associated Press 1980, J8). When asked why he founded the Blue Collar Caucus, Beard explained that "many of us experienced unemployment. Many of us know, from first-hand experience, what public works jobs mean. I shined shoes in Providence. I was a recipient of The Providence Journal Santa Claus Fund" (Tolchin 1977, 13A). Beard was also outspoken about the importance of encouraging working-class Americans to play more of a role in government. "It is a real shame," he often told reporters, "that only two percent of the members of Congress come from the majority of the voters" (Siddon 1977, 2).

Scholars have long recognized that people like Beard—people from what we might call the *working class*—are rare in American political institutions, especially compared to their numbers in the nation as a whole. As Donald R. Matthews (1985, 18) observed more than a quarter century ago, "almost everywhere legislators are better educated, possess higher-status occupations, and have more privileged backgrounds than the people they 'represent.'" Whether this enduring feature of our political process has real consequences, however, remains an open question. Although political observers, philosophers, and policy makers have expressed concerns about the social class makeup of our political institutions since the Founding, political scientists have done little more than speculate about the links between policy makers' *class backgrounds*—their past and present positions in our society's economic or status structures—and the conduct of government. Class-based differences in ordinary Americans' political views are well documented. So, too, are the connections between policy makers' choices and other personal characteristics such as their races and genders. For the past half century, however, scholars of US politics have acted as though the social class divisions that we observe in political opinion surveys, in election results, and in everyday life somehow disappear in our policy-making institutions.

This book provides a long-overdue look at how inequalities in the social class makeup of American political institutions affect public policy in the United States. Using data on US legislatures, I explore how lawmakers from different classes make decisions about the economic issues that have historically divided Americans along social class lines, issues like taxes, business regulations, and the social safety net. My analyses focus both on how legislators from different classes differ in office and on how these individual-level differences influence collective outcomes—how the shortage of people from the working class and the sharp overrepresentation of white-collar professionals affect the economic policies our government enacts.

The findings reported in this book provide the first evidence that the unequal social class makeup of our political institutions affects who wins and who loses in the policy-making process. Like ordinary Americans, lawmakers from different classes tend to think, vote, and advocate differently on economic issues. The numerical underrepresentation of the working class in our legislatures consequently skews economic policy making toward outcomes that are more in line with what more privileged Americans want.

These long-standing realities of American political life have serious implications both for contemporary debates about the government's role in economic affairs and for larger questions about policy making, representation, and political equality in the United States. Scholars, political observers, and those interested in reforming our system of government cannot afford to continue ignoring the fact that the working class is vastly underrepresented in public office, that policies that affect Americans from all walks of life are made by a white-collar government.

What Is Class?

Societies tend to be organized or stratified along widely accepted economic and status dimensions. Some people are well off and well regarded. Others are not. And most observers agree about which people are which. Scholars refer to groups of people who occupy comparable positions on these dimensions as *social classes*. People in a given class tend to have similar interests because of their similar places in society. Some recognize these common bonds and consciously identify with their class. Others are driven by their social endowments to adopt certain habits without giving much thought to how their place in society influences their views and choices.

The dividing lines between social classes in most societies revolve around the labor market, that is, how people earn a living. Broad divisions—like those between the owner of a factory and her employees—are plainly apparent. Finer distinctions are, too. The CEO and the middle manager at a large firm are both part of management, but they fall in different places within that category. The foreman in a factory and the line worker he supervises are both workers, but most observers would say that the line worker belongs to a different (and slightly lower) rank or class. Occupations can be categorized in many ways: by how much money they pay, how much education they require, the amount of authority over others they entail, the amount of accountability to supervisors they demand, how prestigious they are, or—perhaps most famously—their relationship to the means of production. Each of these attributes affects the people in a given line of work in some way (and may affect which people choose a given line of work). Each therefore has the potential to create the shared interests that make classes an important feature of how societies work.

Of course, occupational differences are by no means the only dividing lines between social classes. A person's class is reflected in how she speaks and dresses, the kind of home she lives in, the kinds of recreational activities she pursues, and a wide range of other characteristics. These attitudes and behaviors are an important part of the way class distinctions manifest in everyday life. In general, however, they are strongly associated with how people earn a living. People in similar lines of work lead similar kinds of lives.

Although Americans often dislike talking about class, social class divisions color many aspects of our lives. In the United States, a person's class is one of the best predictors of a variety of behaviors ranging from matters of taste such as entertainment, art, and consumption (Holt 1998) to decisions about where to live (Lott 2002), whom to invite into our social circles (McPherson, Smith-Lovin, and Cook 2001), how to speak (Lamont 1992), and how to raise our children (Anyon 1996). Class predicts significant differences in health outcomes (Carpiano, Link, and Phelan 2008) and incarceration rates (Western and Pettit 2010). It creates material interests that pit people from different classes against one another in a variety of settings (Wright 1997). And it affects how involved people are in civic life (Verba, Schlozman, and Brady 1995, chap. 7), how they think about a wide range of political issues (Campbell et al. 1960, chap. 13; Hout 2008), and how they vote on election day (Berelson, Lazarsfeld, and McPhee 1954; Hout, Manza, and Brooks 1995). We may not like talking about class, but it permeates just about everything we do.

Including holding public office.

The Unequal Social Class Makeup of American Political Institutions

By virtually any measure of class or social attainment, the average policy maker in the United States is vastly better off than the average citizen. The size of the social gap between citizens and their representatives varies somewhat across different political institutions and depends in part on how exactly we measure class. In general, however, politicians tend to be drawn overwhelmingly from the top strata of American society. According to the 2000 census, roughly 65 percent of Americans were raised in families headed by blue-collar workers (manual laborers or service industry workers), 54 percent worked in blue-collar jobs themselves, and 73 percent of people over age twenty-five did not have college degrees (Ruggles et al. 2009). The latest Federal Reserve estimates suggest that the median net worth of American families was $77,300 in 2010 (Bricker et al. 2012). On each of these measures, politicians in every level and branch of American government are considerably better off than the citizens they represent.

Historically, our presidents have been our most privileged leaders (Pessen 1984). At least since the start of the twentieth century, no blue-collar worker has ever become president; every chief executive has been a former business owner, farm owner, lawyer, or skilled professional (CQ Press 2008). Three-quarters of all presidents have had college degrees, and only one president in the last century (Harry Truman) did not. At least eight of the twelve postwar presidents have had a net worth equivalent to $1 million or more today when they took office (McIntyre, Sauter, and Allen 2010). And although many of our presidents grew up in families of modest means—five of the twelve postwar presidents were raised by low-income or working-class parents[1]—even by this measure, presidents significantly outrank ordinary Americans.

The story is essentially the same in the other branches of the federal government. Every seat on the Supreme Court is filled by a lawyer who graduated from Harvard or Yale (Turley 2010). Millionaires currently make up a 5–4 majority (*New York Times* 2010, A11), and only two justices (Clarence Thomas and Sonia Sotomayor) were raised by blue-collar workers.

Even members of Congress—the branch of the federal government often touted as most closely reflecting the nation's diversity—are vastly better off than the people who elect them. Lawyers and business owners, who make up approximately 10 percent of the population, comprise at least half of both chambers, whereas legislators from working-class jobs make up less than 2 percent of Congress. Almost every member today is a college graduate. Only 20 percent grew up in working-class homes. And the median net worth of members of Congress is approximately $1.5 million (Center for Responsive Politics 2012), roughly nineteen times the median net worth of American families.

State and local officials tend to be slightly less privileged, but even in these jurisdictions, most policy makers are considerably better off than the citizens they represent. According to the most recent data available, blue-collar workers make up just 3 percent of the average state legislature (National Conference of State Legislatures 2011) and 9 percent of the average city council (International City/County Management Association 2001). Almost 75 percent of state lawmakers (*Chronicle of Higher Education* 2011) and 68 percent of city council members (ICMA 1991) have college degrees, fewer than in Congress but still far more than among the general public. There are no nationwide surveys of the financial resources and family backgrounds of state and local legislators, but there are signs that these measures are likely skewed toward privilege as well: the median net worth of state lawmakers in Florida in 2008, for instance, was more than $700,000 (Kam and Smith 2008)—just shy of Congress's median net worth at that time.

These inequalities in the makeup of our political representatives even cross party lines. Between 1999 and 2008, the average Republican in Congress had spent about 1 percent of his precongressional career in blue-collar jobs, and the average Democrat had spent about 2 percent, a statistically negligible difference. On some class measures, Democrats are closer than Republicans to the typical American: in the early 2000s, the average congressional Democrat had a significantly lower net worth (approximately $640,000) than the average Republican (just under $1 million). However, even on measures like this one, congressional Democrats are still closer to their colleagues in the GOP than they are to the typical American family (which had a net worth of approximately $120,000 in the early 2000s). Republican politicians may be slightly more privileged, but both parties are, in a descriptive sense, the party of the well off.

Figure 1.1 summarizes how presidents, Supreme Court justices, members of Congress, state legislators, city council members, and ordinary Americans rank on four common measures of social class: occupation (measured as the percentage of individuals who worked in manual labor or service industry jobs), educational attainment (the percentage without college degrees), financial resources (the percentage who were not millionaires), and family background (the percentage who were raised by poor or working-class families).[2] Viewed this way, it is easy to see how the gap between politicians and citizens varies across different class indicators and different political institutions. The most striking feature of figure 1.1, however, is how consistently political decision makers outrank ordinary Americans. Compared to the average citizen, the average politician in each set of institutions was at least 20 percentage points more likely to come from a white-collar (that is, non-working-class) family and at least 40 percentage points more likely to have a college degree, to come from a white-collar occupation, and to be a millionaire. At every point in the policy-making process, people with significant social and economic advantages are running the show.

These imbalances are by no means recent developments. They have persisted, moreover, even as other underrepresented groups have begun to

Figure 1.1 The Unequal Social Class Makeup of American Political Institutions

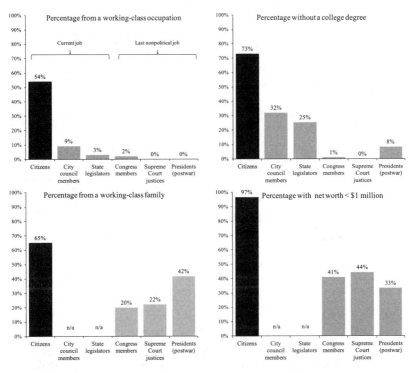

Sources: Data for presidents are from 1946 to 2010. Data on Supreme Court justices are from October 2010. Data on Congress are from 2009 (net worth) and 1999 to 2008 (occupation, education, and family). State legislator data are from 2011 (education) and 2007 (occupation). City council data are from 1991 (education) and 2001 (occupation). Data on citizens are from 2000 (occupation, education, and family) and 2011 (net worth). Note 2 in chapter 1 provides additional details about the sources used in this figure.

break through the glass ceiling. Figure 1.2 plots the percentage of members of Congress who served between 1901 and 1996 who were women, racial or ethnic minorities, and who were from the working class (that is, who last worked as manual laborers, service industry workers, or union officials before entering politics). Although women and minorities were still under-represented at the end of the twentieth century, both groups gained considerable ground during the postwar period. In sharp contrast, working-class Americans—who have made up more than 50 percent of the labor force for at least the last hundred years[3]—have never made up more than 2 percent of Congress.[4]

Figure 1.2 The Demographic Makeup of Congress, 1901–96

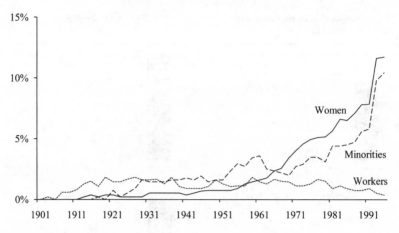

Source: ICPSR and McKibbin (1997).

This long-standing feature of American political life isn't going anywhere any time soon, either. Data on the makeup of state and local legislatures—which tend to foreshadow demographic changes in national offices—suggest that, if anything, working-class representation may decline even further in the short term. In state legislatures, for instance, women's representation skyrocketed from 8 percent to 24 percent between 1976 and 2007, and the share of lawmakers who were black or Latino grew from 9 percent to 11 percent. During the same period, the share of state legislators from blue-collar jobs fell from 5 percent to 3 percent.[5] The path to political office has always been difficult for the working class, and it doesn't seem to be getting any easier.

The Elephant in the Room

These inequalities in the social class makeup of American political institutions raise a number of serious questions about our political process. How do the class backgrounds of our political decision makers affect the policies our government enacts? Do lawmakers promote the interests of their own social class at the expense of other groups, or do they work for the common good regardless of their personal stakes in the issues of the day? Does the numerical representation of a particular social class in our political institutions affect how that class's interests fare in the policy-making process?

Answering these questions should be a high priority. Arguments about the differences between politicians from different classes have a long history in American political thought and in democratic theory more generally.[6] Modern political discourse is awash in commentary about policy makers' class backgrounds. Candidates and officeholders themselves often attribute paramount importance to their social class backgrounds. And questions about the social class makeup of government speak to concerns about political equality that go to the very heart of what we stand for as a country.

To date, however, hard research on the shortage of working-class Americans in our political institutions has been remarkably scarce. Descriptive studies of the class backgrounds of public officials briefly flourished in the 1950s and 1960s (e.g., Beckett and Sunderland 1957; Matthews 1954a, 1954b; Zeller 1954), but follow-up research "to determine the relationship between [policy makers'] social backgrounds and the conduct of government" (Matthews 1954a, 38) never materialized. Donald Matthews's (1985, 17) complaint more than a quarter century ago is no less true today: despite "several decades of unprecedented achievement in legislative research," the link between policy makers' class backgrounds and their choices in office "is still mainly an assertion" (see also Mayhew 2008; Norris and Lovenduski 1995).[7] As it stands, political scientists simply don't know much about how inequalities in the class composition of American political institutions affect policy making in the United States.

Our inattention to this enduring feature of our political process is a serious oversight. Scholars know a great deal about aspects of American civic life that are far newer than white-collar government, like broadcast television and Senate elections. We have produced rich literatures on the numerical underrepresentation of women and racial minorities (e.g., Berkman and O'Connor 1993; Canon 1999; Griffin and Newman 2008; Swers 2002; Thomas 1991; Whitby 1997), but not social classes.[8]

Even the scholars who care about the upper class's oversized influence in American political life haven't paid much attention to the sharply tilted composition of our political institutions. In the last decade, political scientists have made significant strides in understanding why our political process is more responsive to the interests of the wealthy (thanks in large part to organized efforts like the American Political Science Association's Task Force on Inequality and American Democracy). However, most scholars who have confronted this important question have focused on two related culprits: inequalities in routine forms of political participation and inequalities in the organized pressure system. On the one hand, some scholars note, less affluent people are less likely to vote or write letters to their elected officials, which mutes their political influence in serious ways. Summarizing decades of data on numerous forms of political engagement, Schlozman et al. (2005, 69) conclude that "those with high levels of income, occupational status and, especially, education are much more likely to be politically artic- ulate," which has "unambiguous implications for what policymakers hear." A second line of research has highlighted the sharp social class biases in organized political activity, that is, biases in who lobbies, who donates, and who forms interest groups. When Schattschneider ([1960] 1975, 35) ana- lyzed these processes more than a half century ago, he famously concluded that "the flaw in the pluralist heaven is that the heavenly chorus sings with a strong upper-class accent." Since then, the accent has only gotten thicker: unions have declined, business lobbies have become more numerous and more sophisticated, and campaign donations and spending have reached all-time highs (Hacker and Pierson 2010; Winters 2011, chap. 5).

There can be little doubt that, as Jacobs and Skocpol (2005, 1) note, "public officials . . . are much more responsive to the privileged than to aver- age citizens and the less affluent" because "the privileged participate more than others and are increasingly well organized to press their demands on government." However, there may be more to the problem than just partici- pation and organization. Whether our political process listens to one voice or another depends not just on who's doing the talking or how loud they are; it also depends on who's doing the *listening*. To date, scholars who care about wealthy Americans' disproportionate political influence have focused on inequalities in the inputs of the political process—inequalities in who pressures government, either through routine forms of political participa- tion or through larger organizational efforts. What about inequalities in who decides what to do with those inputs—inequalities in who *runs* govern- ment? Who votes and who participates and who donates and who organizes all undoubtedly affect who wins and who loses in US politics. But if we want to understand why affluent Americans wield more political influence than other citizens, we need to pay attention to inequalities in *who governs*, too.

Understanding the effects of government by the upper class could also shed new light on a number of other important questions about US poli- tics. Citizens, journalists, and political scientists have always wondered, for instance, what makes politicians tick, what drives their choices in office. Scholars currently know a great deal about how the political environment— institutions, constituents, political parties, and so on—can shape what pol- icy makers do in office. However, we know relatively little about the origins of policy makers' own views and opinions, the "personal roots" of their decisions (Burden 2007). Politicians' choices (like everyone's choices) reflect some compromise between what they really want and the constraints imposed on them by others, but for at least the last half century, the analysis of those external constraints has been "the dominant theoretical approach for explaining congressional organization and behavior" (Arnold 2004, ix–x) and elite decision making more generally.[9] We still have a lot to learn about where our representatives' own intrinsic motivations come from and how their own values and beliefs influence what they do in office. Understanding how class matters in our political institutions could be an important step toward a more complete picture of what goes on in our representatives' heads.

It could also be a step toward more satisfying answers to long-standing questions about *political power* in the United States. In 1956, C. Wright Mills's *The Power Elite* sparked an energetic debate about the social and economic overlap among political, corporate, and military leaders in the United States. Mills and others (e.g., Domhoff 1967) argued that there was a single overarching class of elites in the United States that directed everything from museums and charities to corporations and governments. *Pluralist* scholars countered that our porous political process "has a built-in, self-operating limitation on the influence of all participants" (Dahl [1961] 2005, 305). How could any group, let alone one as diverse as the elites Mills identified, wield very much power in our expansive, fragmented government? In the end, the pluralists carried the day, at least in the eyes of most political scientists. However, one important piece of evidence was never entered into the debate: neither the pluralists nor the power elite scholars ever tested the basic idea that lawmakers from different classes might behave differently in office (Carnes and Lupu 2012).[10] Although our political process gives citizens and interest groups many opportunities to influence public policy, officeholders have the final say in what government does, and they have a great deal of personal leeway, even in a porous political process with a vibrant pressure group system. Social and economic elites may have diverse views, but if they have different views *on average* than the average citizen, their disproportionate numbers in our political institutions could bias public policy in their class's favor. Power elite theorists never tested this possibility systematically, and in the absence of any hard evidence, political scientists tended to side with the pluralists. This important debate has been at an empirical impasse for decades; understanding how lawmakers from different classes think and behave could help to revive it.

The only consideration that might discourage us from studying the underrepresentation of the working class is the old idea that white-collar

government is a practical necessity, that working-class Americans are unqualified to hold public office. Aren't more affluent leaders *better* leaders—
shouldn't we want them running the country? The idea has deep roots:
during the Founding, Alexander Hamilton (1788) argued that workers'
"habits in life have not been such as to give them those acquired endowments, without which in a deliberative assembly the greatest natural abilities are for the most part useless." Today, many scholars continue to assert
that "leadership is a specialization necessitated by the division of labor in
all societies" (Cohen 1981, 5) and that class markers like education are
"compelling indicator[s] of a leader's quality" (Besley and Reynal-Querol
2012, 552).

Although these ideas resonate with some political observers, they have no
basis in scientific research. There has never been a single empirical study—
not one—that has suggested that working-class Americans are underrepresented in public office because they are poorly suited for the job.[11] To the
contrary, what little evidence there is suggests that blue-collar workers are
underrepresented not because of some deficiency on their part, but because
of discouraging circumstances, like the high cost of running a campaign, the
practical burdens associated with holding office, and the gate-keeping decisions of party leaders and interest groups (Carnes 2012). As I illustrate in
the last chapter of this book, the underrepresentation of the working class in
public office is not a practical necessity. It is not a necessary evil. And, as I illustrate throughout the rest of this book, it has real consequences for public
policy and ultimately for the well-being of working-class Americans.

Many of the most daunting challenges facing our country are issues that
divide Americans along social class lines. Unemployment is high. Inequalities in wealth and income are soaring. Labor rights, tax policies, and the
federal budget are explosive topics. One of the most important contributions scholars of US politics can make to debates about these issues is a
clear understanding of how and why our system of government privileges
the interests of certain classes of people at the expense of others. This book
explores one neglected possibility: the enduring and widespread phenomenon of government by the upper class.

Why Does Class Matter?

My central argument in this book is that *the shortage of people from the working class in American legislatures skews the policy-making process toward outcomes that are more in line with the upper class's economic interests.* Ordinary
Americans from different classes have different political views, especially

on economic issues. So do legislators. Ordinary Americans from different classes care about different kinds of problems. So do legislators. Ordinary Americans from different classes would choose different kinds of economic policies if they were in charge. Legislators *are* in charge, and they often do just that.

Lawmakers' choices are by no means unfettered, of course. To the contrary, most officeholders face a wide range of external pressures when they make decisions. Party leaders attempt to persuade them to toe the line (Aldrich 1995; Cox and McCubbins 1993; Rohde 1991). Interest groups lobby them (Austin-Smith and Wright 1994; Hall and Wayman 1990). And the potential electoral consequences of their decisions are almost always on their minds (Arnold 1990; Mayhew 1974a).

Despite these constraints, legislators often have considerable discretion or leeway (Jacobs and Shapiro 2000; Jewell 1982; Reeher 1996). Lobbyists, party leaders, and other stakeholders frequently have conflicting demands that can leave a lawmaker without a clear best strategic option (Kingdon 1981, chap. 10). Constituents are chronically inattentive to what policy makers do (Delli Carpini and Keeter 1996), and much of the actual work involved in lawmaking happens behind the scenes, where citizens have little oversight (Hall 1996). Many important decisions are further obscured by legislative sleight of hand (Arnold 1990; Mettler 2011). Incumbent re-election rates are high (Gelman and King 1990; Mayhew 1974b), and most officeholders feel secure enough in their positions to risk angering constituents, party leaders, or interest groups from time to time in order to do what they believe is right.

As a result, legislators' choices often reflect their own views. When lawmakers cast their votes, they often consider their own opinions about the issues before them. When they decide which policies to advocate, they often focus on problems that have some personal significance to them. In these instances, legislators from different backgrounds tend to behave differently. This may be because, as Burden (2007, chap. 2) notes, a legislator's past experiences can influence her deeply held values, her knowledge or expertise, her perceptions of her material self-interests, or her general ideological orientation. It may also be because of the reverse: in some instances, legislators may have previously chosen to affiliate with certain groups or to have certain experiences on the basis of their attitudes and beliefs. Whatever the exact causal relationship, lawmakers from different backgrounds often have different political tendencies, and—when they look inward for guidance about an issue or a proposal—they often make different kinds of decisions. As a result, many of the divisions that we observe in other areas of life tend to play out in a similar fashion in our legislatures. Lawmakers are people, too, after all.

In this book, I focus on the links between the class backgrounds of American legislators and domestic economic policies like taxation, business regulation, social spending, and labor laws. These issues have immediate implications for the material well-being of different classes of citizens. They often entail zero-sum trade-offs in which one group pays for another group's benefits. Not surprisingly, they elicit the deepest social class divisions in public opinion (Hout 2008). Figure 1.3 compares manual laborers' average responses on several common survey questions about economic issues to the average responses of professionals and managers.[12] On questions about federal assistance to low-income Americans, government regulation of the economy, employment and standard-of-living guarantees, and labor unions, working-class Americans consistently have more liberal preferences than professionals.[13]

There are many possible reasons why that might be. The first wave of research on how class shapes a person's political views emphasized simple material self-interest. Poor and working-class people, in this view, tend to support more progressive economic policies and more economically progressive parties and candidates because progressive policies make poor and working-class people better off (e.g., Downs 1957, chap. 3). More recently, scholars have embraced a more nuanced view of the links between class and political opinion. Americans from the working class may prefer more progressive policies because those policies benefit them in the short term (Melzer and Richard 1981; Rehm 2010) or because social classes tend to develop political and ideological habits over time (Piketty 1995) or because people tend to associate with other people from their class, which reinforces those habits (Keely and Tan 2008; Manza and Brooks 2008). A blue-collar worker may tend to be more progressive than a white-collar professional because he benefits from progressive economic policies or because most of his friends and coworkers are economic progressives. A CEO may vote Republican because she recognizes that it is in her best interest or because her colleagues are all Republicans.[14]

Either way, her ballot still counts the same. Whatever the reason, Americans from the top social strata tend to see economic issues through a different lens, a more conservative lens, than poor and working-class Americans. And that has real consequences for how they behave in the realm of public affairs.

This book shows that the same is true for politicians. Whether because of self-interest or political habits, legislators from different classes bring dif-

Figure 1.3. Class and Economic Attitudes among US Citizens

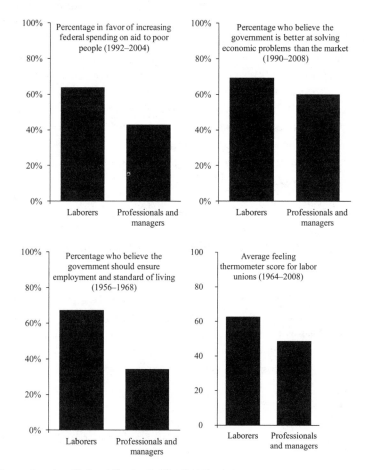

Source: American National Election Studies (2010).

ferent economic attitudes and concerns to the policy-making process. Legislators from the working class are more progressive on economic issues. Legislators from white-collar jobs—especially those from the private sector—are more conservative. And when they have some leeway in how they vote or in the kinds of bills they fight for, they behave accordingly.

Of course, these are not hard-and-fast laws of legislative conduct—there are obvious counterexamples, like Franklin Roosevelt and Ted Kennedy, who came from stunningly privileged backgrounds but nonetheless championed the needs of the less fortunate. The FDRs and Kennedys of the world are the exceptions, however, not the rule. (Perhaps that is part of why they are such memorable figures.) Just as there are many wealthy Americans who care deeply about helping the little guy, there are many lawmakers from privileged backgrounds who fight for the less fortunate. In general, however, more privileged Americans tend to be more conservative on economic issues. And, in general, politicians from more privileged backgrounds tend to be more conservative, too.

These class-based differences in how legislators think and behave have dramatic consequences in the aggregate. Because there are so few lawmakers from the working class, collective decisions in US legislatures tend to be more favorable to the interests of more privileged Americans. Put differently, the *descriptive* or numerical underrepresentation of the working class in our political institutions affects the working class's *substantive representation* (Pitkin 1967)—workers' interests and preferences have less weight in the policy-making process.

The effects on the well-being of working-class Americans are staggering. Business regulations are more relaxed, tax policies are more generous to the rich, social safety net programs are stingier, and protections for workers are weaker than they would be if our political decision makers came from the same mix of classes as the people they represent. These policy outcomes make life harder for the classes of Americans who can least afford it. Government *by* the upper class promotes government *for* the upper class—and government *for* the upper class is often bad for everyone else.[15]

The Evidence

There has always been a school of American political thought that has questioned whether the shortage of people from the working class in our political institutions really matters. When Anti-Federalists charged that the US Constitution would lead to government by the upper class, Federalists argued that the interest of the working class would be "more effectually promoted by [the upper class] than by themselves" (Hamilton 1788). Ever since, there have been political observers who have doubted that imbalances in the social class makeup of our officeholders have any real impact on the policies our government enacts.

This book challenges this school of thought with empirical data on American legislatures: Congress, state legislatures, and city councils. Although social class divisions could exist in any political institution where officeholders have some leeway, American legislatures are ideal laboratories in which to study the role of class in the policy-making process. They are large and diverse. And their members routinely make decisions about economic policy that have far-reaching consequences.

To measure the classes legislators came from, I collected data on the jobs they had before they held office (or in the case of lawmakers in part-time state and local institutions, the jobs they currently have outside of holding office). There are, of course, other ways to measure class—education, income, wealth, family background, and so on—and the question of which is best has a long and somewhat fraught history in the social sciences. As Lareau (2008, 4) notes, even after decades of social class research, "reasonable people [still] disagree about the best way to define the concept." However, most modern class analysts agree that any measure of class should be rooted in occupational data, that is, information about how a person earns a living.

For my purposes, focusing on occupations is both convenient and sensible. It is far easier to collect data on what politicians did for a living than to collect data on other class markers like how they dressed or how much money they made before they held office. What they did for a living, moreover, is arguably the *best* way to measure the classes they came from. As Donald Matthews (1954a, 23) noted in his pioneering research on the class backgrounds of political decision makers, "Probably the most important single criterion for social ranking in the United States is occupation. Although it is by no means a certain index to an individual's social standing in the community, occupation is perhaps the closest approach to an infallible guide." Matthews's insights are just as true today: occupation is still a strong predictor of other measures of class such as income, social status, and the class labels people assign to themselves (Katz 1972, 63; Hout 2008).

Occupations, moreover, are more plausible drivers of what people (or lawmakers) think about public policy than many other class measures like income or education. As Manza and Brooks (2008, 204) succinctly put it:

> Income groups have no common organizational anchor, and . . . current income alone is a poor measure of long-term social standing and life chances. . . .
> Education level is sometimes substituted as a measure of class . . . , although individuals with the same level of educational attainment also do not necessarily have any organizational anchor connecting them outside of their occupational locations. . . . Occupation provides the most plausible basis for thinking about how specifically class-related political micro processes and influences occur. . . . Workplace settings provide the possibility of talking about

politics and forging political identity, and work also provides a springboard for membership in organizations where class politics are engaged: unions, professional associations, business associations, and so forth.

Indeed, occupations are stronger predictors of Americans' political attitudes than many other common social class measures. Composite prestige or "socioeconomic status" measures actually seem to obscure the relationship between political opinion and social class (Weeden and Grusky 2005; Lareau 2008, 12). A person's education level is one of the most important predictors of many forms of civic engagement (Verba, Schlozman, and Brady 1995), but education's effect on how people think about political issues is less clear—some studies find that education is associated with conservative views (Kaufmann 2002) and some find that it is associated with liberal ones (Mariani and Hewitt 2008; Newcomb 1958). Likewise, for people with similar adult social classes, there is little evidence of a statistical link between the social class of the person's parents and their adult political views (Barber 1970; Langton 1969, chap. 2). For every person who worked his way up from a blue-collar childhood to a white-collar adult life and who chose to be a Democrat, there is another who chose to be a Republican. For every Bill Clinton, there is a Richard Nixon.

As for income and wealth—two popular measures of social class—there can be little doubt that they predict important differences in ordinary citizens' political views (e.g., Gilens 2009). For the purposes of measuring where lawmakers came from, however, they have two important drawbacks. First, although it is relatively easy to see how much money legislators earn and how much wealth they have *after* they take office (thanks to financial disclosure requirements that have been in place since the 1970s), it is virtually impossible to obtain hard data on politicians' wealth and income *before* they ran for public office. Even if we could, moreover, those data would probably tell us less about a lawmaker's political opinions than data on *how* they earned their money. Wealth and income are good predictors of a person's place in our economy, but they often conflate people with very different life chances and political socialization experiences. An intern at an investment bank, a skilled machinist, and a graduate student, for instance, earn similar incomes, but if we want to understand how people form political attitudes, it probably wouldn't make much sense to categorize all three as belonging to the same class. Likewise, if we just grouped legislators by income or net worth—or, for that matter, by education level or their parents' social classes—we would miss important differences in how legislators from different occupations think and behave in office. (In the online appendix, I illustrate this point empirically: www.press.uchicago.edu/sites/carnes.) When we meet new people, we seldom ask, "What's your annual income?" or "What was the highest degree you earned in school?" or "What did your parents do when you were growing up?"—partly because it's impolite to ask some of those things, and partly because we all know that we can learn more about a person just by asking, "What do you do for a living?"

The empirical analyses presented here draw on every available source of systematic data on the occupational backgrounds of American lawmakers and on my own original, highly detailed data on the men and women who served in Congress from 1999 to 2008. Following the advice of leading class analysts, I collected information from a half dozen reliable, nonpartisan sources about the prior careers of each of the 783 unique senators and representatives who held office during the 106th through 110th Congresses. With this information, I then computed the proportion of each member's precongressional career spent in each of ten occupational categories:[16] (1) lawyers, (2) farm owners or managers, (3) business owners or executives, (4) business employees, (5) technical professionals (such as doctors and architects), (6) service-based professionals (such as teachers and social workers), (7) military and law enforcement personnel, (8) political office-holders and staffers, (9) workers (manual laborers, service industry workers, farm laborers, and union officials), and (10) other jobs (too vague to classify).[17] To check that past occupations were the best way to measure class, I also gathered data on other common class measures, including education, income, wealth, and family background. The final product is, to my knowledge, the most detailed set of social class data ever compiled for a large sample of US lawmakers.

As figure 1.4 illustrates, the occupational backgrounds of the legislators in my sample varied considerably: for every category (aside from "other occupations"), my sample includes some lawmakers who spent 0 percent of their careers in that line of work and some who spent 80 to 100 percent. Of course, the occupational backgrounds of these members of Congress are strongly biased toward white-collar jobs. Before being elected to Congress, the average legislator in my sample spent more than 30 percent of his working life in politics; more than 20 percent in law; substantial percentages in service-based professions, business ownership or management, other business employment, and technical professions—and spent just 2 percent of his precongressional career in blue-collar work. Even so, with such a large sample of legislators, I can single out many individuals with at

Figure 1.4. The Distribution of Occupational Backgrounds in Congress, 1999–2008

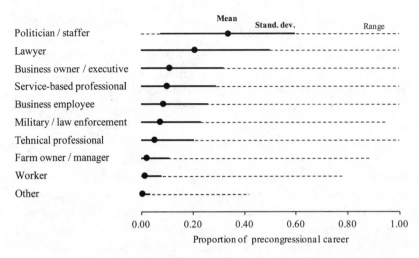

Note: Figure reports the means (dots), standard deviations (bold lines), and ranges (dotted lines) of measures of the proportions of members' precongressional careers spent in each of ten (mutually exclusive and collectively exhaustive) occupational categories. *Source:* Author's data collection.

least some experience in the working class, and a few with a lot. Forty-six (approximately 6 percent) of the 783 members of Congress who served from 1999 to 2008 spent at least some time in blue-collar jobs. Of those, thirty-two spent more than 10 percent of their precongressional careers doing blue-collar work, and thirteen spent more than a quarter of their adult lives in working-class jobs. Although rare, these legislators provide a valuable window into the differences between lawmakers from white-collar professions and those from the working class.

Of course, my data set is limited to one institution and one narrow period of time. As such, I have also examined data compiled by others, including data from the 1990s and 2000s on the aggregate occupational makeup of state legislatures and city councils, a handful of surveys of state and national lawmakers that inquired about their occupational backgrounds and economic attitudes, and a data set called *The Roster of Congressional Office-holders* (ICPSR and McKibbin 1997) that includes occupational information about every member of Congress who served before 1996. (Whereas my data set only includes thirteen legislators who spent a great deal of their careers in blue-collar jobs, the *Roster* data allow us to observe 165 instances in which a legislator in a given congressional session entered politics *directly* from a blue-collar job.) Many of these data sets were not created primarily to study officeholders' class backgrounds. Most therefore use cruder occupational information than my data set (usually just the last job each legislator held) and relatively coarse occupational categories (usually just six to eight). When examined in conjunction with my own data, however, they provide institutional and historical breadth that usefully complements my data set's informational depth. Together, my data and those that existed beforehand give us a more complete picture of the relationship between class and legislative decision making in the United States.

For the purposes of discussion and presentation, throughout this book, I often group the six to ten occupational categories in the data sets that I use into three broader classes: working-class jobs, not-for-profit professions, and profit-oriented professions. *Working-class jobs* are those that provide employees with little material security and that require little capital or formal education. *Profit-oriented professions* are white-collar jobs—jobs that provide moderate to high levels of material security—in which profit is generally the paramount motive, like running a business. And *not-for-profit professions* are white-collar jobs that are not centrally concerned with maximizing profits, like teaching and social work. For the sake of variety, I use the terms *working-class jobs* and *blue-collar jobs* interchangeably (or sometimes simply write *workers*), and for the sake of simplicity, I sometimes use the term *white-collar jobs* to refer to both profit-oriented professions and not-for-profit professions.

These categories seem to capture nicely the major divisions between legislators from different lines of work. People in white-collar jobs (both profit-oriented and not-for-profit) tend to enjoy a great deal more material security than those in blue-collar jobs. Perhaps because they experienced this security—or perhaps because of political habits formed over time and through repeated interactions with people like themselves—lawmakers from white-collar professions tend not to be as supportive of social safety net programs, progressive taxes, and other liberal economic causes as lawmakers from the working class.

Among lawmakers from white-collar professions, moreover, those who worked in profit-oriented professions—business owners, their high-ranking employees, and professionals in other organizations that function like businesses (e.g., farm owners or doctors)—tend to be more conservative on economic issues than lawmakers from not-for-profit professions. This may be because lawmakers from profit-oriented professions had stronger personal incentives to prefer conservative, hands-off economic policies during their working lives, or it may be because they were exposed to stronger cultures of conservative economic thought. Whatever the exact reason, like ordinary Americans in private-sector professions, lawmakers from profit-oriented professions are less likely to support liberal economic policies like business regulations, social safety net programs, and progressive taxes.

Beneath these larger divisions between legislators from the working class, from profit-oriented professions, and from not-for-profit professions, there are also more subtle differences between the narrower occupational categories in my data. A teacher and a city council member are both different from a CEO, but they are also different from one another. To avoid obscuring these differences, throughout this book, I rely on the more detailed six- to ten-category occupational coding schemes in my analyses. When I present my findings, I simply group these narrower occupational categories so that the profit-oriented professions appear first (in my ten-category coding scheme, these are farm owners or managers, business owners or executives, business employees, and technical professionals), the not-for-profit professions appear next (service-based professionals, military and law enforcement personnel, political officeholders and staffers, and lawyers[18]), and the working-class jobs appear last (workers).[19] This presentation style allows readers to see both the larger patterns across legislators from different types of occupations and the more subtle variations between lawmakers from particular jobs.

The first goal of this book is to explore the individual-level relationship between class and legislative conduct. In chapter 2, I use my original congressional data and the *Roster of Congressional Officeholders* data set to determine whether legislators from different classes vote differently on economic issues. Chapter 3 then uses these two data sets to study the links between class and *legislative entrepreneurship*, the kinds of bills lawmakers introduce, how hard they work to see them enacted, and how likely they are to see their proposals advance through the legislative process. The evidence is crystal clear: legislators from different classes behave differently in ways that mirror social class divisions in the public. When lawmakers from the working class cast their votes, they are more likely to vote for progressive policies than legislators from white-collar jobs, especially those from profit-oriented professions. When lawmakers from the working class introduce economic legislation, it is more progressive, and they work harder than other members to see it enacted. Like lawmakers from other historically underrepresented groups, however, legislators from the working class must work twice as hard as other members to pass the same number of economic bills. The shortage of people from the working class in our legislatures biases roll-call voting in favor of the preferences and interests of white-collar Americans and keeps the issues working-class citizens care about off the table in the first place.

But why does class matter so much? In chapter 4, I analyze several surveys of legislators to determine what exactly drives lawmakers from different classes to behave differently. The crucial difference I find is remarkably simple: lawmakers from different classes have different opinions about economic issues. And when they get the chance, they act on them.

Although these differences of opinion are simple, they have dramatic consequences in the aggregate. In chapter 5, I return to the macrolevel question driving this book, namely, how do imbalances in the social class makeup of political institutions affect economic policy? In doing so, I expand my focus to include federal, state, and local legislatures. Although Congress is ideal for research on individual lawmakers, its social class makeup has changed so little over time (see figure 1.2) that it is difficult to draw firm conclusions about how congressional policy would differ if Congress were run by a different mix of people. Chapter 5 uses data on how members of Congress from different classes vote to extrapolate how Congress's class composition might have influenced the outcomes of the most significant economic issues the federal government has confronted in the last decade, including the minimum wage, the Bush tax cuts, and the federal response to the late 2000s recession. I complement this analysis by examining economic policy in states and cities, where the aggregate class composition of policy-making institutions varies considerably from place to place and where, fortunately, other scholars have collected data on the social class makeup of legislatures during selected time periods. Together, these analyses illustrate how individual-level social class differences in our legislatures can have serious consequences for economic policy in the aggregate—how inequalities in the makeup of our representatives affect who ultimately wins and loses in the economic policy-making process.

In chapter 6, I discuss the troubling implications of my findings for our understanding of representation, inequality, and political power in the United States. I conclude by considering a second question raised by the existence of imbalances in the class backgrounds of political officeholders (and given added urgency by the finding that those imbalances are politically consequential), namely, *Why are there so few working-class people in political office in the first place?* Although I stop short of offering a definitive answer here, my findings cast serious doubt on the old idea that the working class is unfit to govern. Just as there have always been people who have questioned whether the social class makeup of our government matters, there have always been people who have maintained that we can't do anything about it. Both arguments are flat wrong. Those of us who care about the oversized influence of the affluent in American politics need to start paying more attention to the fact that our country is run by a white-collar government. And we need to start asking what we can do about it.

TWO

Voting with Class

Men of the most elevated rank in life will alone be chosen. The other orders of society, such as farmers, traders, and mechanics, who all ought to have a competent number of their best informed men in the legislature, shall be totally unrepresented. . . . [Congress] will consist of the lordly and high minded; of men who will have no congenial feelings with the people, but a perfect indifference for, and contempt of them; [it] will consist of those harpies of power that prey upon the very vitals, that riot on the miseries of the community.

—"The Address and Reasons of Dissent of the Minority of the [Constitutional] Convention of the State of Pennsylvania to Their Constituents," 1787

The idea of an actual representation of all classes of the people by persons of each class is altogether visionary. Unless it were expressly provided in the Constitution that each different occupation should send one or more members the thing would never take place in practice. Mechanics and manufacturers will always be inclined with few exceptions to give their votes to merchants in preference to persons of their own professions or trades. . . . They know that the merchant is their natural patron and friend; and they are aware that however great the confidence they may justly feel in their own good sense, their interests can be more effectually promoted by the merchant than by themselves.

—Alexander Hamilton, "Federalist #35," 1788

Debates about the ratification of the US Constitution often centered on questions about the social class makeup of the political institutions the document outlined. Because of the relatively small number of seats in the proposed House of Representatives—the only popularly elected governing body in the original Constitution—congressional districts would have to cover vast areas and include many people. Most observers agreed that these large districts would powerfully advantage candidates with resources, status, and celebrity and would give rise to a "natural aristocracy," a democratically elected government that nonetheless consisted primarily of the upper class. Anti-Federalists cast this feature of the Constitution as an assault on the ideals of popular sovereignty and representative government. The upper class, they claimed, would use its place in our legislatures to promote policies that preserved its privileged place in society. Federalists offered an altogether different portrait of America's democratic aristocracy. In their view, lawmakers from the upper class would work for the common good, either because of the natural affinities between different classes, the superior intelligence and virtue of the upper class, or the Constitution's safeguards against tyranny and faction.[1]

More than two centuries later, these rival perspectives still echo throughout our political discourse. Candidates from the working class often claim to share workers' interests and portray wealthy or business-connected lawmakers as out of touch. Officeholders from privileged backgrounds vigorously deny these accusations. Some reframe their ties to businesses and the wealthy as a sign that they know what's best for the nation as a whole with "slogans such as president Calvin Coolidge's 'the business of the nation is business' or Charles E. Wilson's (Eisenhower's secretary of defense and a former executive at General Motors) statement that 'what was good for the country was good for General Motors and vice versa'" (Witko and Friedman 2008, 72).

If we wish to understand how government by the privileged affects economic policy, we must first settle this old debate. Do lawmakers from different classes actually behave differently in office? Or do they fight for the interests of their constituents, their parties, and so on, regardless of their personal stakes in the issues of the day?

This chapter begins to answer these questions by examining how members of Congress vote on economic legislation. When lawmakers face simple yes-no decisions on issues that affect different classes of Americans differently, do their choices vary by class? To find out, I analyzed data on the class backgrounds and voting decisions of members of Congress, who cast hundreds of roll call votes each year and whose collective choices have enormous consequences for American politics and American society. Using my original data for the 106th through 110th Congresses (1999 to 2008) and other less detailed data on post–World War II Congresses, this chapter shows that lawmakers from different classes do in fact vote differently, that these differences have persisted for the last several decades, and that they persist throughout individual lawmakers' careers. The old notion that politicians from different classes essentially want the same things—that the interests of the mechanic "can be more effectually promoted by the merchant"—is deeply mistaken. On the important economic issues of the day, members of Congress routinely vote with class.

Legislative Voting as a Window into the Importance of Class

Scholars of US politics probably know more about legislative voting than they do about everything else lawmakers do in office put together. And for good reason: voting is important. Chamber or roll call votes are "the final points of decision in an American legislature," "the ultimate arbiter of conflicts which take place within the body," and "the end product of the law-making apparatus" (Kingdon 1981, 4). Predictions about future roll call votes influence lawmakers' choices at earlier stages of the legislative process (Arnold 1990). The outcomes of roll call votes influence the direction of public policy and how legislators fare in the next election (Canes-Wrone, Brady, and Cogan 2002).

Legislative voting is also popular with scholars of US politics because it is relatively easy to study. Reliable information about how legislators vote is widely available. At the congressional level, roll calls are recorded electronically and posted online shortly afterward. Votes happen frequently, which makes it easy for scholars to carry out statistical analyses with large samples. Moreover, because voting entails a choice between a fixed set of discrete options, it is easy to make apples-to-apples comparisons across individuals or groups of legislators. When a lawmaker drafts a new bill or advocates a new issue, she can decide to work on any of a wide range of topics and can decide to tackle them in any of a wide range of ways. When a legislator votes, however, she has the same set of options as every one of her colleagues: vote yes, vote no, or abstain. When legislators cast their votes, they give us all a clear view of where they stand on the issues. And they give political scientists clean-cut data on how they make decisions.[2]

In addition to being politically important and scientifically useful, legislative voting is a natural starting point for research on legislators' personal characteristics for another reason: it provides a *hard test*. Nothing else legislators do is scrutinized as aggressively as roll call voting. Party leaders closely track whether rank-and-file members vote the party line. Interest groups use votes to create composite rankings that identify their friends and enemies in the legislature. Voting is easy to translate into electoral punishment, especially compared to many other forms of legislative activity. It is difficult to craft an attack ad about how a legislator bargained with the Rules Committee on a question of jurisdiction to ensure that a popular bill was sent to a hostile committee; it is easy to say that a rival candidate voted to do something stupid. Under this kind of pressure, legislators are more likely to defer to other political actors—and are therefore less likely to look inward for guidance (Burden 2007, chap. 2; Hall 1996). If legislative voting on a given issue is associated with some personal characteristic of lawmakers, that characteristic is probably even more important during the lower-profile stages of the policy-making process. Differences in voting are politically consequential, easy to measure, and usually only the tip of the iceberg.

Despite the intense scrutiny lawmakers face, they still have some leeway when they cast their votes (Reeher 1996). Lawmakers from different racial groups, for instance, tend to vote differently on a wide range of issues, even after controlling for other things that might influence how they vote, like the party they belong to or the views of their constituents (Canon 1999; Griffin and Newman 2008; Whitby 1997). Likewise, even after accounting for other factors, male and female legislators tend to vote differently on women's issues (Swers 2002); veterans and nonveterans tend to vote differently on defense issues (Gelpi and Feaver 2002); and religious people, parents of schoolchildren, and smokers tend to vote differently on religious issues, educational issues, and smoking issues (Burden 2007).

Scholars generally agree that these patterns reflect differences in legislators' own opinions or *policy preferences*. Surveys of legislators find racial and gender gaps in their political views that mirror racial and gender gaps in how they vote (Barrett 1995; Button and Hedge 1996; Mezey 1978; Thomas and Welch 1991). Casual observations of politicians and campaigns seem to support this idea, too. When former senator Blanche Lincoln ran for Congress for the first time in 1992, she appealed to voters by saying, "I would never ask you to vote for me simply because I am a woman, but it is time for a woman's perspective" (quoted in Burrell 1994, 30). When Texas state legislator Jose Aliseda won office in 2011, he said, "As a Mexican immigrant, I think I bring a different perspective to a lot of things" (quoted in Philpott 2011). Why do lawmakers from different backgrounds vote differently? The most obvious answer is that they have simply retained their social group's unique political opinions, and when they have some leeway in how they vote, they often act on those views (Burden 2007, chap. 2).[3]

Could class work this way? On its face, the idea seems plausible. As chapter 1 noted, Americans from different classes have reported having different economic policy preferences for as long as pollsters have been asking (Campbell et al. 1960, chap. 13; Centers 1953; Hout 2008). Blue-collar workers have always tended to want more generous social programs and stronger workplace protections. Professionals, especially those in the private sector, have always tended to want lower taxes and fewer regulations on businesses. These patterns could be the result of anything from simple self-interest (redistribution, social safety net programs, business regulations, and progressive taxes all have immediate benefits for blue-collar workers and immediate costs for wealthier Americans; Melzer and Richard 1981; Piketty 1995; Rehm 2010) to group identification, socialization, or social network effects (once established, the political dispositions of groups or classes of people tend to be self-reinforcing; Keely and Tan 2008; Manza and Brooks 2008). Whatever the reason, people from different occupations or classes bring different perspectives to the realm of public affairs.

Politicians often say they do as well. House Speaker John Boehner frequently comments on the importance of his career in business; while campaigning in Ohio in October 2010, for instance, he said, "I'm a small businessman at heart. Always will be. . . . Running a small business here in Butler County was one of the proudest times of my life. And it gave me a perspective on our country that I've carried with me throughout my time in public service." Other politicians have made similar claims about their work in everything from science and accounting to public service and blue-collar jobs.[4]

If these arguments capture a more general pattern—if lawmakers from different lines of work tend to bring different political opinions to our legislatures—legislative voting on economic issues may sometimes differ by class, just as voting on racial issues sometimes differs by race and voting on gender issues sometimes differs by gender. Like working-class citizens, legislators from the working class may tend to have more progressive economic preferences and may consequently vote more progressively on economic issues from time to time. Likewise, lawmakers from white-collar backgrounds, especially those from the private sector, may retain their class's more conservative views and consequently tend to vote more conservatively. When pollsters ask ordinary Americans about their opinions on economic issues, people from different classes tend to answer differently. When important economic issues are put to a vote in our legislatures, lawmakers from different classes may vote differently in much the same way.

Measuring the Divisions

Someone visiting a US legislature for the first time probably wouldn't be able to tell whether lawmakers from different classes were voting differently on economic issues. On a typical day, there might only be a few floor votes on substantive issues. The visitor might notice broad differences in how Democrats and Republicans vote and, depending on the issues, perhaps even variations in how women or racial minorities cast their votes. However, any differences between legislators from the working class and those from white-collar jobs would probably be all but invisible. Most legislators' party affiliations are listed alongside their names in official documents, and their races and genders are usually plainly apparent (although not always, especially in the case of race). However, their class backgrounds—the jobs they had before they held office—are virtually impossible to see with the naked eye. Moreover, even if an observer could somehow distinguish the legislators who had been construction workers from those who had run corporations, there might be only one or two former blue-collar workers—in some legislatures, there might be none at all. The day's voting could be sharply divided along class lines, but a visitor might still leave without even a vague sense of the social class divisions that had played out before her eyes.

Determining whether legislators from different classes vote differently on economic issues requires detailed information about the occupational backgrounds of a large sample of legislators and detailed information about their votes on a large sample of economic proposals. A researcher could collect these data in virtually any American political institution in which officeholders have some leeway when they vote. In many respects, however, Congress is the ideal institution for this kind of analysis. The class backgrounds and votes of members of Congress are far easier to measure than those of lawmakers in state and local legislatures. The constraints on members' discretion are greater, too, which provides a harder test of the argument that class matters. The policy stakes are nowhere more serious than in Congress. And Congress has been the subject of debates about the class composition of our political institutions since the Founding.

To measure legislators' class backgrounds, I rely here on the original data set I described in chapter 1—which includes detailed information about the occupational histories of every legislator who served in Congress from 1999 to 2008—and the *Roster of Congressional Officeholders* (ICPSR and McKibbin 1997)—a data set with simple occupational information about every member of Congress who served before 1997. The *Roster* data set's occupation measures have a few drawbacks: they only record the last job listed for each legislator in his or her official (self-edited) biographical profile, and they use less nuanced occupational categories than those in my original data. However, the *Roster* data set's sheer size and unparalleled historical breadth provide opportunities to study the relationship between class and roll call voting in narrow subsets of legislators and in earlier periods of American history, tasks that are difficult or impossible with my smaller, more recent data set.

To measure how legislators from different classes voted on economic issues, I focus on three *composite voting indexes* (scores assigned to legislators based on their choices on a large number of bills): one computed by political scientists, first-dimension DW-NOMINATE scores, and two computed by economic interest groups, the AFL-CIO's congressional voting report cards and the US Chamber of Commerce's *How They Voted* congressional score-cards. If legislators sometimes base their choices on their class-contingent political preferences and sometimes do not, focusing on individual roll call votes would risk exaggerating the importance of class (if the researcher chose to study specific roll calls for which class was especially important, either accidentally or intentionally) or understating the relationship between class and voting (if the researcher happened to study only the votes on which legislators' hands were tied by external factors). Focusing on composite scores based on numerous votes allows us to step back from the idiosyncrasies of particular roll calls and ask whether there is a more general relationship between the classes lawmakers come from and how they vote on economic issues.

The two types of composite scores I use here represent two distinct approaches to measuring legislative voting on economic issues. DW-NOMINATE scores are *ideal point estimates* based on a statistical procedure that analyzes every vote cast in each Congress and identifies the main ideological divisions in the legislature by examining which members consistently voted the same ways. This procedure assigns each lawmaker a number—her DW-NOMINATE score—on a left-right scale that corresponds to the major issues that have traditionally divided the two parties, which tend to revolve around the government's size and role in the market (Poole and Rosenthal 1997). These scores are widely used in research on Congress, are comparable over time and between chambers, and are strongly associated with other composite measures of legislative voting. They have one important drawback for my purposes, however: they can sometimes be influenced by divisive issues that are not strictly economic matters. DW-NOMINATE scores are good measures of legislative voting on economic affairs, but they occasionally capture other major divisions in Congress.

For that reason, I also analyze voting scores computed by the AFL-CIO and the Chamber of Commerce, which only reflect voting on high-stakes economic legislation. Each year, each organization chooses roughly a dozen roll calls that it regards as key votes and assigns each member of Congress a score based on the number of times her vote agreed with the organization's view. These scores are less comparable over time than DW-NOMINATE scores and are only available for the last few decades. However, they provide cleaner measures of how legislators voted on issues with immediate implications for the well-being of different classes of Americans, the issues that tend to elicit the deepest social class divisions in the general public.[5]

To make it easier to compare how these three voting measures differ by class, I have rescaled legislators' DW-NOMINATE and AFL-CIO scores to match the Chamber of Commerce's scale: all three measures have been set to range from 0 to 100, with higher values signifying more conservative voting on economic issues. With these data, we can answer a variety of questions about class and legislative conduct. The next three sections focus on the three that seem the most pressing: Do members of Congress from different classes vote differently on economic issues? Have they always done so? And do legislators from different classes still vote differently after they join the "political class"—do lawmakers who have been in office for many years still remember where they came from?

Class and Legislative Voting Today

Of the 783 men and women who served in Congress from 1999 to 2008, just thirteen had spent a quarter or more of their precongressional working lives in blue-collar jobs. This baker's dozen included four Republicans (Senators Lincoln Chafee,[6] Chuck Grassley, and Orrin Hatch; and Representative Jo Ann Davis) and nine Democrats (Representatives Robert Brady, Julia Carson, Luis Gutierrez, Philip Hare, Stephen Lynch, Mike Michaud, Grace Napolitano, David Obey, and Linda Sánchez). Before taking office, these lawmakers held jobs ranging from farmhand and construction worker to receptionist and restaurant server. Most worked their way up to Congress gradually, working first in blue-collar jobs, then later in white-collar jobs, before eventually running for office.

Most, however, still talk about the importance of their time in the working class. Representative Mike Michaud's congressional website describes him as a legislator who "has taken the experience of his hometown and his experience as a millworker to the floor of the United States Congress. As a working class Mainer, Mike is in a unique position among members of Congress to understand the problems facing real Americans here and around the country." Representative David Obey's online biography similarly focuses on how his working-class roots influenced his views on business regulations:

I remember taking our 20-minute lunch breaks and sitting on the steps on the back porch at the plant and seeing these huge pipes pour this junk into the Wisconsin River. . . . I vowed at the time that if I ever had the chance to do anything to make industry stop using our rivers and streams as liquid dumps I would do it. . . . I also remember that every time I visited my grandmother, who lived on Third Avenue in Wausau, we had to take a rag and wipe off the chairs and the porch swing because they were covered with dust and grime from the junk that was coming out of the smokestack at 3M Company. Today, that doesn't happen anymore, and I am proud to have been able to play at least a small role in bringing that progress about.

The progressive sentiments embodied in this type of rhetoric have long been a common refrain among lawmakers from the working class. But is there more to class than just rhetoric?

The voting records of these thirteen blue-collar legislators suggest that there is. According to the Chamber of Commerce's voting scale, ten of these thirteen members ranked in the most liberal 25 percent of their parties at least once between 1999 and 2008, and four ranked in the most liberal 10 percent. The same was true according to the AFL-CIO's vote scoring system: ten of the thirteen scored in the most liberal 25 percent of their parties at least once, and eight scored in the most liberal 10 percent. Compared to a typical group of four Republicans and nine Democrats, these thirteen legislators had DW-NOMINATE scores that were 3 points (out of 100) more liberal on average, AFL-CIO scores that were 5 points more liberal, and Chamber of Commerce scores that were 6 points more liberal. Differences of this size are striking (especially in light of the many other factors that influence legislator's choices). To move one lawmaker's AFL-CIO roll call score a few points would require changing how she voted on some of the most high-profile economic bills of the year. To move *every* lawmaker's score a few points would mean changing hundreds of votes on monumental economic policies. Although legislators from the working class are rare, those who have held office recently appear to have brought the working class's more progressive economic perspective with them—with potentially serious consequences for economic policy.

The differences between lawmakers from different classes appear even starker when we distinguish between the different white-collar occupations legislators previously held. Figure 2.1 plots average DW-NOMINATE scores, Chamber of Commerce scores, and AFL-CIO scores among the legislators who spent *at least half* of their careers in one of the nine occupational categories I created for this analysis.[7] (No legislator spent more than half of his or her career in the tenth category, "other occupations," so I have ignored it here.) In each panel, these nine categories are grouped into the three broader classes of occupations I discussed in chapter 1, with profit-oriented professional occupations at the top, not-for-profit professional occupations in the middle, and working-class jobs at the bottom. Within each of these three broader groups, the narrower occupational categories are ordered from most liberal to most conservative. (Again, here—and throughout the remainder of the chapter—I have rescaled the DW-NOMINATE and AFL-CIO scores to match the 0-to-100, conservative-to-liberal scale the Chamber of Commerce uses.) The resulting orderings are identical: within each of the two broader classes of jobs that include multiple occupations, legislators from different occupations were ranked the same on all three voting measures.

The patterns evident in figure 2.1 are remarkably similar to the social class divisions that scholars have long observed in ordinary Americans' economic attitudes. On all three voting measures, former technical professionals, business owners and executives, and business employees in Congress consistently voted most conservatively. Farm owners and managers were usually among the most conservative as well, although on the AFL-CIO's voting scale, they more closely resembled former not-for-profit professionals. (This pattern may reflect farmers' precarious economic position: as business owners, they benefit from conservative policies that keep wages low and regulations lax, but because their startup costs are high and their livelihoods are sensitive to fluctuations in the climate and the price of their crops, they may also support some measures that compensate for the unpredictability of the free market.) Lawmakers who spent most of their precongressional careers in working-class jobs, on the other hand, consistently voted the most liberally on economic legislation. And lawmakers from professional occupations not centrally oriented toward the market—military and law enforcement personnel, lawyers, politicians and staffers, and service-oriented professionals—fell somewhere in between. The magnitudes of the differences were especially striking. The occupational groups with the most liberal and most conservative average DW-NOMINATE scores—former blue-collar workers and former technical professionals—differed by 37 points out of 100. On the Chamber of Commerce's voting scale, they were separated by 43 points out of 100. On the AFL-CIO's scale, they differed by 76 points, more than three-quarters of the possible range of scores.[8]

Of course, it is easy to imagine many non-class-related explanations for the patterns documented in figure 2.1. Perhaps legislators' occupations are

Figure 2.1 Class and Economic Voting Scores in Congress, 1999–2008

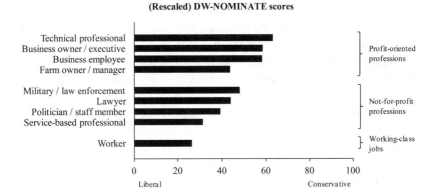

(Rescaled) DW-NOMINATE scores

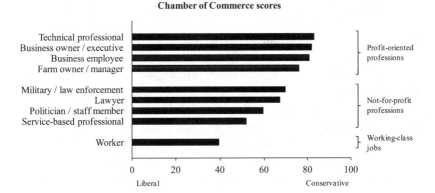

Chamber of Commerce scores

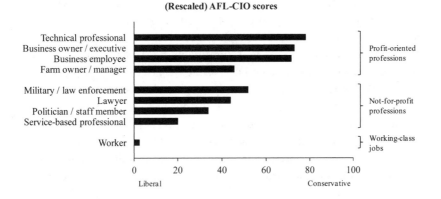

(Rescaled) AFL-CIO scores

correlated with some other politically salient personal characteristic such as party or race or gender. Or perhaps these occupational data are really capturing the effects of some feature of legislators' strategic environments. Perhaps, for instance, working-class congressional candidates do better in elections in liberal states and districts, where members of Congress have strong incentives to vote liberally regardless of their class backgrounds (and, likewise, technical professionals tend to do better in conservative districts, and so on).

To test these possibilities, I estimated a series of statistical models (for the statistically inclined: they were ordinary least squares regressions) that measured the relationship between each legislator's roll call voting scores and the proportion of her career spent in each of the occupational categories in figure 2.1. These models also took into account other aspects of each legislator's own background (party, age, race, gender, and religion), who her constituents were (percent urban, percent white, occupational composition, median household income, union membership, partisan identification, and average political ideology), who donated to her campaigns (total contributions, total corporate contributions, and total labor contributions), and how well she did in her last election (most recent margin of victory).[9] If the relationship between class and roll call voting in figure 2.1 was the result of some other lurking characteristic of legislators or their strategic environments, it should have disappeared in this analysis.

It did not. Table 2.1 lists the coefficients for the occupational measures in my statistical models (to save space, I have relegated the coefficients for the control variables to the online appendix). Because the occupational measures are proportions, the estimates in this table can be thought of as the expected difference (on a 0 to 100 scale) between a lawmaker who previously worked exclusively in the job in question (e.g., business owner) and a lawmaker who previously worked exclusively in the omitted category (lawyer). (For instance, in model 1, the 4.02 in the "Technical professional" row indicates that the average DW-NOMINATE score among legislators who worked exclusively as technical professionals was 4.02 points out of 100 higher or more conservative than the average DW-NOMINATE score of the legislators who worked exclusively as lawyers.) Even after taking into account many alternative explanations—party, constituency, campaign donations, and so on—legislators from different classes still appeared to vote differently in ways that mirrored the social class gaps that public opinion scholars have observed for decades. Legislators who spent more of their professional careers as business owners or executives or as technical professionals had significantly higher, more conservative DW-NOMINATE scores than

Table 2.1 Class and Economic Voting in Congress, 1999–2008

	1	2	3
	(Rescaled)	Chamber of	(Rescaled)
Economic voting measure	DW-NOM	Commerce	AFL-CIO
Profit-oriented professions			
Technical professional	4.02[+]	−5.45[+]	−0.38
	(2.30)	(3.14)	(2.24)
Business owner/executive	2.26*	3.04[+]	2.53
	(1.14)	(1.80)	(1.92)
Business employee	1.54	−0.64	0.88
	(1.13)	(1.95)	(1.84)
Farm owner/manager	0.55	7.07*	8.26*
	(1.84)	(3.07)	(3.20)
Not-for-profit professions			
Military/law enforcement	−0.59	−0.94	−1.05
	(1.29)	(2.15)	(2.00)
Lawyer (omitted)	—	—	—
Politician/staff member	−1.04	−2.44[+]	−3.06*
	(0.87)	(1.47)	(1.44)
Service-based professional	−3.07**	−2.91	−2.90[+]
	(1.15)	(1.84)	(1.76)
Working-class jobs			
Worker	−5.66*	−11.55**	−9.65*
	(2.42)	(3.73)	(3.95)
(Controls not reported)			
N	2,626	2,594	2,594
R^2	0.93	0.80	0.93

Note: [+] $p < 0.10$, * $p < 0.05$, ** $p < 0.01$, two tailed. Standard errors are clustered by legislator. Lawyer is the omitted occupational category. Coefficients for control variables and for the "other occupations" category are omitted. All three outcome variables are scaled so that they range from 0 to 100, with higher values signifying more conservative voting.

those who worked exclusively as attorneys (the omitted category); those who spent more of their careers as service-based professionals and blue-collar workers had significantly more liberal voting scores. On the AFL-CIO and Chamber of Commerce scales, farm ownership was significantly associated with more conservative voting, and working-class jobs were associated with significantly more liberal voting. The gaps between lawmakers from different classes were often smaller in these models than in figure 2.1, but the same general patterns were still apparent. With one exception,[10] each of the models reported in table 2.1 suggested that legislators who spent more of their careers in blue-collar jobs tended to vote significantly more liberally than those who spent more of their careers in each of the four professional, profit-oriented occupations.[11]

The social class divisions documented in these statistical models were striking. According to the first model in table 2.1, legislators who worked exclusively in the most progressive occupational group, blue-collar workers, had estimated roll call scores about 10 points (out of 100) more liberal than those who worked exclusively in the occupational group with the most conservative scores, technical professionals. On the Chamber of Commerce and AFL-CIO scales, blue-collar workers and farm owners were estimated to be the most ideologically distinct: legislators who worked exclusively in these occupational categories differed by approximately 18 points on both measures. Although these social class gaps were smaller than the divisions documented in figure 2.1, they were still enormous by legislative voting standards. According to model 1, the average difference between a former blue-collar worker and a former technical professional (the technical professional's roll call score was approximately 10 points more conservative) was more than twice the size of the expected difference between black and white members (whites were 4 points more conservative) and more than one-third the size of the gap between Democrats and Republicans (Republicans were 28 points more conservative). The 10-point class gap was just shy of the 13-point difference between a legislator who represented the most ideologically liberal constituency (by my measure, California's ninth district, which includes portions of the Bay Area, Oakland, Piedmont, and Berkeley) and one who represented the most conservative constituents (Louisiana's seventh congressional district) and the (nonsignificant) 11-point difference between a legislator who represented a district where blue-collar workers made up of majority of their constituents and one who represented a district where business owners or executives were in the majority. It was more than five times the size of the gap between legislators who represented the districts with the highest and lowest median incomes and approximately ten times the size of the gender gap (male legislators were 1 point more conservative) and the gap between Catholic and Protestant lawmakers (less than 1 point). It was larger than the difference between a legislator who represented the most union-dense constituency in the country and one who represented a constituency with no union members (5 points more conservative). And it was larger than the expected gap between the legislator who received the most money from labor unions and the members who received nothing from unions (who were 7 points more conservative).[12]

Moreover, the statistical models reported in table 2.1 assume that class does not influence any of the other variables I have controlled for. If a legislator's occupational background was part of what drove her to identify with her party, to receive campaign contributions from certain groups, or to run for office when and where she did, the models reported in table 2.1 will mistake some of the "class effect" for a "party effect," a "donor effect," or a "constituent effect." (This may well be the case: legislators who spent more of their careers in working-class jobs were more likely to be Democrats; to receive money from labor groups; and to represent constituents who were urban, unionized, Democrats, and liberals.) If anything, the models in table 2.1 probably underestimate how much class matters; they are probably the *lower bound* of the relationship between class and roll call voting.[13]

It is difficult to know which is closer to the truth, this lower bound or the gaps documented in figure 2.1, which does not account for anything else that might influence legislators' choices (this is the *upper bound*, the largest effect anyone could possibly attribute to class). For our purposes, however, a little uncertainty on this point is not a problem. Even if we assume that a legislator's class has no effect on any other aspect of who she is or her strategic environment—even if we take the lower-bound estimates in table 2.1 at face value—the answer to the question at issue in this chapter is the same. Just as citizens from different classes tend to have different views about economic policy, legislators from different classes tend to make different choices when they vote on economic proposals. White-collar professionals in Congress tend to vote as if they are "small businessm[e]n at heart." Lawmakers from the working class tend to vote as if they have "taken . . . [their] experience as . . . millworker[s] to the floor of the United States Congress."[14]

And those differences in voting are large enough to have real consequences. If there were a lobbyist or a wealthy constituent who could move legislators' economic roll call scores by 10 to 18 points, we would probably regard that person as one of the most significant players in Washington politics. When important economic issues are put to a vote in Congress, class matters at least that much—maybe more.

Just as ordinary citizens are less sharply divided by class on social issues, the social class divisions among legislators were considerably murkier when I examined noneconomic measures of how legislators voted. Table 2.2 presents the results of three regression models estimated using the data on legislators' occupations and the control variables from table 2.1. The models in table 2.2, however, predict how legislators scored on three common measures of roll call voting on noneconomic issues: second-dimension DW-NOMINATE scores (which capture the *none*conomic issues in Congress that cut across the traditional left-right divisions on economic

Table 2.2 Class and Voting on Noneconomic Issues in Congress, 1999–2008

	1a	2a	3a
Noneconomic voting measure	(Rescaled) 2nd-dim DW-NOM	(Rescaled) NEA	(Rescaled) ACLU
Profit-oriented professions			
Technical professional	2.81	1.12	−3.58
	(2.75)	(2.63)	(4.10)
Business owner/executive	2.35	3.47[+]	3.39
	(2.02)	(1.82)	(2.22)
Business employee	5.13*	2.29	1.53
	(2.23)	(2.04)	(2.52)
Farm owner/manager	9.51[+]	0.60	12.62**
	(5.27)	(4.39)	(4.06)
Not-for-profit professions			
Military/law enforcement	0.62	−1.30	7.47*
	(3.68)	(2.32)	(3.09)
Lawyer (omitted)	—	—	—
Politician/staff member	−1.07	−1.79	0.87
	(1.83)	(1.52)	(2.22)
Service-based professional	−1.45	−0.83	−5.65*
	(2.27)	(2.08)	(2.86)
Working-class jobs			
Worker	−4.38	−3.06	−14.67*
	(5.53)	(5.18)	(6.38)
(Controls not reported)			
N	2,594	1,565	2,593
R^2	0.84	0.91	0.80

Note: $^+ p < 0.10$, $^* p < 0.05$, $^{**} p < 0.01$, two tailed. Standard errors are clustered by legislator. Lawyer is the omitted occupational category. Coefficients for control variables and for the "other occupations" category are omitted. All three outcome variables are scaled so that they range from 0 to 100, with higher values signifying more conservative voting.

issues), roll call scores computed by the National Education Association (which speak to the possibility that lawmakers from the working class might be less supportive of education), and scores computed by the American Civil Liberties Union.

Progressive reformers sometimes worry that lawmakers from the working class—although more liberal on economic issues—would vote more conservatively on social or moral issues like gay marriage, abortion, and so on. The data suggest that these concerns are probably overblown. In Washington—where public policy is often cast in simple left-right terms—the social class divisions on these three noneconomic issues were actually similar to the social class gaps on economic issues (albeit smaller and less precise). On all three measures (which I have rescaled like the measures in table 2.1—they range between 0 and 100, and lower values signify more liberal votes), legislators who spent more time in working-class jobs tended to be slightly (although usually not statistically significantly) more progressive, that is, farther to the left on the DW-NOMINATE second dimension, more supportive of education, and more progressive on civil liberties issues. When it comes to the economy, Americans have always been divided by class in predictable and understandable ways. However, on noneconomic issues—especially so-called moral issues—the class gap has typically been smaller and more volatile. Although working-class Americans tend to be more conservative on social issues, those views tend to take a backseat to economic considerations in the voting booth (see, for instance, Bartels 2008, chap. 3). Likewise, if legislators from the working class harbor conservative social preferences, they seem to take a backseat to the larger left-right divide in Washington when legislators cast their votes. Like ordinary citizens, legislators routinely vote with class—on economic issues.

Class and Legislative Voting during the Postwar Period

Of course, Congress is an evolving institution. As chapter 1 noted, members of Congress have always been drawn overwhelmingly from the upper class (see figure 1.2). However, we cannot simply assume that class was as important in the 1990s or the 1980s or the 1950s as it is today. Class divisions in public opinion tend to evolve over time (Hout, Manza, and Brooks 1995). During the 1990s, some scholars even argued that historical changes like the rise of the welfare state, the diversification of the occupational structure, and across-the-board increases in living standards had brought about the "death" of class politics in advanced democracies (Clark, Lipset, and Rempel 1993). In the wake of the late 2000s recession and its political aftermath (including the Tea Party movement and the Occupy Wall Street protests), class politics are undoubtedly alive and well in the United States. But we can't simply jump to the conclusion that class has always been important in our legislatures just because class is important today. The decade covered by my original data set was a period of significant economic volatility: income and wealth inequalities soared, a housing bubble burst, a financial crisis ensued, and a Great Recession began. Does class matter as much when the economic climate is calmer? Has class always been a dividing line in Congress, or does the relationship between class and legislative voting fluctuate over time?

Figure 2.2 Class and Legislative Voting in Postwar Congresses

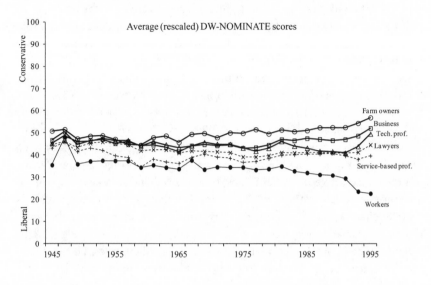

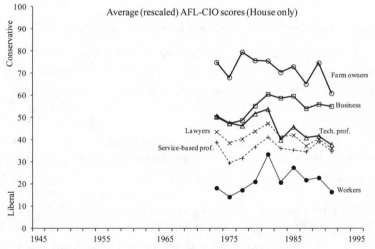

Figure 2.2 uses the *Roster* data set to plot how the average DW-NOMINATE and AFL-CIO scores of legislators from different classes fluctuated in every Congress between 1945 (when World War II ended and large-scale public opinion research began) and 1996 (the last year covered in the data set). Because the *Roster* data set's occupational measures are not as detailed as the measures I collected, I have grouped legislators' former occupations into

seven categories: technical professionals, business owners *and* employees, farm owners, lawyers, politicians (not pictured in figure 2.2 to save space), service-based professionals, and workers. Also, because electronic records of interest group voting scores are scarce for this period, figure 2.2 does not include Chamber of Commerce scores and only includes AFL-CIO scores for legislators in the House of Representatives.

Throughout the postwar period, the relationship between class and roll call voting was remarkably similar to what we see in more recent Congresses. In every Congress since World War II, legislators last employed in working-class jobs (signified by a thin black line) had more liberal average DW-NOMINATE scores than legislators from profit-oriented professions (signified with thick black lines). With the exception of one term in the late 1940s and another in the late 1960s, the gaps were always equivalent to at least 10 percent of the DW-NOMINATE scale, that is, 10 points out of 100. And, if anything, they appeared to be growing: from the 1980s to the end of the data set in 1996, the gap between former workers and former farm owners in Congress expanded by about 15 points (although some of this difference was undoubtedly driven by the well-documented polarization between Republicans and Democrats; see McCarty, Poole, and Rosenthal 2006, chap. 2). AFL-CIO scores in the House followed a similar trajectory. From the 1970s (when the AFL-CIO first began calculating scores) through the 1990s, members of Congress from the working class consistently had scores at least 20 points more liberal than legislators who had been businesspeople or technical professionals and at least 40 points more liberal than those who had been farm owners.

As in my more recent data set, these class-based differences in legislative voting do not appear to be the result of other differences in legislators' backgrounds or strategic environments. Because the *Roster* data set is so large, I first simply sliced it into smaller groups (i.e., Democrats vs. Republicans, white legislators vs. black legislators) to see whether taking other characteristics into account in that fashion could "explain away" the voting differences between legislators from different classes. The first panel in figure 2.3 plots average rescaled DW-NOMINATE scores for all House members in the *Roster* data set from each occupational background. The subsequent panels plot the same averages but divide members into subgroups based on other factors that might influence their choices: party identification, gender, and race; the legislator's vote margin in the last election; the partisan makeup of the legislator's district (measured as the Republican share of the two-party vote during the last presidential election); and the racial composition, median family income, and median age of the legislator's constituents.[15]

Figure 2.3 Class-Based Differences in Roll Call Voting on Economic Issues in the US House, by Legislator and District Characteristics

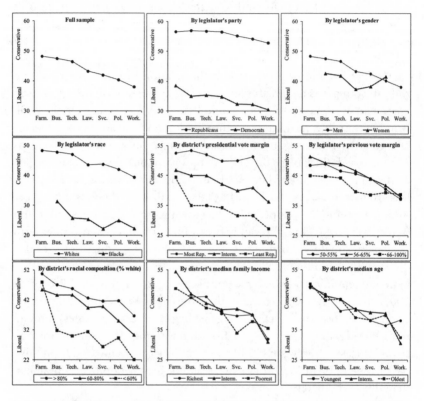

Note: Dots represent average rescaled DW-NOMINATE scores for the group in question. Because of data limitations, the first five panels were based on data from 1901 to 1996, the panel labeled "By district's presidential vote margin" was based on data from 1953 to 1996, and the remaining panels were based on data from 1963 to 1996. Results were omitted if there were fewer than ten observations for a given group in the pooled data set.

Although many of these factors predict striking differences in how legislators vote—see, for instance, the gulf between Republicans and Democrats in the second panel—none of them appears to be behind the social class differences documented in the first panel. Even controlling for the economic makeup of the district did little to account for the social class of the legislator. As the middle panel in the bottom row of the figure illustrates, lawmakers from districts with high and low median incomes differed little in how they voted—the three lines essentially overlap—and distinguishing between rich and poor districts did little to "explain away" the differences between legislators from different classes. Regardless of how I divided the legislators in the *Roster* data set, the same basic pattern emerged: farm owners, businesspeople, and technical professionals tended to vote more conservatively than lawyers, service-based professionals, politicians, and especially workers.

Statistical models that controlled for all of these factors at once reached the same conclusions. Table 2.3 presents the results of two regression models that relate legislators' DW-NOMINATE and AFL-CIO scores to data on their previous jobs and to control variables that captured several of the legislator's other characteristics (party, gender, race, and age); the partisan leanings of the legislator's constituents (the Republican share of the two-party vote during the last presidential election); the racial composition, median

Table 2.3 Class and Economic Voting in Postwar Congresses

	4	5
Economic voting measure	(Rescaled) DW-NOM	(Rescaled) AFL-CIO
Time frame	1963–96	1971–92
Profit-oriented professions		
Technical professional	1.17	2.48
	(0.75)	(2.00)
Business owner/employee	0.99*	2.02
	(0.41)	(1.70)
Farm owner/manager	3.54**	13.14**
	(0.81)	(3.04)
Not-for-profit professions		
Lawyer (omitted)	—	—
Politician/other	−0.04	−0.57
	(0.44)	(1.63)
Service-based professional	−0.82	−2.54
	(0.58)	(1.77)
Working-class jobs		
Worker	−1.47	−4.05
	(1.44)	(3.42)
(Controls not reported)		
N	7,422	4,244
R^2	0.78	0.72

Note: [+]$p < 0.10$, *$p < 0.05$, **$p < 0.01$, two tailed. Standard errors are clustered by legislator. Lawyer is the omitted occupational category. Coefficients for control variables are omitted. Both outcome variables are scaled so that they range from 0 to 100, with higher values signifying more conservative voting.

family income, and median age of the member's constituents; and the legislator's vote margin in the last election.[16]

Taking all of these factors into account at the same time still didn't explain away the relationship between class and economic policy voting in Congress. The coefficients in table 2.3 reflect the average difference between a legislator who last worked in the occupation in question and a legislator who last worked in the omitted occupational category, lawyer. (Similar to table 2.1, the estimate for technical professionals in the first column—1.17—suggests that the average former technical professional's rescaled DW-NOMINATE scores was 1.17 points higher than the average lawyer's score.) Both models in table 2.3 found that legislators who had been farm owners, businesspeople, and technical professionals voted the most conservatively on economic questions; that former workers cast the most liberal votes; and that former lawyers, politicians, and service-based professionals fell somewhere in between. Two occupational groups (business owners/employees and farm owners/managers) were statistically distinct from the omitted category (lawyers), and many were nearly significant. Moreover, both models found that legislators from the working class were significantly more progressive than legislators from profit-oriented professions.

The estimated differences in economic voting in table 2.3 were smaller than those in table 2.1. This may be because the class gap in roll call voting was genuinely smaller from 1945 to 1996 than it was between 1999 and 2008 or, more likely, because the occupational measures in the *Roster* data set are less precise than those in my data set.[17] In either case, the models in table 2.3 suggest that legislators from different classes voted differently on economic issues during the second half of the twentieth century, that the differences in their voting patterns were similar to what we observe in more recent data, and that those differences were not simply the result of other factors that influence how they vote. On the DW-NOMINATE scale, former workers' roll call scores were approximately 3 points out of 100 more liberal than those of former businesspeople and technical professionals and 5 points more liberal than those of former farm owners. On the AFL-CIO scale, the differences were more than twice as large, 7 and 17 points. Legislators from different classes who are otherwise similar—who have similar personal characteristics and who represent similar constituents—tend to vote differently on economic issues.

We can even see these differences when we compare legislators from different classes *who represent exactly the same constituents*. Figure 2.4 plots the results of two simple *matching analyses*. The top panel graphs the *differences* in legislators' DW-NOMINATE scores according to the regression model re-

Figure 2.4 Three Measures of Class-Based Differences in Legislative Voting

Comparing members of Congress from different classes
(controlling for legislator and district characteristics)

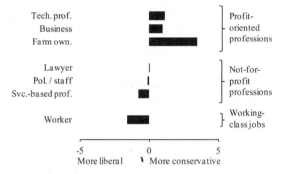

Comparing House members from the same district, the same
party, and different classes (who served back-to-back)

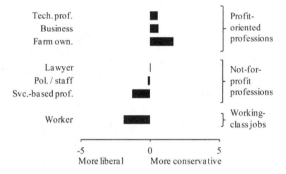

Comparing senators from the same state, the same party, and
different classes (who served at the same time)

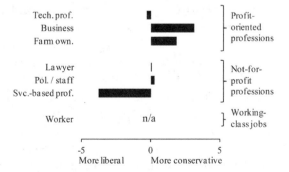

Note: Bars report estimated differences in legislators' (rescaled) DW-NOMINATE scores.

ported in column 4 of table 2.3. The next two panels graph the average differences between legislators from the same party who represented the same state or district but who came from different classes. House members never represent the same constituents at the same time, so I used the *Roster* data set to identify every instance since World War II of a member of the House being replaced (because she resigned, died, or was voted out) by someone from the same party but from a different occupational background. For the Senate, where two legislators represent every state at the same time, I simply identified every case in which the senators from a given state were from the same party but came from different occupations. For both the House and Senate, I then computed the average difference between a lawyer and each of the other occupations (e.g., how much would we expect the representative's DW-NOMINATE score to change if a lawyer replaced or was replaced by a technical professional; how much difference would we expect between a senator who was a lawyer and a senator from the same party and state who was a technical professional).[18] All three panels in figure 2.4 can be interpreted the same way: they display the estimated difference in economic roll call voting between lawmakers from different classes, using lawyers as the reference group.

All three approaches produce the same basic result. Whether we examine regression models with heaps of control variables (which have their drawbacks; see Achen 2005) or simply compare similar legislators from different occupations, the gaps in their voting patterns are almost identical. The history of Congress provides us with relatively few opportunities to make the kinds of comparisons summarized in the matching analysis in figure 2.4; since World War II, only 564 House members fit the criteria (replacing or being replaced by another legislator from the same party but from a different occupation, where one was a lawyer), and there have been only 1,129 instances of two senators from the same state and party but from different classes serving during the same congressional term.[19] Even so, these results were squarely in line with everything else we have seen in this chapter: compared to a lawyer from the same party who represented the same constituency, a former profit-oriented professional tended to vote more conservatively, a former not-for-profit professional tended to vote more liberally, and a former worker tended to vote most liberally of all. Regardless of how we look at the data on economic voting in postwar Congresses, class matters.

Far from being a flash in the political pan, social class divisions in legislative voting on economic issues have been remarkably stable since World War II. They are not recent developments, nor are they "dying" in our legislatures. Class-based differences in citizens' economic preferences have been around at least since the 1940s. So have class-based differences in how legislators vote.

The Enduring Imprint of Class

How long do those differences last, though? When politicians talk about their former jobs, they often suggest that what they did before they held office had a lasting effect on their political perspectives; as John Boehner said of his experience as a businessman in Ohio, "it gave me a perspective on our country that I've carried with me throughout my time in public service." So far, this chapter has assumed that lawmakers do just that, that they continue to act on the political preferences characteristic of their class even after they begin careers in public service. When John Boehner became a politician, the argument goes, he ceased many of his business activities, but he still retained the political perspective characteristic of businesspeople. Likewise, when Edward Beard, the house painter from Providence, was sworn into Congress, he left painting behind, but he continued to see public affairs through the eyes of a blue-collar worker.

Those who are skeptical that the social class makeup of our legislatures matters often argue the opposite, that policy makers—especially those from the working class—forget what it was like to be accountants or scientists or house painters as they get accustomed to being politicians. Congressman Beard was pointedly criticized along these lines from the moment he took office; as one opinion columnist said during his first term, "Beard genuinely earned only $9,000 as a painter before coming to Congress, but now he is learning, like many congressmen, how to live on $57,500 and still not make ends meet" (Kondracke 1977, S9). If politicians enjoy prestige, material comfort, and the many intangible perks associated with white-collar jobs, do they all eventually resemble white-collar professionals, regardless of where they came from? Are those from the working class co-opted—"assimilated and committed to the institutions and values of the dominant socioeconomic group" (Domhoff 1967, 5)—as they trade in overalls and lunch boxes for suits and cloth napkins?

One way to answer these questions is to compare members of Congress who are new to politics to those who have served longer. If lawmakers forget where they came from over time, the differences between legislators from different classes should be large early in their careers, but lawmakers who have been in office a while should act about the same regardless of class.

Figure 2.5 graphs DW-NOMINATE scores for postwar legislators in the *Roster* data set who last worked as farm owners, businesspeople, and

Figure 2.5 The Stability of Class-Based Differences in Legislative Voting

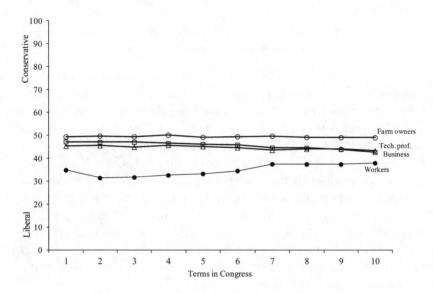

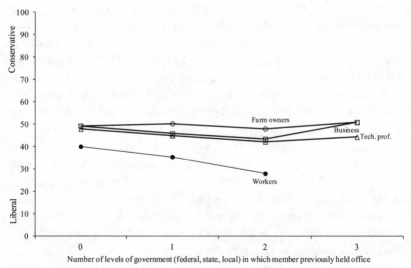

Note: This figure plots average (rescaled) DW-NOMINATE scores for members of Congress who served between 1945 and 1996.

technical professionals (the three professional, profit-oriented occupational categories in the *Roster* file) and workers (the one working-class occupational category). In this figure, legislators are subdivided by two measures of prior political experience: the number of terms the member had served in Congress (top panel) and the number of levels of government—federal, state, and local—in which the member had previously held office (bottom panel).

Neither time in Congress nor work in other political institutions seemed to matter much. As the top panel of figure 2.5 illustrates, the gap between former workers and former profit-oriented professionals is essentially the same (or perhaps even slightly wider) after five terms (ten years) in Congress. In their tenth terms—almost two decades after entering Congress—former workers and former profit-oriented professionals appear slightly more similar than they did when they first took office, but their voting scores are still different. If co-optation occurs, it moves at a glacial pace. The bottom panel of figure 2.5 is even less supportive of the they-forget-their-roots hypothesis. Members of Congress with more prior experience in other political institutions actually appear to be *more* divided along social class lines than those for whom Congress is a first political office.[20]

Statistical models tell the same story. In table 2.4, I have added political experience measures to model 4 in table 2.3 (which captured social class differences in DW-NOMINATE scores in the *Roster* data set, holding constant several of the legislators' other personal traits and strategic considerations). Each model in table 2.4 adds one of the political experience measures from figure 2.5—the number of terms the member had served in Congress in model 6, the number of levels of previous government service in model 7—and the interaction between that measure and each occupational variable. The coefficient for the experience measure itself (–0.16 in model 6, and –0.47 in model 7) tells us how time in office affects all members (the difference is modest). As before, each occupational measure illustrates the difference between legislators from that occupation (e.g., farm owners) and those from the omitted category (lawyers). And the variables that interact experience with occupation tell us how class-based gaps in roll call voting differ for members with more prior political experience (e.g., the –0.15 for "Technical professional × political experience" in model 6 suggests that the 4.12 point gap between former technical professionals and former lawyers shrinks by just 0.15 points every term the member serves).

Like figure 2.5, these statistical models found little evidence that legislators are co-opted by the experience of holding office. Only one occupational experience interaction term was statistically significant; we would

Table 2.4 Class, Political Experience, and Economic Voting in Postwar Congresses

	6	7
	Terms in Congress	No. of levels of gov't prior
Political experience measure	(1–35)	(0–3)
Profit-oriented professions		
Technical professional	4.12**	3.93*
	(1.00)	(1.53)
Technical professional × political experience	−0.15	−0.32
	(0.15)	(0.83)
Businessperson	1.35	3.23**
	(0.94)	(1.22)
Businessperson × political experience	−0.05	−2.01*
	(0.14)	(0.90)
Farm owner/manager	1.43**	1.22
	(0.52)	(0.79)
Farm owner/manager × political experience	−0.11	−0.26
	(0.08)	(0.56)
Not-for-profit professions		
Politician/other	−0.44	0.97
	(0.56)	(1.05)
Politician/other × political experience	0.07	−0.70
	(0.09)	(0.72)
Service-based professional	−0.78	−0.14
	(0.62)	(1.08)
Service-based professional × political experience	−0.02	−0.65
	(0.11)	(0.85)
Working-class jobs		
Worker	−2.60	−2.02
	(1.73)	(2.27)
Worker × political experience	0.16	0.48
	(0.15)	(1.19)
Political experience	−0.16**	−0.47
	(0.06)	(0.31)
(Controls not reported)		
N	7,422	7,411
R^2	0.78	0.78

Note: $^+p < 0.10$, $^*p < 0.05$, $^{**}p < 0.01$, two tailed. The dependent variable in each model is the legislator's rescaled DW-NOMINATE score. Standard errors are clustered by legislator. Lawyer is the omitted occupational category. Coefficients for control variables are omitted.

expect about that much by chance alone. Moreover, most were tiny. Model 6, for instance, suggested that a member of Congress from a working-class job would have to serve seventeen terms (thirty-four years) before the difference in his votes on economic policies would vanish; the average legislator during this period served only five terms.

The original data that I collected are less well suited than the *Roster* data set to measuring changes over time; the time frame for my data set is too

Table 2.5 The Stability of the Working-class Difference, 1999–2008

	8	9	10
Economic voting measure	(Rescaled) DW-NOM	Chamber of Commerce	(Rescaled) AFL-CIO
Profit-oriented professions			
Technical professional	3.46	−6.86*	−0.13
	(2.36)	(3.20)	(2.29)
Business owner/executive	1.77	1.85	2.78
	(1.14)	(1.74)	(1.98)
Business employee	1.58	−0.68	0.83
	(1.12)	(1.95)	(1.86)
Farm owner/manager	0.16	5.98[+]	8.41*
	(1.79)	(3.10)	(3.25)
Not-for-profit professions			
Military/law enforcement	−0.16	0.13	−1.27
	(1.24)	(2.06)	(2.04)
Lawyer (omitted)	—	—	—
Politician/staff member	2.38*	6.17**	−4.81*
	(1.20)	(2.06)	(2.24)
Service-based professional	−3.37**	−3.68*	−2.78
	(1.13)	(1.86)	(1.77)
Working-class jobs			
Worker	−1.35	−9.82	−15.92[+]
	(5.79)	(9.97)	(9.29)
Worker × years in politics	−0.23	−0.15	0.30
	(0.24)	(0.49)	(0.33)
Years in politics	−0.13**	−0.33**	0.07
	(0.03)	(0.06)	(0.06)
(Controls not reported)			
N	2,626	2,594	2,594
R^2	0.93	0.80	0.93

Note: [+] $p < 0.10$, * $p < 0.05$, ** $p < 0.01$, two tailed. Standard errors are clustered by legislator. Lawyer is the omitted occupational category. Coefficients for control variables and for the "other occupations" category are omitted. All three outcome variables are scaled so that they range from 0 to 100, with higher values signifying more conservative voting.

short, and there are simply too few cases to parse the sample in the ways that figure 2.5 and table 2.4 do. However, simpler tests using my data reach similar conclusions. Models 8, 9, and 10 in table 2.5 mirror models 1, 2, and 3 in table 2.1 (the regression analysis using my original data set). In each of the corresponding models in table 2.5, I have simply added a variable that captures the number of years the member worked in politics at any level of government before coming to Congress and a term interacting that measure of political experience with the proportion of the member's career spent in working-class jobs. If working-class people lose their distinctly progressive economic orientation as they spend more time in politics, this interaction term should be positive and statistically significant. It is not. In model 10, the coefficient has the expected sign but falls far short of statistical or substantive significance; in models 8 and 9, the coefficient actually has the opposite sign, suggesting that former workers become more progressive the longer they hold office.

No matter how we look at the data, legislators who have been in office longer seem to be just as divided by class as political newcomers.[21] Policy makers from blue-collar backgrounds change classes when they enter politics, but they do not appear to change their policy perspectives. Neither do business owners, technical professionals, or legislators from other lines of work. The processes that give rise to class-based differences in legislative voting continue to operate long after lawmakers enter public life.

Representational Inequality in "Ayes" and "Nays"

In 2003, Representative Linda Sánchez and Representative Loretta Sánchez became the first sisters to serve in Congress simultaneously. In many respects, the two were similar: they were raised by the same parents, they attended the same schools, their races and genders were the same, they belonged to the same political party, and they both represented mostly Hispanic urban congressional districts in California with similar median incomes and similar partisan compositions. The two sisters differed sharply, however, in one important respect. Representative Linda Sánchez spent nearly all of her precongressional career as a blue-collar worker, labor lawyer, and union organizer. Representative Loretta Sánchez spent nearly all of her precongressional career as a financial analyst in the private sector.

Political observers immediately noticed that the two sisters brought distinct perspectives to office. *Congressional Quarterly*'s profile of Linda Sánchez noted, for instance, that "though they are both Democrats, Linda . . . is no political clone of Loretta. . . . Before coming to the House, Linda practiced civil rights and labor law; Loretta was a businesswoman with an MBA."[22] Indeed, their voting records clearly reflected distinct economic perspectives. Compared to her businesswoman sister, Linda's votes on economic issues were more liberal: from 2003 to 2008, the former union organizer's AFL-CIO scores were 3 points more liberal on average, her Chamber of Commerce scores were 11 points more liberal, and her DW-NOMINATE scores were 7 points (out of 100) further to the left. It is difficult to know whether the two sisters chose different careers because they had different political views to begin with or whether they developed different views in their different careers (or both). Whatever the reason, the labor advocate and the financial analyst thought differently about the government's role in economic affairs—and often voted accordingly.

Congress rarely gives us opportunities to study the behavior of lawmakers whose former occupations are so different and who are so similar in so many other respects. However, the findings presented in this chapter suggest that the differences between Representatives Linda and Loretta Sánchez are typical of the distinctions between lawmakers from different classes. Like ordinary citizens, legislators from the working class tend to favor greater government intervention in economic affairs, whereas lawmakers from professional, profit-oriented occupations tend to support more conservative economic policies. On many (though certainly not all) economic roll calls, they consequently tend to vote differently. These patterns have been remarkably stable over the past several decades and are remarkably stable throughout legislators' careers.

Since the Founding, scholars and political observers have debated whether legislators from different classes behave differently in office. And since the Founding, the defenders of government by the upper class have argued that lawmakers from different backgrounds behave about the same in office. This chapter's analysis of congressional roll call voting provides the first rigorous test of those arguments, the first attempt to bring hard evidence to bear on the question of whether lawmakers from different classes actually behave the same. The evidentiary bar was set high—this chapter analyzed the most constrained form of legislative conduct in the most heavily scrutinized legislature in the world—but the verdict sharply refuted the old idea that our lawmakers' class backgrounds are irrelevant. Contrary to Alexander Hamilton's expectations, the merchant and the mechanic in Congress do not appear to have harmonious views about the government's role in the economy. The unequal numerical or *descriptive representation* of classes in our legislatures promotes inequalities in their *substantive represen-tation*, the extent to which their interests prevail, at least when legislators cast their votes.

It is difficult to say much with certainty about the larger effects of these trends—that is, how policy outcomes might have differed if the class com-position of Congress were equal to that of the nation as a whole—because the data used in this chapter focus on individual decisions, not collective choices. Taken at face value, however, the results presented here suggest that class-based differences in individual legislators' choices likely have sig-nificant consequences in the aggregate. Although the average member of Congress in my original data set voted with the AFL-CIO approximately 53 percent of the time, a regression model like the one in the third column of table 2.1 suggests that if the class composition of Congress were identi-cal to that of the nation as a whole, the average member would have sup-ported the AFL-CIO's position between 58 percent of the time (if the model is estimated with controls, as in table 2.1) and 79 percent of the time (if it is estimated without controls), which translates into approximately one to six more major progressive economic policy outcomes in each Congress (assuming that the AFL-CIO supports approximately two dozen bills every two years).[23] Similarly, whereas the members of Congress in my data set voted with the Chamber of Commerce an average of 67 percent of the time, regression models suggest that a class-balanced Congress would have voted with business interests on just 49 percent (without controls) to 62 percent (with controls) of bills, which translates into about one to four fewer major probusiness policies in each Congress. Class-based differences in legislative voting on economic issues—coupled with inequalities in the social class makeup of Congress—appear to matter enough to push policy in a con-servative direction on at least a few major economic bills each year. Over the course of the last half century, these inequalities have probably tilted the policy-making process toward conservative economic outcomes on dozens of high-stakes economic initiatives.[24]

Of course, this chapter has focused only on roll call voting, the final stage of the legislative process. Most of the actual work involved in creating public policy takes place long before the votes are cast, in committees and caucuses, in one-on-one interactions, and in the offices of individual mem-bers working to promote a proposal or a cause.

In these prevote stages of the policy-making process, a legislator's actions are often less visible to constituents and less closely scrutinized by party leaders and interest groups. And because legislators face less oversight—and therefore enjoy more leeway—their own views, experiences, and back-

Figure 2.6 Discretion and Class Voting in the US Senate

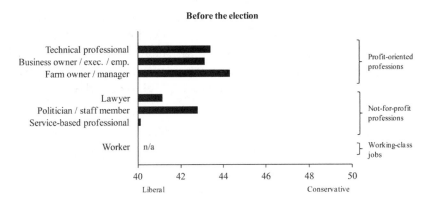

Before the election

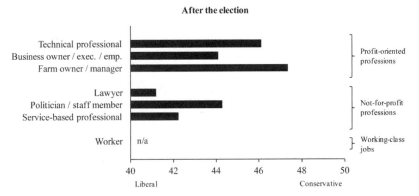

After the election

Note: Bars report estimates from regression models (using *Roster* data from 1963 to 1996) that related senators' (rescaled) DW-NOMINATE score to their previous occupations and to several legislator controls (party, age, race, and gender) and constituency controls (Republican vote share in the last presidential election, percentage white, median age, median income, and senator's own vote share in the last presidential election). Because there were no senators from the working class during this time frame, the workers bar is omitted in this figure.

grounds are likely to matter far more than they do when legislators cast their votes.

Even during the voting stage, discretion seems to bring out legislators' personalities. Figure 2.6 compares class-based differences in senators' DW-NOMINATE scores during the last two years of their six-year terms, when their reelection campaigns are imminent (top panel), and the first two years of their terms (bottom panel), when they have roughly half a decade before they will face the voters again. The differences are crystal clear. As elections near, senators differ less by class when they cast their votes. When elections are a long way off, however, senators have more leeway—and their votes depend more on who they are and where they came from.

In the prevote stages of the legislative process, lawmakers often enjoy this kind of leeway regardless of whether elections are coming up. Analyzing how they vote is a good way to begin understanding the dynamics of class and legislative decision making, but what legislators do before the votes are cast is just as important—and even more sharply divided by class.

THREE

Before the Votes Are Cast

More than three years after we entered the worst economic slump since the 1930s, a strange and disturbing thing has happened to our political discourse: Washington has lost interest in the unemployed. . . . No jobs bills have been introduced in Congress, no job-creation plans have been advanced by the White House and all the policy focus seems to be on spending cuts. So one-sixth of America's workers—all those who can't find any job or are stuck with part-time work when they want a full-time job—have, in effect, been abandoned.

—Paul Krugman, "The Forgotten Millions," March 17, 2011

The best point at which to manage conflict is before it starts.

—E. E. Schattschneider, *The Semisovereign People*, 1960

On January 6, 1983—in the wake of the late 1970s energy crisis and the early 1980s recession—Representative Joseph Minish, a former labor organizer from New Jersey, introduced a bill in the US House entitled the National Development Act. The bill proposed to create a federal corporation that would lend funds to businesses and local governments, help expand job-creating companies and public works projects, and get unemployed Americans back to work. Minish was serious about seeing the proposal through to enactment: the bill was drafted in a way that ensured that it would be referred to the committee he chaired, and he assembled a coalition of eighteen cosponsors, more than the average for the bills that were proposed during that Congress (which averaged nine cosponsors) and the bills that were enacted (which averaged fourteen cosponsors). Despite these efforts, the subcommittee that was assigned to review the National

Development Act of 1983 tabled it after only a single hearing. The bill was never heard from again.

Minish's experience was by no means unusual. Each year, members of Congress introduce thousands of bills. Many care deeply about their proposals and work hard to shepherd them through committee hearings, floor debates, and roll call votes. Most members only occasionally see their legislation enacted, however. More than 88 percent of the almost 138,000 bills proposed between 1979 and 2008 stalled in committee. Just 10 percent were passed in the chamber in which they were introduced, even fewer were passed in both chambers, and fewer still were signed by the president and formally enacted (Adler and Wilkerson 2011).

The bills lawmakers advocate and the process by which their proposals are weeded out collectively constitute a powerful form of *agenda control* in our legislatures. If no legislator is willing to propose a given policy, it cannot be considered or debated. If a policy's sponsor is unwilling or unable to move the proposal through the legislative process, it will never reach the floor, let alone be enacted.

If we wish to understand how lawmakers from different classes differ in office, we cannot simply focus on roll call voting. What happens before the votes are cast is just as important. This chapter explores the relationship between class and *legislative entrepreneurship* on economic issues, the work lawmakers do to guide new economic proposals through the legislative process. Although this work is only a small part of what lawmakers do behind the scenes—which ranges from attending committee hearings and party caucuses to corresponding with constituents and meeting with lobbyists—legislative entrepreneurship is a uniquely illuminating activity. It gives us a clear view of the kinds of problems and policies that are important to lawmakers. It reveals how much of their time and resources they are willing to invest in those issues. And it shows us how much power each lawmaker has over the political agenda in our legislatures.

As with roll call voting, legislators from different classes appear to bring different perspectives when they introduce new economic legislation. Those from the working class are especially energetic: the economic bills they introduce are more progressive, and they invest significantly more effort in them than other members. Like other historically underrepresented groups, however, the concerns raised by lawmakers from blue-collar backgrounds often fall on deaf ears: legislators from the working class must work twice as hard as other members to pass the same number of economic bills. Policy makers from the working class bring a unique voice to the prevote stages of the legislative process, but in our white-collar government, they must shout to accomplish what other politicians can do with a whisper.

Legislative Entrepreneurs

Most of the work involved in the legislative process happens long before a proposal reaches a floor vote. Some legislator or group of legislators must first identify a problem and a suitable policy to address it (Kingdon [1984] 2011). They must then draft a bill that will be appealing to a large number of their colleagues and to key gatekeepers in the legislative process like committee chairs and party leaders. They must keep tabs on the bill as it moves through committees and lobby on its behalf when it faces opposition. They might also help ensure that the proposal receives a warm audience by assembling a coalition of cosponsors and other lawmakers who know about the proposal and who can be trusted to support it. When the bill arrives in a committee or subcommittee, more legislators enter the fray. Committee members research and debate the proposal's merits. They hold hearings with experts. They amend the bill, sometimes substantially. They then recommend how the chamber as a whole should proceed.

Lawmakers expend scarce resources when they participate in these prevote stages of the legislative process (Hall 1996). Legislative entrepreneurs, "advocates for proposals or for the prominence of an idea" (Kingdon [1984] 2011, 122), often incur the highest costs. Designing legislation, building coalitions, tracking bills, and badgering other members take time and energy, two of the scarcest resources a legislator has. They also require staff support and sometimes outside consulting. At various stages of the process, a legislative entrepreneur may have to trade in the intangible currency of favors, for instance, by agreeing to support another lawmaker's position on a different bill in exchange for that legislator's support on her own proposal. By choosing to advocate a given policy, moreover, an entrepreneur links her reputation to the issue (Wawro 2000). Some of these costly activities are sometimes partially offset by sympathetic lobbyists and interest groups, who might help draft legislation, mobilize support both inside and outside Congress, and investigate how various proposals could affect a legislator's chances of winning the next election (Hall and Deardorff 2006; Hansen 1991; Wright 1995). These kinds of assistance seldom go very far, however. Legislative entrepreneurs must usually sacrifice large amounts of their limited resources if they hope to see their proposals succeed.

Their efforts, however, are no guarantee of success. To the contrary, a bill can be defeated at many points in the legislative process. If a committee does not report a bill to the larger chamber (and if it is not discharged from the committee by other means), the bill cannot be considered on the floor. Bills that are reported are placed on the legislative calendar; if they are tabled, filibustered, or scheduled too late in the year, they may never be put to a vote. Bills that come to a vote may be defeated. Those that are passed may not be passed by the other chamber or may not survive the conference committee. Legislative entrepreneurs can take steps to increase the odds that their bills advance through each stage of the process: those who develop greater expertise on an issue (Moore and Thomas 1991), recruit more cosponsors (Krutz 2005), steer their bills to committees on which they serve (Takeda 2000), and make more floor speeches on behalf of their proposals (Anderson, Box-Steffensmeier, and Sinclair-Chapman 2003) are more likely to see their legislation succeed. Even so, the policy-making process does not always reward effort; many legislative entrepreneurs passionately champion their ideas only to see them fall by the wayside time and again.

Because of the high costs and uncertain rewards, lawmakers face important trade-offs when deciding whether to advocate a new issue or proposal. No one can be involved in every fight, and some issues are harder to promote than others. Legislative entrepreneurs must choose their battles carefully.

Scholars of legislative politics have typically focused on three aspects of these choices: *legislative goals*, the policy outcomes legislative entrepreneurs hope to achieve; *legislative effort*, how hard legislative entrepreneurs work to promote their proposals; and *legislative effectiveness*, their ability to move their proposals through various stages of the process. Two legislators with the same goal on some issue may differ dramatically in their willingness to use their scarce resources to advocate that goal. Of course, these differences may not amount to much if neither legislator can keep her proposal trudging forward through the long slog by which a bill becomes a law. To understand legislative entrepreneurs, at a minimum, we must know what they are trying to accomplish, how hard they are working, and how often they succeed.

All three seem to depend in part on who they are. Whereas roll call voting is highly visible, closely monitored by a wide range of interest groups, and easy to translate into punishment at the polls, legislative entrepreneurship often happens behind the scenes, where legislators have considerable discretion and often work on issues and problems that matter to them on a personal level. Legislators sometimes sponsor bills, work on committees, and participate in floor debates in the hope of building reputations that constituents, donors, and interest groups will view favorably (Koger 2003; Weingast and Marshall 1988). However, they can also easily reframe, downplay, or ignore these kinds of activities. When lawmakers decide which legislative initiatives to spearhead and how much effort to devote to them, political considerations are often less important than personal ones (Burden 2007; Hall 1996).

The two most important personal considerations seem to be how much legislators *know* about a given issue and how much they *care* about it. Hall (1996) finds that lawmakers tend to participate in the prevote stages of the legislative process when they have some specialized knowledge about the issue in question or some personal interest in it. Burden's (2007) quantitative analyses and Mayhew's (2000) historical research reach similar conclusions. Krehbiel's (1991) and Fenno's (1973) well-known studies of committee assignments find that expertise and interest in good policy are often central to members' choices. Even Schiller (1995, 201)—who focuses on the external considerations that sometimes compel legislators to introduce bills—acknowledges that the main driver of legislative entrepreneurship is "a set of personal and political goals that stem from [a legislator's] personal interests."

As a result, many of the same demographic characteristics that predict how legislators think and vote also predict the kinds of bills they introduce. Black lawmakers work harder than their white colleagues to promote legislation on issues that affect the black community (Bratton and Haynie 1999). Women in our legislatures work harder to promote legislation on women's issues (Little, Dunn, and Deen 2001; Swers 2002). Religious lawmakers work harder to promote legislation on religious issues (Burden 2007, chap. 5). When a legislator takes up a cause and fights for it, we often get a clear view of who she really is and what's really important to her.

Who she is may also be a factor in whether she wins that fight. Lawmakers from the social groups that have historically dominated our policy-making institutions tend to be more effective at moving their proposals through the policy-making process, whereas legislative entrepreneurs from historically underrepresented groups often struggle to influence the political agenda. Black lawmakers are more likely to advocate legislation on racial issues than their white colleagues but are less likely to see their proposals enacted (Bratton and Haynie 1999). Female legislators are more likely to sponsor bills on women's issues but are less likely to move their proposals through the various stages of the legislative process (Takeda 2000, chap. 7). The causes of these inequalities in legislative effectiveness are still something of a mystery to scholars of legislative politics.[1] They could reflect differences in legislative entrepreneurs' abilities to build coalitions or lobby key gatekeepers in the legislative process. They could occur because lawmakers from historically underrepresented groups pursue goals that are less attractive to their colleagues. Or, as one study of the experiences of women of color in Congress suggests (Hawkesworth 2003), they could be the result of prejudice against "outsiders."

Whatever their causes, these inequalities in legislative effectiveness can seriously complicate how a group's interests are represented in the policy-making process. What goes onto the agenda in our legislatures depends on what individual members know about and care about, but it also depends on what the legislature as a whole is willing to consider. When a group is better represented descriptively—when people from that group hold more seats in our legislatures—that group's concerns are voiced more often. However, that doesn't guarantee that other lawmakers will listen. The interests of historically underrepresented groups are often quietly screened out of the legislative process early on, behind the scenes, when almost no one is watching.

The Role of Class

When lawmakers talk about the proposals they've spearheaded, they often point to their occupational or social class backgrounds as the inspirations for their legislative entrepreneurship. In his official biography, Senator Jim Webb—a decorated Vietnam veteran—notes that his work in the military was an important factor in his decision to take the lead on legislation benefiting recent veterans:

> Arriving in the Senate with long experience in military and veterans affairs, on his first day in office Webb introduced a comprehensive 21st century GI Bill for those who have been serving in our military since 9/11, and within 16 months had guided the most significant veterans legislation since World War Two through both houses of Congress.[2]

Representative Sue Myrick's "Issues and Legislation" website discusses her background in business in similar terms:

> As a former small business owner herself, Rep. Myrick understands the challenges facing small businesses. She believes the government needs to get off the backs of business owners and let them spend their valuable time and money creating jobs—not struggling to comply with excessive and expensive

government regulations. . . . Rep. Myrick is committed to passing legislation that gives entrepreneurs incentives to invest and create jobs, and small business owners the resources to expand.[3]

The online biography of Representative Lois Capps—a former nurse—highlights how her "extensive healthcare background informs her work in Congress," saying:

> She is a respected and effective leader in Congress, especially on issues . . . related to public health. Mrs. Capps has successfully spearheaded and passed legislation specifically to: address the national nursing shortage, detect and prevent domestic violence against women, curb underage drinking, improve mental health services, provide emergency defibrillators to local communities, bring CPR instruction to schools, and improve Medicare coverage for patients suffering from Lou Gehrig's disease.[4]

And the online biography of Representative Robert Brady—a former union worker—emphasizes his roots in organized labor and his support for legislation benefiting less privileged Americans:

> Born and raised in Philadelphia, Brady graduated from St. Thomas More High School, found employment as a carpenter and was soon part of the leadership of the Carpenters' union. He continues to be a member of both the Carpenters' and the Teachers' unions. . . . Brady has been an unwavering advocate for legislation that supports the well-being of financially disadvantaged communities. He has sponsored or co-sponsored legislation that promotes affordable housing, as well as strategies to ensure that all Americans have access to quality healthcare and life-saving prescription drugs.[5]

Each of these statements boils down to the same basic idea: legislators from a given class care more about the problems facing that class and are more likely to advocate solutions to those problems (which often benefit the rest of us, too).

The notion that class influences legislative entrepreneurship has never been tested systematically. However, its core assumption—that people care more about the problems that affect their own social class—finds clear support in data on the political attitudes of ordinary Americans. Figure 3.1 uses responses to the American National Election Study (ANES) to plot the percentage of laborers and the percentage of managers and technical professionals who reported that they viewed social welfare or labor issues

Figure 3.1 Occupational Differences in the Percentages of Americans Who Viewed Social Welfare or Labor Issues as the Most Important Problem Facing Our Country, 1960–2000

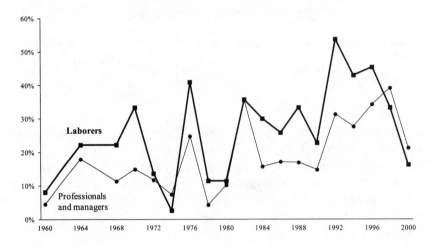

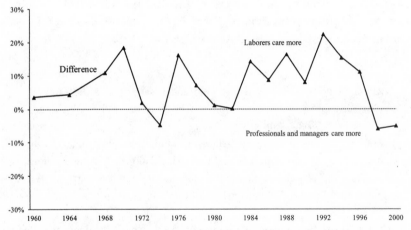

Source: American National Election Studies (2010).

(issue categories created by the ANES that include unemployment, urban decay, unions, health care, and the minimum wage) as the most important problem facing our country. For most of the last half century, workers have been more likely—sometimes dramatically more so—to regard these kinds of bread-and-butter domestic economic issues as paramount. On average, the share of workers who care about these problems has been 7 percentage points higher than the share of professionals, a striking finding considering the open-ended nature of the question.[6] On issues that affect businesses but have less immediate consequences for working-class Americans—issues like foreign investment, tariffs, and international trade deficits—the opposite has been true. During this period, professionals and managers were approximately 12 percentage points more likely than laborers to say that these issues were the most important problems facing our country.[7] For many observers, these findings won't come as much of a surprise. Americans care more about the problems that directly affect people like themselves, people in their own social classes.

If lawmakers have the same tendencies—if they care more about the issues that affect the classes they came from—it should also come as no surprise that "a former small business owner . . . understands the challenges facing small businesses" or that a former carpenter is "an unwavering advocate for . . . the well-being of financially disadvantaged communities." We should expect legislators who have more direct experience with a problem or a policy to invest more effort proposing and promoting bills that address it. Former farmers should care more about the problems facing farm owners and should work harder than other legislators to advocate proagriculture proposals. Former social workers should care more about social programs. Former businesspeople should work harder promoting probusiness proposals. And former blue-collar workers should work harder on legislation that protects the working class.

In light of what we know about the legislative effectiveness of historically underrepresented groups, however, we cannot assume that these efforts will count equally in our legislatures, that legislative entrepreneurs from different classes will be equally effective at passing legislation. Like female and minority lawmakers, lawmakers from the working class have been sharply underrepresented in our political institutions for generations. There are good reasons to suspect that legislative entrepreneurs from the working class may face many of the same obstacles as female and minority legislative entrepreneurs.

In other settings, working-class people who find themselves among white-collar Americans often feel like they don't belong, like they are outsiders in some important sense. Sennett and Cobb's (1973, 20–21) study of workers in Boston in the late 1960s found many examples, including "Frank Rissarro," a former butcher turned bank loan officer who despite being "not in any way ashamed of his working-class past [nonetheless] feels passive in the midst of his success because he feels illegitimate, a pushy intruder." Ryan and Sackrey (1984, 5) recall Rissarro in their pioneering research on college professors from blue-collar backgrounds, who routinely report feelings of "malaise and discomfort" in their "new, higher, station."

For whatever reason, white-collar settings are foreign turf for people from the working class.

If our legislatures are anything like our banks and our universities—if lawmakers from the working class are somehow outsiders in our white-collar government—their efforts to promote new issues and pass new legislation may not go as far. If their careers exposed them to less equal-status contact with managers, owners, and other professionals, they may settle for less in negotiations with members from those backgrounds. If lawmakers from white-collar jobs don't care much about the problems facing working-class Americans, legislators from the working class may face an uphill battle as they attempt to promote legislation that addresses those problems. And if lawmakers from white-collar backgrounds feel some prejudice against working-class people (as some studies maintain; see Beck, Whitley, and Wolk 1999; Naples 1997), they may be less willing to give a legislative entrepreneur from the working class a break. Legislative entrepreneurship on behalf of the working class may be more than simple issue advocacy. It may be a fight.

The rhetoric about lawmakers from the working class often hints at as much. Speaking about trade legislation, Representative Philip Hare—who previously worked in a clothing factory and a labor union—noted "I didn't come out here to be a backbencher. . . . Somebody's got to stand up for the American worker."[8] Former cabdriver Representative Luis Gutierrez's tenacious work on behalf of immigrants and the working class led supporters to dub him "El Gallito," which roughly translates, "the little fighting rooster." Obituaries for Representative Julia Carson—a former waitress, secretary, and union worker—praised her with titles such as "Mourners Bid Adieu to 'People's Champ'" and "Congresswoman Gave Voice to Disadvantaged." Legislative entrepreneurs from the working class are not simply portrayed as "committed to passing legislation" or "respected and effective leader[s]." They are "champs" and "fighter[s]" who "stand up for the American worker" when no one else will. They give a "voice to the disadvantaged" that our political process wouldn't hear otherwise.

Is there any truth to this rhetoric, to the idea that legislative entrepreneurs' goals, effort, and effectiveness differ by class? Just as past research has little to say about the links between class and roll call voting in our legislatures, scholars of legislative politics have been mostly silent about how lawmakers' class backgrounds influence their conduct during the prevote stages of the legislative process. If we wish to understand the differences between legislative entrepreneurs from different classes—and, hence, how inequalities in the social class makeup of our legislatures affect the kinds of issues they tackle—we will simply have to find out for ourselves.

Measuring Legislative Entrepreneurship

As chapter 2 explained, it is relatively easy to measure roll call voting. Roll call data are accurate and publicly available and have been analyzed extensively. Measuring legislative entrepreneurship is far harder. The behavior is open ended, and there is no natural way to quantify it. There are no widely accepted composite scores that capture the ideological content of legislators' policy proposals.[9] No interest groups rate members of Congress on the legislation they advocate, how hard they work to see it passed, or how often they succeed.

Instead, the scholars who study the prevote stages of the legislative process have devised several techniques for measuring legislative participation in general and legislative entrepreneurship in particular. Hall's (1996) approach—using detailed records of committee deliberations, staff interviews, and floor activity to gauge the extent and aim of each member's involvement in the passage of each bill—is the gold standard. As Wawro (2000, 26) notes, however, it is "incredibly costly to obtain" this kind of data, even for a small number of proposals. For larger samples of bills, it is virtually impossible.

A more common alternative is to study legislative entrepreneurship using blunter but more readily available quantitative measures. Activities like proposing legislation and speaking on the floor can be counted and coded relatively easily using legislative research archives like the Library of Congress's THOMAS website. Scholars interested in small subsets of bills often collect original data on the legislators who sponsored or cosponsored them, who worked to promote those bills in committees, and who participated in floor debates (e.g., Burden 2007; Swers 2002). Scholars interested in larger samples of legislation usually limit their attention to the legislators who formally sponsored each bill (Anderson, Box-Steffensmeier, and Sinclair-Chapman 2003; Cox and Terry 2008; Schiller 1995; Takeda 2000; Woon 2008; Whitby 2002). A bill's sponsor is almost always a leader on the proposal: she typically gathers information, builds a coalition, guides the legislation forward, and handles correspondence related to the bill. Unlike other measures of legislative entrepreneurship, moreover, reliable data on the bills members have sponsored are readily available. Focusing on a bill's sponsors can overlook other legislative entrepreneurs who worked to promote the bill and, of course, data on the bills legislators introduce are not the same as data on the bills they would *really like* to introduce (Hall 1992). Nevertheless, for research on large samples of legislation, bill sponsorship data strike a useful balance between quantity and quality.

To measure the links between class and legislative entrepreneurship, I rely here on Adler and Wilkerson's (2011) data on the bills introduced in Congress between 1979 (the first year that bills could have an unlimited number of cosponsors, a rule change that ended the practice of repeatedly introducing the same bill) and 2006 (the last year for which the database currently includes information about the policy issues addressed in each bill). For each bill introduced in each congressional term, Adler and Wilkerson recorded who sponsored the proposal, how many legislators joined as cosponsors, and the main issue addressed in the legislation. To single out the economic proposals, I focused on the bills that Adler and Wilkerson classified as dealing with agriculture; banking, finance, and commerce; community development and housing; education; government operations; labor, employment, and immigration; macroeconomics; social welfare; and transportation.[10]

To measure legislative effectiveness, I simply used Adler and Wilkerson's data to compute the number of economic bills proposed by each legislator that were reported out of committee, the number that were passed in one chamber of Congress, and the number that were ultimately enacted.[11] And to measure legislative effort, I computed the number of cosponsors each legislator recruited for all of the economic bills she introduced in a given Congress. A legislator who introduces a bill has usually already invested a great deal of time and energy in the proposal (Price 1972). However, legislators sometimes introduce bills to appease some constituency or interest group without investing any real effort in them. To avoid counting bills like these, I focused on cosponsorship rates, which tend to reflect how hard a legislative entrepreneur has worked to build support for her proposals (Wawro 2000, 30–31)—and which cannot easily be faked for the sake of appearances.

Measuring members' legislative goals was less straightforward. Adler and Wilkerson's database records the issue area each bill addresses (e.g., macroeconomics) but not which side it takes (e.g., liberal, conservative, middle of the road). Given the sheer volume of the legislation in question (more than 3,600 economic bills were introduced in the 109th Congress alone) and the ambiguity associated with deciding what exactly constitutes a conservative or liberal economic policy, it was not feasible to code the political intent of each bill in this sample independently. Instead, for the small number of economic bills that reached final passage votes on the chamber floor, I computed the *partisan difference* in those votes, the percentage of Republicans who voted yea on the bill minus the percentage of Democrats who did so. Because of data limitations, I could only compute these measures for the 106th through 109th Congresses (1999 to 2006). Very few bills actually reach final passage in any given Congress (of the 36,940 bills introduced during this time frame, just 1,004—or about 3 percent—were eventually put to a vote), so it is difficult to make strong inferences with these data. However, they provide us with a glimpse at the relationship between class and the economic goals legislative entrepreneurs pursue.[12]

To measure the classes that legislators came from, I relied primarily on data from the *Roster of Congressional Officeholders* data set (ICPSR and Mc-Kibbin 1997), the larger but less detailed biographical data set that I used to analyze roll call voting during the postwar period in chapter 2. The *Roster* data set's strength is its breadth: with it, I can analyze legislative entrepreneurship in every Congress from 1979 to 1996. With my smaller but more detailed original data set, I can only study bills proposed between 1999 (when my data set begins) and 2006 (when the bill proposal data end). Measuring legislative entrepreneurship with quantitative data on bill introductions introduces a great deal of statistical imprecision into my analysis—introducing a bill is a good proxy for legislative entrepreneurship, but not a perfect one (Hall 1996, chap. 1)—and I am therefore reluctant to interrogate this subset of my original data as aggressively as I did the whole data set when I analyzed roll call voting (which is measured essentially without error). For the sake of comparison, in the sections that follow, I present statistical models that use both the *Roster* data set and my original data, and I use my data set to analyze the partisan differences in final passage votes on the bills members introduce, which were only available for the time frame covered by my data set. For the most part, however, I focus here on what the larger *Roster* data set can teach us about class and legislative entrepreneurship.

The Policies Legislators Propose

The first lesson seems to be that the economic goals legislative entrepreneurs pursue differ by class in essentially the same way that roll call voting on economic issues differs. Many of the bills that are introduced in Congress are clearly motivated by the social class backgrounds of their authors. Congressman Harold Johnson from California, a former district chair for the Brotherhood of Railway Clerks, frequently introduced nuanced revisions to

Figure 3.2 Partisan Differences in Final Passage Votes on Economic Legislation, by Sponsor's Occupational Background, 1999–2006

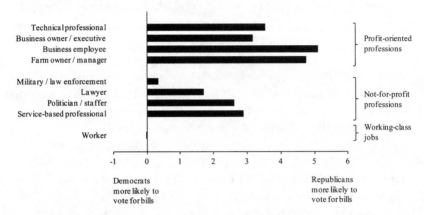

Note: Partisan differences in final passage votes were measured as the percentage of Republicans who voted in favor of the bill minus the percentage of Democrats who did so. For each member, I computed the average partisan difference on all of the bills he or she sponsored that reached a final passage vote. I then averaged these values for lawmakers in each occupational category. *Source:* Adler and Wilkerson (2011); author's data collection.

federal transportation regulations designed to enhance worker safety, such as H.R. 7488, a 1980 bill "to amend title 49 [on transportation], United States Code, to provide additional criminal penalties for safety violations" on the part of employers. Congressman Peter Hoekstra from Michigan, who spent nearly all of his precongressional career as a business executive, often introduced probusiness and antiunion legislation, such as H.R. 2656, a 1997 bill to "prohibit Federal funding for the election of officers and trustees of the International Brotherhood of Teamsters," and H.R. 3098, a 2001 bill to "amend the Internal Revenue Code of 1986 to classify office furniture as 5-year property for purposes of accelerated depreciation."

A more systematic analysis points to the same conclusion. Figure 3.2 plots the average partisan difference in final passage votes on the bills introduced by lawmakers from different classes. As in chapter 2, I have grouped legislators into nine categories (nested in three broader classes) based on detailed information about their occupational backgrounds. The ideological pattern across the three larger categories is fairly straightforward. Like roll call voting, on average, the economic bills introduced by lawmakers from profit-oriented professions—former businesspeople, former farm owners, and so on—were the most conservative. The economic bills proposed by former not-for-profit professionals—former politicians and former service-based professionals such as teachers and social workers—were generally more liberal. And the economic legislation proposed by the one former blue-collar worker who saw a proposal reach a final passage vote between 1999 and 2006 (Congressman Mike Michaud, a former union worker) was more liberal still. It is important to be cautious when interpreting these findings; with so few cases, these results can only be suggestive. Nevertheless, they are squarely in line with the idea that legislative entrepreneurs from different classes pursue different goals.

They also differ in how hard they work to advance those goals. Figure 3.3 uses the *Roster* data set (which has less nuanced occupational categories) to plot the total numbers of cosponsors that legislators recruited for their economic proposals. Viewed this way, lawmakers seem to take the lead on issues they know about from experience, and lawmakers from the working class seem to expend exceptional effort (perhaps to combat biases against their legislative agendas). By this measure, former farm owners worked more than twice as hard as other members to pass agricultural legislation (top left panel). Service-based professionals—an occupational category that includes teachers and social workers—worked substantially harder than any other group on social welfare proposals (bottom row, center column). White-collar professionals of all stripes worked harder to pass legislation on banking, finance, and domestic commerce (top row, center column). And former blue-collar workers worked harder on bills related to labor, employment, and immigration (middle row, right column)—a category with obvious implications for poor and working-class Americans—and government operations (middle row, middle column)—a category that includes a wide range of size-of-government issues as well as bills affecting several federal departments that deal with domestic economic affairs, such as the Department of Labor and the Department of Commerce.

Overall, legislators from the working class appear to deserve their reputation for tenacity. Even when I add up legislative effort across all nine issue areas, no other class of legislative entrepreneurs came close to matching the effort that former blue-collar workers devoted to their economic causes. As the top panel of figure 3.4 illustrates, between 1979 and 1996, the average lawmaker from a white-collar background recruited a total of approximately 60 to 80 cosponsors on her economic bills (or about 10 per bill). The bills introduced by former workers, on the other hand, averaged roughly 150 cosponsors (or about 25 per bill). On economic issues, lawmakers from the working class clearly "didn't come out here to be . . . backbencher[s]."

How did they manage to devote so much more effort to their economic proposals than other legislators? There are only so many hours in the

Figure 3.3 Class-Based Differences in Legislative Effort (Cosponsorship Counts), by Issue Area, 1979–96

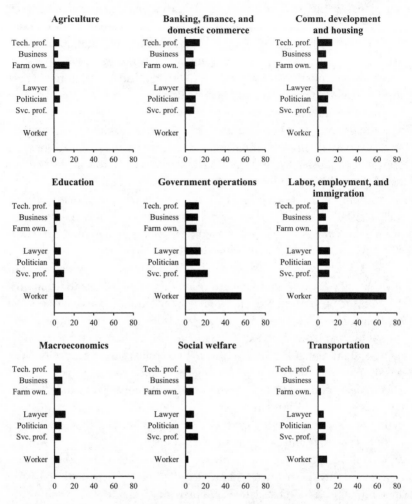

Note: Bars report the average number of cosponsors that the legislators from a given occupation recruited for bills they introduced on the issue in question. *Source:* Adler and Wilkerson (2011); ICPSR and McKibbin (1997).

day—how did lawmakers from the working class recruit twice as many cosponsors? The bottom panel of figure 3.4 suggests an answer: lawmakers from the working class devoted considerably more effort to their economic proposals and considerably less effort to everything else. Whereas their economic legislation tended to attract about twice as many cosponsors as other members' economic bills, their noneconomic legislation tended to attract about half as many. Legislators face trade-offs when they decide which issues to advocate. Those from the working class seem to simply devote more of their limited legislative resources to economic policy.

Many of the class-based differences in legislative effort documented in figures 3.3 and 3.4 fell short of conventional levels of statistical significance, although with such coarse issue categories and such imperfect measures of legislative effort and legislative class, this should hardly come as a surprise. Moreover, most of the gaps in figures 3.3 and 3.4 were still evident in statistical models that controlled for other characteristics besides legislators' class backgrounds. The large difference in legislative effort on economic issues documented in figure 3.4 was especially robust. Figure 3.5 displays the

Figure 3.4. Class and Legislative Effort (Cosponsorship Counts) on Economic and Noneconomic Issues, 1979–96

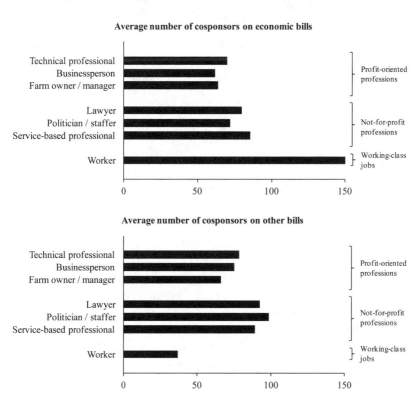

Note: Bars report the average number of cosponsors that the legislators from a given occupation recruited for bills they introduced on the issue in question. *Source:* Adler and Wilkerson (2011); ICPSR and McKibbin (1997).

Figure 3.5. Predicted Legislative Effort (Cosponsorship Counts) on Economic Bills

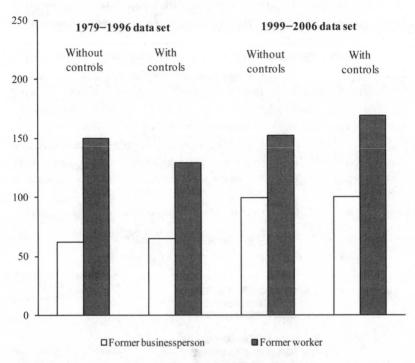

☐ Former businessperson   ■ Former worker

Note: Bars report estimates from negative binomial models (reported in the online appendix) relating cosponsorship counts to legislators' occupational backgrounds, with and without control variables.

numbers of cosponsors on economic bills we would expect a typical former worker and a typical former businessperson (a category that was generally representative of other white-collar professionals in these analyses) to recruit, according to statistical models (negative binomial regressions, which are reported in their entirety in the online appendix).[13] The figure displays results using both the *Roster* data set and the portion of my original data set for which bill proposal data are available. Using each data set, I estimated one statistical model that only related legislative effort to legislators' occupations ("Without controls") and a second model ("With controls") that also controlled for the personal and strategic factors that I controlled for in chapter 2 (e.g., the legislator's party, race, and gender and the partisan, racial, and ideological makeup of her constituents) as well as four other factors that predict legislative effort: how long the legislator has been in office (Campbell 1982; Whitby 2002), whether she chairs a committee

(Wawro 2000), the number of committees she serves on (Schiller 1995), and whether her party is in the majority (Koger 2003; Woon 2008).[14]

Controlling for these other factors made essentially no difference: with or without controls, legislators who previously worked in blue-collar jobs tended to recruit substantially more cosponsors to their economic legislation. The gap between former workers and legislators from other classes often fell just shy of conventional levels of statistical significance, which may reflect the scarcity of legislators from working class or, more likely, the imprecision introduced by using data on cosponsorship counts to measure legislative effort. In general, however, the findings summarized in figure 3.5 were nearly identical to those in figure 3.4. Even after accounting for a wide range of alternative explanations for legislative effort, legislative entrepreneurs from the working class work substantially harder than other members to advance their economic proposals.

The Policies Legislators Pass

If the agenda-setting process in our legislatures were unbiased with respect to lawmakers' class backgrounds—if every legislator who invested a certain amount of effort could expect to pass a certain number of bills—then legislative entrepreneurs from the working class should have passed about twice as many economic bills as other members. If, on the other hand, legislative entrepreneurs from the working class work harder than other members because they have to overcome more hurdles in the agenda-setting process—if they must shout to be heard in our white-collar legislative branch—then despite their exceptional effort, they should have passed about as many bills as other legislative entrepreneurs.

The evidence suggests that they must shout to be heard. Although members of Congress from the working class work twice as hard as other members to pass their economic proposals (at least in the way we can measure, cosponsorship counts), they do not succeed at moving their legislation forward any more often than their colleagues. Figure 3.6 plots the average numbers of economic bills that legislators in the *Roster* data set saw reported out of committee (top panel), passed in one chamber (middle panel), and enacted (bottom panel). In general, passing legislation is extremely difficult: in a typical congressional term, a legislator from the most effective occupational group, lawyers, could expect to see just 0.8 economic bills reported out of committee, 0.7 passed in one chamber, and 0.4 enacted, on average. The enactment rates in these analyses tend to be lower than the passage rates in part because the same bill is sometimes passed under different bill

Figure 3.6. Effectiveness at Three Stages of the Legislative Process, 1979–96

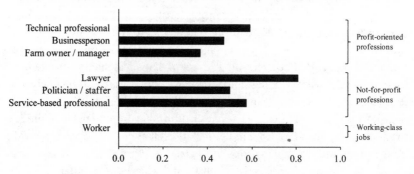

Average number of economic bill proposals reported out of committee

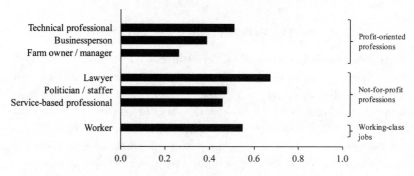

Average number of economic bill proposals passed in one chamber

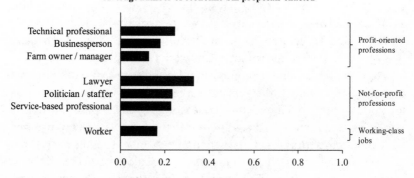

Average number of economic bill proposals enacted

Source: Adler and Wilkerson (2011); ICPSR and McKibbin (1997).

numbers in the House and Senate but enacted under only one of the two numbers. (If H.R. 123 and S. 4 are identical proposals that both pass in their respective chambers and are eventually signed into law, both of the bills will be counted as "reported out of committee" and as "passed by one chamber," but only one will be counted as "enacted."[15]) Even so, passing legislation is clearly an arduous process.

In general, members of Congress who work harder tend to celebrate victory more often (Anderson, Box-Steffensmeier, and Sinclair-Chapman 2003; Krutz 2005; Matthews 1960; Moore and Thomas 1991). Legislative entrepreneurs from the working class, however, seem to face unique obstacles. From 1979 to 1996, former workers saw on average just 0.8 economic bills reported out of committee in each Congress, slightly fewer than the average lawyer and only about 25 percent more than legislators from most other occupational backgrounds. Former workers saw just 0.6 economic bills passed in one chamber and just 0.2 bills enacted, figures that were comparable to those for other members. Despite their exceptional legislative effort on economic issues, lawmakers from the working class were no more likely to see their economic proposals become law than legislators from white-collar backgrounds.

Why don't legislative entrepreneurs from the working class pass more bills? The data do not suggest an easy answer. It isn't that legislators from the working class are bad at building coalitions—they recruit more cosponsors than anyone. And they don't seem to be making other strategic missteps behind the scenes, either. In the *Roster* data set, the average lawmaker from a business background served on 2.3 committees at any given time, about the same as the average lawmaker from the working class, who served on 1.8. About 8 percent of former businesspeople were committee chairs, about the same as former workers, 7 percent of whom chaired committees. Crafting a bill so that it will be referred to your own committee is a good idea: legislators from business backgrounds introduced, on average, 2.7 economic bills per term that were referred to a committee they served on and an average of 0.2 that were referred to a committee they chaired. Legislators from the working class did the same or better: they introduced an average of 4.5 economic bills per term that were referred to committees they served on and an average of 0.2 bills that were referred to committees they chaired.

The most important difference between lawmakers from the working class and other legislators appears to be their legislative goals: they tend to introduce more progressive economic policies than legislators from white-collar backgrounds. However, this ideological difference does not seem to explain the working-class "effectiveness penalty," either. Between 1979 and

1996, the members of Congress from business backgrounds whose DW-NOMINATE scores fell in the most liberal 10 percent of all members enacted more than twice as many bills (0.54, on average) as former workers who were just as liberal (who averaged just 0.24 enactments). Ideology doesn't seem to be behind the gap.

Statistical models that account for a wide range of legislator characteristics point to the same puzzling conclusions. Using a series of negative binomial regressions, I measured how the number of economic bills each legislator in the *Roster* data set advanced through each stage of the policy-making process (committee report, passage in one chamber, and enactment) differed for lawmakers from different classes, controlling for two measures of legislative effort: the total number of economic bills each member proposed and the total number of cosponsors who endorsed those bills.[16] I also controlled for (1) *the personal and strategic considerations* that I controlled for in chapter 2, like the member's party, race, and gender, and the characteristics of the member's constituents; (2) *the four factors that influence legislative effort*—seniority, chairing a committee, serving on numerous committees, and belonging to the majority party—which also influence legislative effectiveness (Anderson, Box-Steffensmeier, and Sinclair-Chapman 2003; Hibbing 1991; Takeda 2000; Volden and Wiseman 2008); and (3) *two other factors that predict legislative effectiveness* (Adler and Wilkerson 2005; Frantzich 1979; Krutz 2005; Moore and Thomas 1991), how ideologically extreme the member is (which I measured by computing the absolute value of the distance between the member's own DW-NOMINATE score and the DW-NOMINATE score of the median member of Congress) and how many of the member's economic bills were referred to her own committees. If there is something wrong with lawmakers from the working class that offsets their exceptional legislative effort—if they aren't senior enough, aren't centrist enough, aren't on the right committees, and so on—the link between class and legislative effectiveness should have disappeared when I controlled for these factors.

Even after accounting for this wide range of explanations, my statistical models (reported in their entirety in the online appendix) suggested that former workers in Congress were less effective at passing legislation than we would expect on the basis of how hard they work. Each regression model found that legislative entrepreneurs from the working class were less likely than other members to see their bills reach the stage of the legislative process in question, and these class-based differences in legislative effectiveness were almost always statistically significant at conventional levels. That is, former workers were significantly less effective at moving bills through

Figure 3.7. Predicted Bill Passage Rates at Three Stages of the Legislative Process, 1979–96

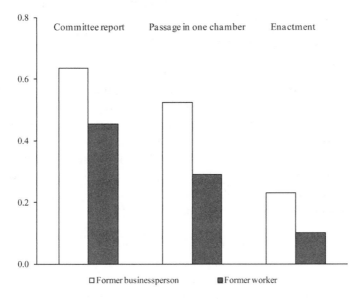

Note: Bars report estimated numbers of bills passed from negative binomial models (reported in the online appendix) relating bill passage counts to legislators' occupational backgrounds and additional control variables. These estimates assume that the legislator proposed ten bills and recruited twenty cosponsors for each one.

each stage of the legislative process than we might expect based on the constituencies they represented, the formal leadership positions they held, how hard they worked, and a host of other factors.

Figure 3.7 illustrates the difference in the number of bills a former businessperson in Congress and a former blue-collar worker could expect to advance to each stage of the legislative process in a given Congress, according to my statistical analysis. The estimates in this figure assume that each member introduced ten economic bills and recruited twenty cosponsors on each proposal.[17] The pattern in the results is unmistakable: legislative entrepreneurs from the working class were less likely than members from business backgrounds (and the other occupational backgrounds not depicted here) to see their bills reported out of committee, passed, and enacted. Although legislative entrepreneurs from the working class build extensive coalitions of cosponsors—and, likely, work harder to support their proposals in other ways not measured here—the bills they introduce are killed off at an exceptionally high rate.

It's possible that their bills are shot down more often because legislative entrepreneurs from the working class fall short in some way that I cannot measure. However, the bulk of the available evidence suggests that these lawmakers are taking the right steps, that they are often coming up empty-handed for reasons beyond their control. Working-class members of Congress are less effective—they pass fewer bills—but they do not appear to be less politically adept in ways that we can measure, that is, less well situated in committees or less capable of assembling legislative coalitions. Something else, something outside of the control of legislators from the working class, seems to be frustrating their policy ambitions.

Identifying the culprit is unfortunately beyond the scope of what I can accomplish with the data in this chapter. Perhaps legislators from white-collar backgrounds don't understand or don't care about the problems facing blue-collar Americans. Perhaps they care, but they care about other issues and policies even more. Or perhaps they don't see lawmakers from the working class as credible policy entrepreneurs; as Carpenter (2010, 830) notes, "where the policy realm . . . is composed of a professional discipline . . . ideas that originate from outside these networks are likely to be resisted."[18]

Although there is no smoking gun yet, the facts of the case are clear enough. Legislators from the working class face unique challenges in the prevote stages of the legislative process, the stages that ultimately determine which issues and problems our legislatures address. By all indications, blue-collar legislative entrepreneurs bring a unique perspective to our legislatures: they introduce more progressive bills, they focus on issues relevant to the needs of ordinary Americans, and they work hard to see their proposals pass. They are rare in most political institutions, however, and their perspectives are weeded out of the legislative process at a higher rate than those of other members. Although their disproportionate effort largely offsets this bias (and may in fact be a response to it), lawmakers from the working class must fight harder than other members to be taken seriously in our white-collar government.

Leaving the Working Class Off the Agenda

How does an idea's time come? Why do some issues rise to the top of the political agenda while others do not? When the congressional scholar John W. Kingdon posed these questions to policy makers in Washington in the late 1970s, few could give him a clear answer. One replied bluntly, "You're the political scientist, not me" (quoted in Kingdon [1984] 2011, 1).

As Kingdon went on to show, ideas have narrow windows of opportunity, and they have the best chances of making it onto the national agenda when they have energetic advocates in the policy-making process who are prepared to fight for them when the political climate, the policy-making environment, and the real-world conditions are right.

What happens, though, when a social group has few or no advocates in our policy-making process, when almost no one in government truly understands the group's needs and perspectives? Kingdon's argument paints a bleak picture of how that group's interests will fare. It is extremely difficult to launch a new idea, to get policy makers interested in a new proposal, and to get the political process to tackle a new problem. Without advocates ready to capitalize on rare windows of opportunity, Kingdon's work suggests that a social group's needs could be largely left off the national agenda.

The findings presented in this chapter support this troubling conclusion. Although the evidence is imperfect, the kinds of class-based divisions that we observed in roll call voting appear to exist in the prevote stages of the legislative process as well, the stages at which problems are identified, proposals are put forth, and the legislative agenda is set. Legislators from different classes bring different concerns and interests to the policy-making process. They focus their efforts on different causes, and they propose legislation that pursues different goals.

If every legislative entrepreneur's efforts were translated into policy outcomes in roughly equal measure, these differences—coupled with the sharp numerical underrepresentation of the working class—would already be bad news for blue-collar Americans. As this chapter has shown, however, the news gets even worse. Legislative entrepreneurs from the working class move about half as many bills through Congress as we might expect on the basis of their legislative effort. Their exceptionally hard work on behalf of their economic proposals largely offsets this bias—they celebrate about as many legislative victories as other members—but the odds are against them from the start.

As with race- and gender-based inequalities in bill passage rates, the causes of these class-based differences in legislative effectiveness are still unclear. Lawmakers from blue-collar backgrounds often claim that they face an uphill battle as they attempt to convince our white-collar legislatures to take the working class's needs seriously. The evidence in this chapter is squarely in line with that idea, but more work will be necessary before we understand exactly why that is.

Regardless of their causes, class-based inequalities in legislative effectiveness have unambiguous consequences for the substantive representation of the working class. By the time members of Congress cast their votes, the bills before them are already sharply slanted in favor of the concerns of white-collar Americans. Lawmakers who care about workers rarely get to show it on the floor; the differences in how legislators from different classes vote on economic proposals (which we saw in chapter 2) probably mask even greater variation in their opinions about economic issues (which we will see in chapter 4). The differences between lawmakers who were business own-ers and those who were blue-collar workers would probably be even greater if more bills introduced by former blue-collar workers made it to the floor, if the legislative agenda focused on more of the issues that working-class Americans care about. By the time the votes are cast, however, the fight has usually been over for months—the working class has lost before it ever had a chance to throw a punch.

In an op-ed column in March 2011 entitled "The Forgotten Millions," Paul Krugman lamented how "no jobs bills [had] been introduced in Con-gress" in the wake of the late 2000s recession and that instead "all the pol-icy focus seem[ed] to be on spending cuts." Krugman characterized these outcomes as "a strange and disturbing thing" and a sign that "Washington has lost interest in the unemployed." The analyses in this chapter suggest that there was nothing "strange"—nothing unusual, unfamiliar, or sur-prising—about them. Lawmakers who are personally acquainted with the realities of working-class life—including the painful consequences of unem-ployment—are rare, and the unique perspectives these lawmakers bring are weeded out of the policy-making process early on. The few lawmakers from the working class can shout for only so long. It should come as no surprise when their voices are drowned out.

FOUR

Class, Opinions, and Choices

The Democratic Congressional Campaign Committee, through a spokeswoman, charged that [Congressman John Boehner] "epitomizes the smoked-filled, back-room, special-interest deal making that turns off voters about Washington." Mr. Boehner . . . and his lobbyist allies ridicule such criticism as politically motivated by desperate Democrats. His actions, they say, simply reflect the pro-business, antiregulatory philosophy that he has espoused for more than three decades, dating back to when Mr. Boehner . . . ran a small plastics company in Ohio.

—"A G.O.P. Leader Tightly Bound to Lobbyists," *New York Times*, September 11, 2010

A man doesn't change a whole lot just because he has been elected to the Senate. If he's been a small-town lawyer, or a banker, or a businessman he is going to think and act like one when he gets to the Senate.

—Washington lobbyist, quoted in Donald R. Matthews, *U.S. Senators and Their World*, 1960

If you follow politics, you've probably heard the accusation: candidate so-and-so is out of touch. He doesn't understand the concerns of people like me. He's a wealthy businessman. He's an ivory tower egghead. He doesn't know how many houses he owns. He gets $300 haircuts. He windsurfs. How could he possibly know what's best for the rest of us? He doesn't even know how a grocery store checkout works.

Accusations like these have a long history in American politics. But should we take them seriously? Are politicians who live privileged lives really so *out of touch,* so oblivious to the needs and views of ordinary Americans? The idea seems to resonate with American voters, at least judging by how often political observers trot it out during campaign season. Then again, lawmakers have vast informational resources—there are legions of constituents, interest groups, and experts who would gladly help affluent lawmakers learn how the other half lives. Are white-collar politicians really so naive about the working class's needs?

My findings in the last two chapters could certainly be interpreted in those terms. When members of Congress cast their votes on economic issues, those who were white-collar professionals often vote like white-collar professionals, and those who were blue-collar workers often vote like blue-collar workers. When members of Congress introduce new economic bills, those from the working class propose more progressive legislation and work harder to see it enacted. Perhaps, one might argue, that's because former white-collar professionals in Congress don't understand the problems facing working-class Americans (and vice versa).

Then again, lawmakers from different classes might behave differently for another reason altogether. As I have argued throughout this book, legislators from different classes might simply have different concerns and different political preferences—they might care about different problems and have different opinions about how to solve them. This explanation is less racy (saying a candidate disagrees with some of her constituents on policy questions will grab fewer headlines than saying a candidate is detached or oblivious), but it fits the findings in chapters 2 and 3 just as well. Even if white-collar lawmakers knew exactly what working-class Americans need and want, they might still choose to work on other issues because they care more about those problems or choose to vote for different policies because they think those policies are better. Lawmakers from white-collar backgrounds might not be uninformed or out of touch—their concerns and opinions might simply be somewhat *out of step* with the concerns and opinions of the working class.

How we make sense of the fact that legislators from different classes behave differently—how we think about the causes of class-based gaps in legislative conduct—is important to our general understanding of class and representation. It is also important as we begin to think about how reformers could promote greater political equality. If social class divisions in how legislators behave are the result of differences in what legislators know, we might be able to close those gaps with the kinds of outreach programs that interest groups already use to educate legislators about the policy preferences of the less fortunate. If, on the other hand, the gaps are the result of differences in what legislators *think*, differences in their opinions about economic policy, reform may be more challenging. Before we can move forward, we need to know whether legislators from different classes behave differently because they don't know what people from other classes want or because they simply prefer other policies. Are they out of touch, or out of step?

Evaluating these competing explanations is no small task. To do so, we need data on lawmakers' class backgrounds and decisions (as in chapters 2 and 3), and we also need a way to measure what's going on inside their heads. This chapter makes the most of the information that exists. To my knowledge, there have been just three national surveys of US lawmakers that have asked about their occupational backgrounds and about how they make decisions on economic issues: a nationwide survey of state legislators conducted in 1995, Project Vote Smart's ongoing state-level *Political Courage Test,* and Miller and Stokes's *American Representation Study,* a one-of-a-kind survey that asked members of the House of Representatives in 1958 a detailed series of questions about their choices in office. These three data sets capture only a sliver of the larger universe of lawmaking in the United States. However, they provide us with a rare glimpse at how legislators' class backgrounds have influenced their decisions over the course of the last half century. And together they tell a coherent story about why class matters in our legislatures.

Part of my argument in chapters 2 and 3 was that lawmakers from different classes bring different opinions or perspectives to public office, that they vote differently and introduce different kinds of bills because they actually think differently about economic issues. In this chapter, I lay out the evidence for this view, for the idea that differences in legislators' opinions— and not the kind of ignorance that politicians often accuse one another of—are behind class-based differences in legislative action. There is little evidence that lawmakers are out of touch with other classes: regardless of where they came from, legislators seem to understand what different classes of constituents want. However, they also bring their own views to the legislative process, and when they have some leeway, they often act on them. Lawmakers from different classes behave differently in office because they are more in step with their own class ideologically—and therefore less in step with other classes that have different opinions about economic issues. Our white-collar government is not ignorant about the needs of the working class. It simply views those needs through white-collar lenses.

Out of Touch, or Out of Step?

Researchers have long recognized that knowledge and opinion are very different things. Knowing means understanding something in some factual sense. Having an opinion means having an attitude or a disposition toward it. The two are obviously related: a person can't have an opinion about something unless she knows at least a little about it (although we all know people who have opinions about things they know *almost* nothing about). However, knowing and having opinions are truly distinct processes: learning new information and forming favorable or empathetic views actually engage different parts of our brains (Keysers 2011). Being out of touch with a group, not knowing about its concerns or opinions, is truly distinct from being out of step with it, not sharing those views.

Often it can be hard to tell the difference, however—especially in the world of politics, where many decision makers keep their motives close to the vest. If a legislator votes for a bill that makes corporations worse off, did she do it because she didn't know how the bill would affect them, or because she believed that the bill's benefits outweighed the costs that companies would have to shoulder? Was she out of touch with the corporate community, or was her opinion on this issue just out of step with what companies wanted? If a legislator votes against a proposal to increase the minimum wage, did she do it because she didn't know how hard it is to make ends meet on the old minimum wage? Or did she understand the realities of living on the minimum wage but still think that increasing it would be bad public policy? Was she out of touch with low-wage workers, or was her opinion just out of step with what they want? Lawmakers seldom give us straight answers to questions like these.

Up front, it may not matter much; regardless of the legislator's motives, she voted the way she did, the bill's fate was what it was, and the effect on the group was the same. In the long run, however, an out-of-touch lawmaker and an out-of-step lawmaker pose very different challenges. If a legislator is just out of touch with a group, that group may be able to educate her about its needs. The group can write letters to the legislator, issue press releases, write policy memos, and so on. If what the legislator knows (or doesn't know) is the problem, the group may have a fighting chance. If the legislator's own views are out of step with the group's preferences, however, the odds that she will be kinder to the group in the future are considerably slimmer. Lawmakers seldom change their minds—they "die in their ideological boots," as one scholar put it: "once elected to Congress, members adopt an ideological position and maintain that position throughout their careers" (Poole 2007, 435). A group facing an out-of-step legislator may not be able to do much with the standard tools of lobbying and issue advocacy; interest groups are better at mobilizing their friends than converting their enemies (Hall and Wayman 1990), and elections seem to be more useful for replacing out-of-step legislators than changing their minds (Lee, Moretti, and Butler 2004). The group's only option may be to try to replace the legislator with another candidate who shares its goals.

Determining why lawmakers from different classes behave differently, then, is about more than just understanding why a legislator's background might influence her behavior in office.[1] The unequal social class makeup of our legislatures tilts the policy-making process in favor of outcomes that are more in line with the needs of white-collar professionals and less in line with the needs of working-class Americans. However, if lawmakers from a certain class tend to behave a certain way simply because of what they know—because they are in touch with their own class and out of touch with others—it might be possible to offset the bias against the working class by simply educating former white-collar professionals in Congress about the needs of working-class Americans. The standard tools that working-class advocates already use might just need to be amplified: there might simply need to be more proworker organizations writing more white papers and more constituents writing more letters explaining how the proposals before their lawmakers will affect the working class. On the other hand, if legislators from different classes have different political preferences and priorities, trying to educate or persuade them may not accomplish much. Reducing the policy bias against the working class may require more significant change. It may require electing more lawmakers who share the working class's political opinions. It may require giving working-class Americans a real seat at the table.

Existing evidence generally supports this more difficult alternative. Although politicians often accuse one another of being out of touch with ordinary Americans—of not knowing what they want or what they need—our legislatures are actually astoundingly well equipped to keep lawmakers informed about their constituents. Members of Congress receive hundreds of letters, phone calls, and e-mails from citizens every day. If they want to know what other constituents think, they can survey the people they represent, or they can review any of the hundreds of political opinion surveys that are conducted every year. If they want an organized group's perspective, they can easily speak to any of the thousands of interest groups that have permanent offices in Washington, DC, or read those organizations' published reports. Legislatures are *designed* to provide lawmakers with information (Krehbiel 1991; Mayhew 1974a). Members can ask a committee to hold hearings to solicit expert input. They can assign their staff members to do research for them. They can turn to one of Congress's nonpartisan research divisions, like the Government Accountability Office (GAO), which employs droves of talented statisticians, scientists, and the like. They can even employ outside consultants to sift through the information for them.[2] When legislators want to know something, they can usually find the information relatively easily. When lawmakers from different classes vote differently or introduce different bills, most probably know exactly what they're doing.

Some legislators may be out of touch, but most probably simply have different personal views about the issues before them. When a legislator makes a decision, there are many other actors whose views can constrain her choices: constituents, lobbyists, party leaders, colleagues, and so on. Nevertheless, lawmakers sometimes have some leeway. Many of their choices are difficult to trace back to them. Many times, other actors may have conflicting demands that leave lawmakers without a clear best choice. And many legislators are willing to risk angering constituents, party leaders, and interest groups from time to time in order to do what they think is right. As a result, legislators often look inward for guidance—they often choose to do what they think is best. When legislators from different classes behave differently, it may simply be because they have different views and opinions about economic policy.

The scholars who have studied other legislator characteristics like race and gender have generally agreed that differences of opinion are the main reason why lawmakers from different backgrounds tend to make different choices in office. In *The Personal Roots of Representation*, Burden (2007, chap. 2) argues that legislators' policy preferences are the key factor linking their backgrounds and their decisions.[3] In her illuminating study of gender-based gaps in legislative conduct, Swers (2002, 5, 13) attributes those gaps to factors like the "unique experiences of women in relation to the home and the workplace" and the "empathy produced by shared experiences and identification with the interests of a group" (see also Little, Dunn, and Deen 2001; Mezey 1978; Thomas and Welch 1991). In research on the differences between lawmakers of different races and ethnicities, most studies similarly argue that, for instance, "white and black state legislators . . . think about issues related to race and inequality in very divergent ways" (Button and Hedge 1996, 215). Although it is certainly possible that gender- or race-based differences in legislative conduct reflect gender- or race-based differences in what legislators know, most of the available evidence points to the conclusion that these gaps are the result of differences of opinion.[4]

Following suit, many groups interested in advancing the policy goals of women or racial minorities have recently begun complementing traditional education and advocacy activities with programs that attempt to elect more women or racial minorities to public office (e.g., EMILY's List). Educating lawmakers is relatively straightforward, but what lawmakers know isn't always the problem. Sometimes it's what lawmakers believe. And when that can't be changed, it is often more productive to simply try to elect someone else.

Are white-collar lawmakers out of touch with the experiences of working-class Americans, or are their views out of step with what the working class wants? Does the social class bias in lawmakers' choices reflect what they know or what they believe? Should working-class organizations be trying to educate legislators who oppose them, or trying to replace them?

Inside the Mind of a Member of Congress

To readers who closely followed the methodological discussions in the preceding chapters, it will come as no surprise that it is difficult to determine why lawmakers from different classes behave differently in office. Determining *whether* they behave differently required data on their class backgrounds (some of which had to be collected from scratch) and data on their choices in office. To know *why* they do so, we also need additional information that is even harder to come by: data on what legislators are actually thinking.

How can scholars get inside policy makers' heads? The standard tool of modern public opinion research—the political survey—is difficult to use when the subjects are politicians. Lawmakers—and especially members of Congress—have enormous workloads, very little free time, and few incentives to cooperate with scholars interested in probing how they make decisions.

Even with the recent explosion of quantitative research on legislative politics, to the best of my knowledge, there have only been three national surveys of US lawmakers that can shed light on the factors behind class-based differences in legislative conduct. Two are surveys of state legislators. In 1995, a study called the *State Legislative Survey* asked a national sample of state lawmakers about their occupations and their personal beliefs about the government's role in economic affairs (and a variety of other issues). And for the past few years, Project Vote Smart—a nonpartisan, nonprofit organization dedicated to keeping voters informed about elected officials—has collected information about state legislators' work histories and has surveyed candidates for state office about their views on several issues, including economic policy (I focus here on the most recent wave of these *Political Courage Test* surveys, those from 2012, that were administered to legislators in each state's upper chamber).[5] Like most studies of state lawmakers, the *State Legislative Survey* and the *Political Courage Test* do not include information about how legislators voted or the kinds of bills they introduced. At any given time, legislatures in different states are working on different issues and bills, which makes it extremely difficult to create a single measure of state legislators' choices that is comparable across states (Shor and McCarty 2011). Still, these two data sets can tell us a great deal about what lawmakers from different classes know, and what they think.

Research using a third data set can tell us how what they know and what they think affect what they do. In 1958, Warren E. Miller and Donald E. Stokes fielded the *American Representation Study*, a confidential, in-person survey of 146 randomly selected members of the House of Representatives in the outgoing Eighty-Fifth Congress and the incoming Eighty-Sixth. The survey asked dozens of questions—including items about the jobs legislators had, their personal opinions about economic issues, and the groups they kept in touch with. Afterward, Miller and Stokes added objective data on how each legislator voted on various roll calls (but not the bills they introduced, unfortunately[6]) and data on the characteristics of the constituents each member represented. No survey before or since has included as much information about how legislators from different classes make choices about economic issues—no other study can tell us as much about the processes behind class-based divisions in our legislatures.[7]

Just one caveat is in order about the *American Representation Study*: its age. In the 1960s and 1970s, the survey was at the center of a flurry of research on representation and congressional decision making (e.g. Achen 1977; 1978; Alpert 1979; Cnudde and McCrone 1966; Erikson 1978; Eulau and Karps 1977; Gross 1978; Miller and Stokes 1963; Norpoth 1976; Stevens, Miller, and Mann 1974; Stokes 1970; Weissberg 1978). Fifty-some years after it was administered, however, we might wonder whether it can still teach us anything about class and legislative conduct. There are several reasons to think that it can. For one, the class composition of Congress is roughly the same today as it was when the survey was conducted. Figure 4.1 compares legislators' main occupations[8]—the primary measure of a lawmaker's social class in the *American Representation Study*—and my more recent data on the occupational backgrounds of members of the 106th through 110th Congresses (1999 to 2008).[9] Aside from a decrease in former lawyers and an increase in former politicians, the class backgrounds of contemporary members of Congress are roughly the same as those of the legislators who held office a half century ago.[10] The same classes of people who governed Miller and Stokes have governed us ever since.

Figure 4.1 The Occupational Backgrounds of Members of Congress, 1957–60 and 1999–2008

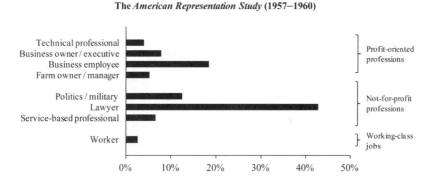

The *American Representation Study* **(1957–1960)**

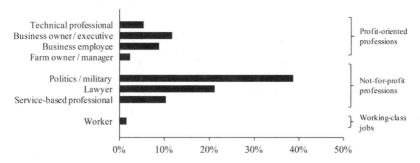

Author's original data (1999–2008)

Note: Several of the occupational categories in the *American Representation Study* are renamed here to correspond to the labels in my data (see chapter 4, note 8). *Source:* Miller and Stokes ([1958] 1984); author's data collection.

Over time, those classes have voted essentially the same, too. The top panel of figure 4.2 plots class-based differences in the *American Representation Study*'s composite economic roll call voting measure (a count of the number of conservative votes each member cast on a set of seven high-profile economic roll calls in each of the two Congresses during the study's time frame).[11] The bottom panel plots class-based differences in AFL-CIO scores (which, when rescaled, can also be thought of as a count of the number of conservative votes each member cast) among the legislators in my original data set (from figure 2.1 in chapter 2). The social class divisions in how members of Congress voted in the 2000s were nearly identical to those in the late 1950s: in both data sets, legislators from profit-oriented

Figure 4.2 Class and Roll Call Voting on Economic Issues, Then and Now

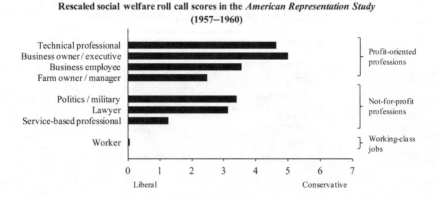

Rescaled social welfare roll call scores in the *American Representation Study*
(1957–1960)

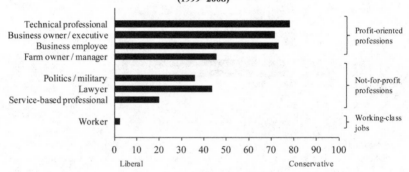

Rescaled AFL-CIO scores in the author's original data set
(1999–2008)

Source: Miller and Stokes ([1958] 1984); author's data collection.

professions tended to vote most conservatively on economic issues, those from not-for-profit professions tended to vote more liberally, and those from the working class tended to vote more liberally still.[12] The *American Representation Study* may be old, but by these measures, we would hardly know it.

Even so, the governing environment has changed in important ways since the 1950s: unions have declined, interest groups have proliferated, media coverage has expanded, the legislative workload has increased, and the cost of campaigning for public office has exploded. However, the basic features of the legislative process that make politicians' own backgrounds so important are still the same. Today's lawmakers routinely face tough choices and competing pressures from a wide range of political actors, just as they did in the 1950s. They often base their decisions on these external influences, but they sometimes base their choices on their own views, just as they did in the 1950s. It should come as no surprise that Miller and Stokes's (1963) classic summary of the *American Representation Study*, "Constituency Influence in Congress," has been cited more than 1,400 times in the half century since it was published—including more than one hundred times in the last year alone. Washington has changed a great deal since the 1950s and 1960s, but legislators face many of the same challenges they faced a half century ago. The *State Legislative Survey* and the *Political Courage Test* may be younger, but the *American Representation Study* still has a lot to teach us, too.

The Importance of Opinions

All three surveys agree on one point: lawmakers from different classes bring distinct political opinions with them to public office. Figure 4.3 plots each survey's measure of legislators' own economic opinions. The *American Representation Study* asked a series of questions about several controversial government spending programs (public housing, public works programs, government investment in atomic power, and federal aid to public schools), which the authors of the study then used to assign each legislator an economic attitude score between zero and four (which I have reversed in figure 4.3, so that higher values signify more conservative views). The *State Legislative Survey* asked a single probing question about economic issues—"[Should we] cut taxes, even if it means deep cuts in government programs?"—and allowed legislators to answer on a 1 to 5 scale, where 1 corresponded to "agree strongly" and 5 corresponded to "disagree strongly." (Again, I have reversed the scale in the figure so that lower values correspond to more liberal positions.) And the *Political Courage Test* asked state legislators whether they would prefer to cut, maintain, or increase funding for several government programs. Figure 4.3 plots the average percentage who said they would maintain or cut spending on four common social programs: K–12 education, higher education, health care, and welfare.[13]

In all three studies, the same basic social class divisions were evident.[14] Regardless of when the survey was conducted, whether it was done at the federal or state level, how it asked about legislators' economic preferences, or whether it was confidential (the *American Representation Study* and the *State Legislative Survey* were, the *Political Courage Test* wasn't), lawmakers from different classes reported having different opinions about the appropriate role of government in economic affairs. Those from profit-oriented professions tended to have the most conservative views. Those from

Figure 4.3 Social Class Divisions in Legislators' Economic Views in the Late 1950s, the Mid-1990s, and the Early 2010s

US House members, 1957–1960

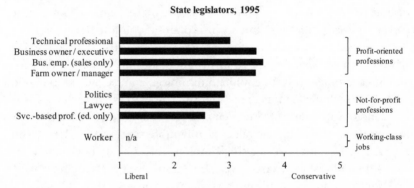

State legislators, 1995

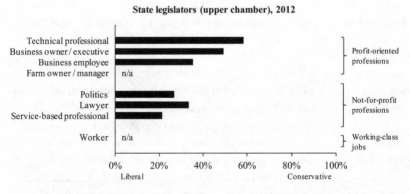

State legislators (upper chamber), 2012

Note: The top panel reports average scores on a series of questions about contemporary economic issues. The middle panel reports average scores on a single question about the trade-off between cutting taxes and providing government services. The bottom panel reports the average percentage of legislators who would prefer not to increase funding to each of four types of social programs. *Source:* Miller and Stokes ([1958] 1984); Carey, Niemi, and Powell (1995); Project Vote Smart.

not-for-profit professions tended to have more liberal opinions. And in the one survey with enough working-class legislators to single them out—the *American Representation Study*—lawmakers from the working class tended to be among the most liberal.[15] The gaps in legislators' opinions were often dramatic: the difference between lawmakers from the most liberal class and those from the most conservative class in the *State Legislative Survey* was more than 20 percent of the possible range of its economic variable. In the *Political Courage Test*, it was close to 40 percent. In the *American Representation Study*, the average legislators from the two most distinct classes differed by more than half of the economic attitude scale.

Moreover, the patterns documented in figure 4.3 were remarkably similar to the differences in roll call voting and bill introductions documented in chapters 2 and 3. They were also remarkably similar to the differences in ordinary Americans' economic perspectives. And they were remarkably stable over time: like ordinary Americans, the differences in the economic views of lawmakers from different classes are essentially the same today as they were in the 1950s.

Like the social class gaps in how legislators vote on economic issues, the gaps in how legislators think about economic issues did not appear to be driven by other factors, like the legislator's party or constituency. For each survey, I estimated statistical models (presented in the online appendix) that controlled for every potential "lurking" variable that was available in the data set (including the legislator's party, by far the best predictor of legislative conduct, and any other personal and political factors the survey had data on). Each statistical model reached the same basic conclusions as figure 4.3.[16] Even after accounting for other factors that might explain why legislators have certain economic views, the economic attitudes of lawmakers from the working class and not-for-profit professionals were significantly more liberal than those of lawmakers from profit-oriented professions in the *American Representation Study* and the *State Legislative Survey*—and the gaps were just shy of conventional significance levels in the *Political Courage Test*.

Did these differences in how legislators think help explain the differences in how they behave? The *American Representation Study* was the only survey of the three that included data on legislators' actual choices. However, it answered the question forcefully: class-based differences in lawmakers' economic attitudes accounted for the entire social class gap in how they voted on economic issues. Figure 4.4 summarizes the results of three statistical models.[17] The first ("No controls") simply measured how liberally or conservatively lawmakers from different classes voted according to Miller and Stokes's composite measure of economic voting, without controlling for

Figure 4.4 Can Legislators' Own Opinions Explain the Social Class Gap in How They Vote on Economic Issues?

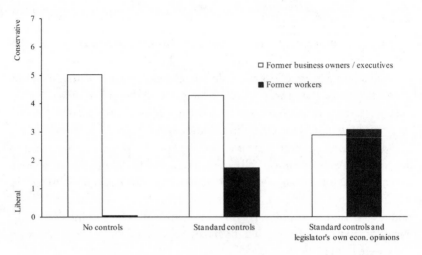

Note: Bars report average predicted roll call scores based on regression models that control for a legislator's last occupation and, where noted, standard controls for other characteristics of the legislator and her constituency and controls for the legislator's own economic policy opinions. The online appendix lists the complete occupational coefficients for each model. *Source:* Miller and Stokes ([1958] 1984).

any other factors. (For simplicity, figure 4.4 plots only the predicted roll call scores of the two classes of lawmakers who tended to vote most differently on economic issues: those who were blue-collar workers before holding office and those who were business owners and executives. Coefficients for all the occupational groups are reported in the online appendix.) The second model ("Standard controls") added additional control variables for several other factors that might influence how a legislator votes on economic issues: the legislator's personal characteristics (party, race, gender, and age), her constituent's characteristics (region, average economic attitudes, Republican vote share in the last presidential election), the legislator's vote margin in her last election, and her perceptions of several characteristics of her district (its racial and partisan makeup). Many of these factors influence how legislators vote on economic issues, and together they helped account for close to half of the gap between how former business owners and former workers in Congress voted on economic issues. Even after controlling for all of these considerations, however, lawmakers from different classes still voted differently.

Controlling for legislators' own views about economic issues accounted for the other half of the gap. The third statistical model summarized in figure 4.4 ("Standard controls and legislator's econ. preferences") controlled for the variables in the second model and the measure of legislators' own views on economic issues from figure 4.3 (as a set of indicator variables). Once I accounted for how lawmakers personally felt about economic issues, the social class gap in how they voted on economic issues vanished. As the third pair of bars in figure 4.4 illustrates, the difference between how the two most economically polarized classes of lawmakers voted was essentially zero (although there were still modest differences between representatives from a few other classes in the full regression model). Lawmakers from different classes tend to think differently about economic issues, and, as a result, they sometimes behave differently in office.

There has never been another survey like the *American Representation Study*, but if a researcher were to replicate it today, she would probably reach the same conclusions about the links between class, opinions, and choices. As chapters 2 and 3 showed, lawmakers from different classes behave differently today, just as they did in the 1950s. As the *State Legislative Survey* and the *Political Courage Test* showed, lawmakers from different classes think differently today, just as they did in the 1950s. And as we know just by listening to modern campaign rhetoric, lawmakers often claim that their backgrounds shape their views and choices today, just as they did in the 1950s. Those from the working class claim that they bring a working-class perspective to office, and those from business backgrounds claim that their "actions . . . simply reflect the pro-business, antiregulatory philosophy" that they developed in that line of work.

The governing environment has changed in important ways in the last half century, of course. However, those changes have not altered two fundamental realities of legislative decision making: lawmakers sometimes base their choices on their own views, and those views are sometimes shaped by the kinds of jobs they had before they held office. Modern lawmakers are ideologically in step with the classes they came from and ideologically out of step with other classes, and they occasionally act accordingly. Just as they always have.[18]

Who's Out of Touch Now?

Of course, there have always been at least a few out-of-touch politicians, too. Being out of touch, however, does not seem to be unique to any particular class. And it doesn't seem to help explain why lawmakers from different classes behave differently in office.

Measuring which legislators are out of touch is naturally challenging. There are no universally accepted indicators, and when people accuse politicians of being out of touch, they seldom specify exactly what that means. The *American Representation Study* and the *State Legislative Survey* each included a few items that seem to tap this concept: items that asked which groups legislators think about when they make decisions, how legislators perceive their constituents, and how legislators spend their time. These measures seem to capture different aspects of what it means to be in touch. None of them, however, help explain why legislators from different classes behave differently in office.

Several of them are not even clearly divided by class. Figure 4.5 plots legislators' responses to a simple open-ended question in the *American Representation Study* that asked which groups or individuals each legislator thought about when deciding how to vote on roll calls.[19] Lawmakers were allowed to list as many groups as they cared to; some mentioned as many as seven. Figure 4.5 plots the percentages of legislators who thought about each of eight classes: farmers, businesses, unions, local businesses, government administrators or service workers, educators, the lower class, and professionals.

If being out of touch means not thinking about a group's needs—and if legislators from one class are out of touch with people from others classes—we would expect the measures summarized in figure 4.5 to be sharply divided by class. Former business owners should have been thinking about the views of business owners and not about the opinions of workers. Former blue-collar workers should have been thinking about the working class, not businesses.

As figure 4.5 illustrates, however, legislative decision making is far more complex. Former farm owners in the House of Representatives gave a lot of thought to farmers—more than half said that farmers' views were important when they cast their votes—but legislators who had been service-based professionals and blue-collar workers also reported that they took farmers' views into account. Most legislators from profit-oriented professions said that they considered the interests of businesses when they cast their votes, but most lawmakers from the working class reported that they took local businesses' interests into account, too. Representatives who had been farm owners and business owners were actually more likely to say that they took the interests of labor unions seriously than representatives from the working class. Legislators tended to report that they thought about their own

Figure 4.5 The Groups House Members Think about When They Cast Their Votes

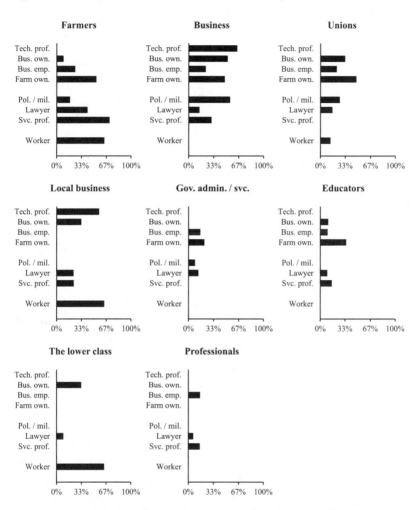

Note: In each panel, the bars illustrate the percentage of House members from each occupational category who said that they regarded the group in question as important when casting their roll call votes. *Source:* Miller and Stokes ([1958] 1984).

class when voting, but many thought about other classes, too. More than 60 percent of the House members from the working class in the *American Representation Study* reported that they considered the interests of the lower class when casting their votes, but most also reported that they considered the needs of farmers and local businesses. More than half of the former business owners in the sample reported that they considered the interests of businesses when they voted in Congress, but roughly a third also reported that they considered the interests of unions and the lower class. By this measure, members of Congress were usually in touch with their own class, but most were also in touch with many other classes, too.

Of course, members of Congress might exaggerate how much they think about certain classes when they make decisions, either intentionally (to appear more evenhanded than they really are) or unintentionally (if they do not realize how out of touch they really are). Figure 4.6 plots three other measures from the *American Representation Study* that are harder to exaggerate. Two asked about the legislator's perceptions of the amount of political activity by unions and businesses in their home district.[20] If legislators from business backgrounds are out of touch with the working class, they may not notice union activity as often and may therefore underestimate the role of unions in politics (and likewise for lawmakers from the working class and business activity).[21] The third measure asked what legislators thought their typical constituent's views were on several economic issues.[22] If legislators are out of touch with other classes, they may systematically mischaracterize public opinion in their districts—perhaps being out of touch means not realizing that constituents from other classes see public policy differently.

As figure 4.6 illustrates, there is little evidence that legislators' perceptions of the role of business and labor in their districts depended on their class backgrounds. Lawmakers were roughly equally likely to perceive business as active regardless of the class they came from, and lawmakers from working-class backgrounds were actually *less* likely than other members to perceive unions as active in their districts.

The one thing legislators from different classes perceived differently was the economic ideology of their constituents. As the bottom panel of figure 4.6 illustrates, lawmakers from the working class tended to perceive their constituents as more liberal, and lawmakers from white-collar professions tended to see them as more conservative, especially lawmakers from profit-oriented white-collar jobs. These differences, moreover, were still evident in statistical models that controlled for the *actual* economic attitudes of each legislator's constituents. In this sense, lawmakers from different classes were out of touch: they tended to exaggerate how much their constituents' views mirrored their own.

However, this perceptual difference did not appear to be responsible for the social class gap in how legislators voted. Figure 4.7 plots the difference between how legislators who were business owners and blue-collar workers voted on economic issues (the same way figure 4.4 did). This time, however, instead of controlling for legislators' own economic opinions, I controlled

Figure 4.6 House Members' Perceptions of Their Districts

Legislators' perceptions of business activity in their districts

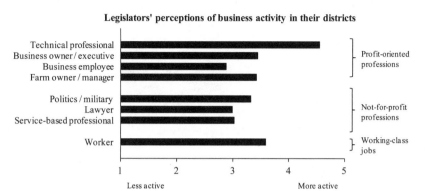

Legislators' perceptions of labor activity in their districts

Legislators' perceptions of constituents' economic attitudes

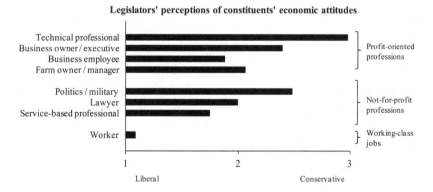

Source: Miller and Stokes ([1958] 1984).

Figure 4.7 Can Measures of Whether Legislators Are "Out of Touch" Explain the Social Class Gap in How They Vote on Economic Issues?

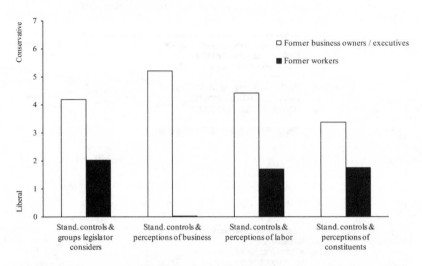

Note: Bars report average predicted roll call scores based on regression models that control for a legislator's last occupation; standard controls for other characteristics of the legislator and her constituency; and, where noted, the groups the legislator thinks about when casting her votes, the legislator's perception of the strength of business or labor in her district, and the legislator's perception of her constituents' views on economic issues. The online appendix lists the complete occupational coefficients for each model. *Source:* Miller and Stokes ([1958] 1984).

for the groups they thought about when voting ("Stand. controls & groups legislator considers"), their perceptions of how politically active business and labor were in their districts ("Stand. controls & perceptions of business" and "Stand. controls & perceptions of labor"), and their perceptions of their constituents' views on economic policy ("Stand. controls & perceptions of constituents"). None of these factors could account for the gulf between how lawmakers from the working class and lawmakers from business backgrounds voted on economic issues. Even the measure of lawmakers' perceptions of their constituents' economic views—which was sharply divided by class—did little to explain why lawmakers from different classes behave differently in office. If legislators really are out of touch with other classes (and the *American Representation Study* doesn't provide much evidence of that to begin with), being out of touch doesn't seem to be behind the differences in legislative conduct documented throughout this book.

More recent measures of whether legislators are in touch with their constituents tell the same basic story. The *State Legislative Survey* did not ask about the groups legislators consider when making choices or about how legislators perceive their constituents, but it did ask several questions about how legislators spend their time that seem to indicate which lawmakers are generally in touch with their constituents. One question directly asked how much time lawmakers spend keeping in touch with their constituents (as opposed to campaigning, drafting legislation, fund-raising, etc.). Another asked how much time lawmakers spend doing casework for constituents. A third question asked how many days state legislators spend in their home districts during a typical week of the legislative session. These measures tapped the most general sense in which lawmakers from one class or another might be out of touch: if legislators from certain classes are less engaged with their constituents overall, we might think that being out of touch was an important part of the social class divisions in our political institutions.

As figure 4.8 illustrates, there were essentially no differences between lawmakers from different classes on any of these measures. Lawmakers who were business owners reported spending just as much time keeping in touch with their constituents as lawmakers who were educators. Those who were lawyers reported doing just as much casework for their constituents as those who were farm owners. Those who were career politicians spent about as much time back in their home districts as those who were business employees.[23]

These lawmakers probably were not exaggerating in the hopes of winning votes. A separate question asked, "When there was a conflict between what you felt was best and what you thought the people in your district wanted, did you think you should follow your own conscience or follow what the people in your district wanted?" More than half of the legislators in the sample indicated that they were more likely to do what they felt was best. These lawmakers were not just pandering to constituents when they answered the survey. They were explaining how they really make decisions in office. And their answers did not reveal any meaningful social class divisions in who was more in touch.

Accusing a politician of being out of touch may sometimes be an effective campaign strategy, and the accusation may sometimes be warranted. But we would seriously misinterpret the social class divisions in legislative conduct documented in this book if we attributed them to white-collar lawmakers simply being out of touch with their working-class constituents, or vice versa. When lawmakers from different classes make different choices, it is not because one class is out of touch overall, or because lawmakers from a given class are ignorant about what other classes of Americans want

Figure 4.8 The Time State Legislators Spend on Their Constituents

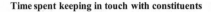

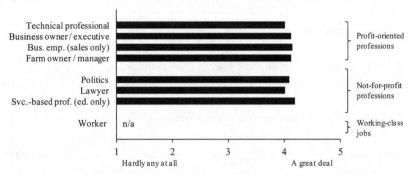

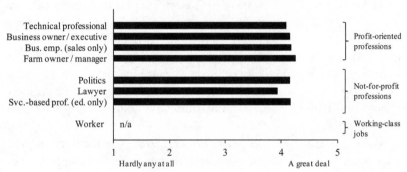

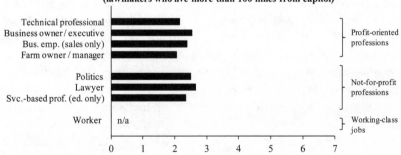

Source: Carey, Niemi, and Powell (1995).

from government. It is because lawmakers from a given class are more ideologically in step with that class and therefore somewhat out of step with others. It is because, as one observer elegantly put it, a lawmaker who has "been a small-town lawyer, or a banker, or a businessman . . . is going to think and act like one" in our legislatures. And that has very different implications than the idea that white-collar lawmakers just don't know enough about the working class.

Out-of-Step Government

American political thinkers have never been seriously troubled by the possibility that a politician might occasionally draw on her own opinions when making choices in office. To the contrary, in *The Federalist #10*, Madison described this process as one of the benefits of representative democracy. The government created by the Constitution, he argued, would

> refine and enlarge the public views, by passing them through the medium of a chosen body of citizens, whose wisdom may best discern the true interest of their country. . . . Under such a regulation, it may well happen that the public voice, pronounced by the representatives of the people, will be more consonant to the public good than if pronounced by the people themselves.

To Madison, the great threat to democracy was not legislators who consulted their own views from time to time, but rather the possibility that "men of factious tempers, of local prejudices, or of sinister designs, may, by intrigue, by corruption, or by other means, first obtain the suffrages, and then betray the interests, of the people." To Publius—and to many democratic theorists before and after him—the Constitution's virtue was that it gave lawmakers enough leeway to use their own judgment, but not so much that they could undermine the public good.

The findings reported in this chapter suggest that Madison's model of delegated authority is less of a normative slam dunk than *The Federalist #10* made it out to be. Our lawmakers are undoubtedly preferable to the "men of factious tempers" Madison described, but they are not the pure "medium . . . of wisdom" he envisioned, either. Political observers like Madison were not troubled by the thought of lawmakers using their own judgment because they assumed that lawmakers would be fair and impartial arbiters of the greater good. Legislators do not, however, simply "refine and enlarge the public views." They bring their classes' political opinions with them to office.[24] Because our legislatures are so imbalanced along social class lines, the opinions of the blue-collar workers who make up the majority of the population are all but excluded from this process. The views lawmakers refine and enlarge are not those of the public; they are those of white-collar Americans. This state of affairs is certainly better than one in which lawmakers base their choices on "local prejudices" and "sinister designs," but it isn't perfect, either.

It is certainly more of a challenge to the ideal of political equality than if white-collar lawmakers were simply out of touch with the working class. Many of the informational techniques that working-class interest groups currently use would be more than enough to educate lawmakers about the conditions facing American workers. Reports, memos, testimonials, and websites only work, however, if lawmakers are willing to learn. If information isn't the problem—if lawmakers from different classes bring different political opinions to office—getting the word out won't do much good. As this chapter has shown, lawmakers from different classes bring different perspectives to public office. And once they get there, they seldom change their minds. If a group wants our legislative process to take the working class's interests to heart, educating white-collar lawmakers probably won't be enough. Giving the working class more of a voice in the legislative process may require getting more working-class Americans into our legislatures.

The stakes are high: as the next chapter illustrates, the shortage of working-class people in public office has real consequences for policy outcomes, consequences that directly and negatively affect the material well-being of working-class Americans. We are right to be thankful that our white-collar lawmakers are not people "of factious tempers" or, for that matter, people who are ignorant about how the other half lives. But the white-collar perspectives that drive their choices still powerfully disadvantage the class of Americans who can least afford it.

FIVE

Economic Policy Making in Class-Imbalanced Legislatures

Individuals, it must be recognized, are of great importance—but their importance stems from their actual or potential relationship to groups. . . . Individual leadership can be understood only in its relationship to group activities.

—Bertram M. Gross, *The Legislative Struggle: A Study in Social Combat,* 1953

It is well to remember that the total outcome, and not just the various members' roll call positions, is what will have consequences for the public which Congress represents. What matters to the prisoner is not how the members of the tribunal voted but whether he is to be released or shot.

—Warren E. Miller and Donald E. Stokes, *Representation in the American Congress,* 1969

In the late 1990s, the New Jersey AFL-CIO launched a program to identify and train union members who were interested in running for public office. The centerpiece of the program was an annual "Labor Candidates School," a two-day course held in mid-August that covered topics ranging from fund-raising and managing campaign staff to targeting voters and developing messages. The school was a runaway success. According to the union, the program currently "enjoys a 76% win rate electing rank-and-file union members to public office for a total of 685 election victories." Graduates of the candidate school serve in virtually every level of the New Jersey government, from fire districts and school boards to county commissions and even the state legislature.

The basic premise of the candidate school is an idea that resonates with the findings outlined in the preceding chapters, the idea that officeholders from different classes bring different perspectives to office, that "no one can represent working families and their unions better than working people themselves." However, most of the materials that the New Jersey AFL-CIO uses to publicize the program focus not on the choices made by individual union-affiliated officeholders, but on the larger legislative victories labor candidates have won. The union does not advertise the voting records of their candidate school graduates or list the bills they have introduced; it focuses on the policies they have helped to enact, from raising the minimum wage and increasing pensions for public employees to reforming worker compensation laws and stopping the outsourcing of state contracts. "As a result of labor's successful program to recruit, train, mentor, and support union members' election campaign efforts," the candidate school website boasts, "labor's success in the legislative arena has grown substantially and many statewide pro-worker policies and laws have been implemented."[1] These legislative accomplishments were, of course, the result of countless individual actions by the lawmakers the program has supported. But those individual actions are not the New Jersey Labor Candidates School's claim to fame. Public policy is what people really care about.

The first goal of this book has been to determine whether lawmakers from different classes bring different economic opinions to the legislative process and make different choices on economic issues. These analyses were an important first step, but they were motivated by a larger and more consequential question, the question of whether the shortage of people from the working class and the overrepresentation of white-collar Americans in our legislatures affect the economic policies our government enacts. To begin understanding the effects of our class-imbalanced political institutions, we needed to know whether individual lawmakers from different classes behave differently in office. To finish answering the question, we need to know whether those individual-level differences actually amount to anything. On the margin, lawmakers from different classes tend to think and vote differently on issues like taxation, social spending, and business regulation. But studying lawmakers' individual choices is no substitute for studying public policy itself (Clinton and Lapinski 2008; Gilens 2012, chap. 2; Hacker and Pierson 2011). Are the social class divisions in how legislators behave large enough to influence policy outcomes? Would the final results of high-stakes economic initiatives really be all that different if our legislatures were made up of the same mix of classes as the people they represent?

The inequalities in the makeup of our legislatures that make these questions worth asking also make them difficult to answer. There are enough individual legislators from the working class that, with a little work, we can see how they differ from other lawmakers. However, entire political institutions made up of large numbers of working-class people are practically unheard of in the United States. In the past hundred years, Congress—the legislature that has been the primary focus of the previous chapters—has never drawn more than 2 percent of its members from the working class (see figure 1.2 in chapter 1). If an institution's class composition never changes, we cannot measure how legislative outcomes differ when different classes rule. We can't say how congressional policy fluctuates when Congress is made up of large numbers of working-class people because Congress has never been made up of large numbers of working-class people.

There are, however, other ways to approach this question. We can use information about how individual members of Congress from different classes behave to project how certain legislative initiatives might have panned out in a more class-balanced version of the institution. Or we can expand our focus to other legislatures—we can compare economic policy across state and local governments, where the social class makeup of legislatures varies considerably from place to place.

This chapter takes both approaches. Using the congressional data from chapters 2 and 3, I simulate whether several recent high-stakes economic policies would have passed if Congress had had the same class composition as the nation as a whole. Using data on states and cities, I also examine the real-world relationship between the social class makeup of a legislature and a consequential and often bitterly contested economic policy, social welfare spending.

The social class divisions in how lawmakers think and behave documented in the preceding chapters add up to a lot in the aggregate. The shortage of people from the working class in our legislatures and the overrepresentation of white-collar Americans means that tax policies are more regressive, business regulations are more probusiness, and social safety net programs are thinner. Who wins and who loses in this country depends in large part on who governs.

Representation and Policy Making

There are at least three factors that determine whether the shortage of people from a given social group will affect the policies that a legislature enacts. The first is just how underrepresented the group is. If a group is dramatically underrepresented, there is a stronger chance that equal representation would change the institution's collective decisions than if the group is just one or two members short. The second is the size of the difference between how legislators from that group behave and how other lawmakers act. If legislators from the group in question vote about the same or introduce the same kinds of bills as other members, the shortage of that group shouldn't affect policy much; if they have different opinions and behave differently, however, the underrepresentation of the group is more likely to affect collective decisions. The third is the relationship between the first two factors, whether the differences between legislators in the group in question and other lawmakers grow or shrink as the group holds more and more seats. When there are more lawmakers from a certain group, their awareness of their shared interests could be heightened. On the other hand, if members of an underrepresented group behave differently because they feel like outsiders, they might actually behave more like other members when they have more seats at the table.

Together, the four preceding chapters strongly suggest that the unbalanced social class makeup of our legislatures has serious consequences for economic policy. As chapter 1 noted, working-class Americans are sharply underrepresented at all levels of government; they make up more than half of the labor market but hold only a tiny percentage of the seats in most political institutions. And as chapters 2 through 4 showed, moreover, lawmakers from different classes differ dramatically in how they think, vote, and advocate on economic issues. Lawmakers from the working class have more progressive views about economic issues, and it shows in how they vote on economic legislation and in the kinds of economic bills they introduce.

There are no obvious reasons to think that these differences would be less pronounced in legislatures that are more balanced by class. To the contrary, political observers have long argued that lawmakers from the working class would stand out *more* if they weren't so outnumbered—that in white-collar institutions like Congress they are often co-opted, "assimilated and committed to the . . . values of the dominant socioeconomic group" (Domhoff 1967, 5). This idea finds some support in the research on other underrepresented groups—when female lawmakers make up larger shares of legislatures, they tend to be more distinct from male lawmakers, not less so (Berkman and O'Connor 1993; Thomas 1991). Some scholars have even argued that underrepresented groups must reach a "tipping point" or a "critical mass" before they start behaving differently and influencing public policy (for a useful review, see Childs and Krook 2008). In legislatures with large numbers of working-class people, lawmakers from the working class might actually behave more differently than they do in institutions like Congress.

Of course, these observations only amount to circumstantial evidence: we can't be certain on the basis of what we've seen in the preceding chapters that the social class divisions in how legislators behave actually affect the policies our government enacts. In American legislatures, collective decisions are not simply the average of individual members' preferences or choices (Krehbiel 1998, chap. 4). There are many plausible scenarios in which adding more working-class people to a legislature would not affect the policies it enacts. If equalizing the social class makeup of an institution reduced overall support for a probusiness bill by 10 percent, that change would only matter if the bill was within 10 percent of the number of votes needed to pass. If the bill had the support of 75 percent of the legislature to begin with—or 25 percent—the change in the institution's class composition would have no impact on the fate of the bill.

Although it seems likely that the social class divisions in lawmakers' choices documented in the preceding chapters are large enough to influence the policies our legislatures enact, we cannot simply make a leap of faith on this point. If we wish to know how our white-collar government influences economic policy, we need to know whether economic policy would be any different in a class-balanced legislature.

What Would a Class-Balanced Congress Have Done?

In the last decade, Congress has passed a flurry of landmark economic legislation. Major tax cuts. Corporate accountability laws. A minimum wage hike. And, of course, the myriad policies enacted in response to the Great Recession: measures to stabilize the housing and financial markets, stimulate economic growth, and extend unemployment and medical benefits.

Would Congress have enacted different policies if it had been made up not of white-collar professionals, but of people whose class backgrounds mirrored those of the nation as a whole? The question is an interesting hypothetical; because the social class makeup of Congress changes so little over time, we cannot directly observe how federal legislation changes when the class composition of the Capitol changes. We can, however, make an educated guess based on how individual lawmakers from different classes behave in office.

When an issue is put to a vote in Congress, every member's ballot counts the same. But what if the weight attached to a member's vote depended on the class she came from? What if the votes of members from overrepresented groups—business owners, lawyers, and other white-collar professionals—counted for less and the votes of members from underrepresented groups like the working class counted for more? Would Congress still have passed the same bills?

The answers to these questions cannot tell us whether Congress would have actually enacted different policies, of course—the legislative process is vast and messy and highly strategic, and we cannot know for certain how lawmakers' incentives might differ in a class-balanced legislature. We can, however, answer a more modest question: Are the class-based differences we see in individual members' choices at least large enough to affect collective decisions in Congress *if we assume* that nothing else about lawmakers' strategic incentives would be different in a class-balanced Congress? Is it at least *plausible* that the social class divisions that we observe in our legislatures could matter in the aggregate?

To find out, I examined data on consequential economic legislation passed between 1999 and 2008, the time frame for which I have original, high-quality data on the social classes that members of Congress came from. To avoid potentially biasing my result by selecting the bills to study myself, I focused on the laws that the congressional scholar David Mayhew has designated *important enactments*. Mayhew identified these bills by searching year-end news accounts of Congress's major accomplishments, which typically appear in the *New York Times*, the *Washington Post*, and a handful of other newspapers and magazines (see Mayhew 2005, 202–4).[2] Using this approach, Mayhew concluded that fifty-six bills passed between 1999 and 2008 were important enactments. Of those, fifteen were directly related to domestic economic policies such as taxation, business regulation, antipoverty programs, or social spending. Table 5.1 lists these fifteen bills and Mayhew's descriptions of them.

Most of the economic legislation on Mayhew's list had relatively straightforward implications for the well-being of different classes of Americans. The bill limiting a company's liability for Y2K-related computer glitches that passed in the 106th Congress shifted responsibility for the harmful effects of computer bugs away from businesses and onto consumers. The post-Enron corporate accountability measure that passed in the 107th Congress created new regulations that limited how a company can conduct business. The minimum wage increase that passed in the 110th Congress was undoubtedly more beneficial to workers than employers (despite measures in the bill that provided tax breaks for small businesses). And the Bush administration tax cuts that passed in the 107th and 108th Congresses were undoubtedly more beneficial to businesses and wealthy Americans (despite modest tax breaks for middle- and working-class citizens).

Not surprisingly, legislators from different classes often voted differently on these fifteen bills.[3] More than two-thirds of the lawmakers who spent most of their precongressional careers as business owners voted against in-

Table 5.1 Important Economic Enactments in Congress, 1999–2008

Years	Bill number	Description	Summary
1999–2000	HR 775	Y2K liability limits	Limited firms' liability for new-millennium computer mix-ups
	S 900	Banking reform	Authorized cross-ownership of banks, brokerages, and insurance companies
	HR 4577	Development tax incentives	Provided $25 billion over 10 years for development in poor locales
2001–2	HR 1836	2001 Bush tax cuts	Provided $1.35 trillion over 10 years, cut rates, phased out the estate tax, eased the marriage penalty, and expanded the child tax credit
	HR 3763	Corporate accountability	Regulated the accounting industry and cracked down on corporate fraud (after the collapse of Enron)
2003–4	HR 2	2003 Bush tax cuts	Provided $350 billion in tax cuts for families, investors, and businesses
	HR 4520	Corporate tax overhaul	Provided $143 billion in tax breaks for businesses over 10 years offset by loophole closures and revenue increases
2005–6	S 5	Class action reform	Shifted class-action suits to federal courts, which made it harder to bring them against businesses
	S 256	Bankruptcy reform	Made it harder for consumers to shed their debts
	HR 4	Pension reform	Shored up often-shaky private retirement programs for 44 million workers and retirees
	HR 6111	Gulf drilling	Opened 8.3 million acres of the Gulf of Mexico to oil and gas drilling
2007–8	HR 2206	Minimum wage increase	Raised the minimum wage to $7.25 per hour and created $4.84 billion in tax breaks for small businesses
	HR 3221	Housing relief	Included $300 billion authorization to ensure home mortgages; rescued and tightened regulation of Fannie Mae and Freddie Mac
	HR 1424	Wall Street bailout	Provided a $700 billion bailout for the financial sector and $150 billion in tax breaks
	HR 5140	Economic stimulus	Provided a $168 billion economic stimulus package, with rebates to taxpayers and tax incentives for business

Source: Mayhew (2005, chap. 2) and http://pantheon.yale.edu~dmayhew/data3.html (accessed August 3, 2010).

creasing the minimum wage to $7.25 per hour; three of the four legislators serving at the time who had worked primarily in blue-collar jobs voted to raise wages. Ninety-two percent of former business owners favored the bill that limited businesses' liability in the event of Y2K-related mishaps, 97 percent favored the 2001 Bush tax cuts, and 86 percent favored the 2003 Bush cuts. None of these bills received a single vote from a legislator from the working class. Of the fifteen enactments, only two—a banking reform measure and the 2008 housing bailout bill—won the support of a majority of both former business owners and former workers.

All fifteen of the these bills passed with strong majorities in our actual, white-collar Congress. If, however, we simply weight legislators' votes differently according to their occupational backgrounds, several of these policies would not have passed in a simulated, class-balanced Congress. Using a procedure similar to the one scholars use to reweight respondents in public opinion surveys, I assigned each legislator who spent at least half of her career in one of the occupational categories from chapters 2 and 3—farm owners and managers, business owners and executives, business employees, technical professionals, military and law enforcement personnel, politicians and staffers, lawyers, service-based professionals, and workers—a simple weight based on the numerical representation of her class in Congress and in the population as a whole (measured using the 2000 census). For instance, lawyers are twenty times more numerous in Congress than in the general public, so I counted each of their votes as just one-twentieth of a vote. Likewise, I counted a vote cast by a legislator from the working class as twenty-five votes, since people from the working class are twenty-five times more numerous in the population as a whole than they are in Congress.[4]

With legislators reweighted in this fashion, six of the fifteen enactments—40 percent of the major economic legislation passed between 1999 and 2008—would not have received a majority vote in my simulated, class-balanced Congress (to say nothing of supermajoritarian voting rules) and therefore would not have become law. All six, moreover, were conservative or probusiness economic policies. The bill limiting businesses' responsibility for Y2K-related computer malfunctions would have received just 34 percent of the vote in a class-balanced Congress. A development tax incentive measure (a Republican-sponsored proposal mostly comprising tax breaks for businesses) would have received only 28 percent of the vote. A Republican-sponsored overhaul of the corporate tax code would have received 39 percent. The $700 billion bailout of the financial sector in 2008—which unions vigorously protested for not doing more to prevent the kind of risky lending that caused the crisis in the first place—would have received just 24 percent of the vote. And the 2001 and 2003 Bush tax cuts—which dramatically shifted the federal tax burden away from rich citizens (see Bartels 2008, chap. 6; Massey 2007, chap. 5)—would have had the support of only 36 percent and 33 percent of the members of a class-balanced Congress. The social class divisions in how legislators vote are indeed large enough to affect the outcomes of some of the most significant economic policies in recent history.

More sophisticated methods of weighting members pointed to the same basic conclusion. One important limitation of the simple approach described above is that by weighting members from different classes differently, it also reweights any attribute that is correlated with class, like the legislator's party or the characteristics of her constituents. The differences between the actual outcome of each bill and the weighted outcome listed above could reflect some other difference that has nothing to do with the class backgrounds of legislators. What we really need to know is whether each bill would have passed in a Congress with a balanced social class makeup *but the same mix of other legislator and constituency characteristics.*

As a simple test, I estimated a series of statistical models (logistic regressions) that related each member's vote on each bill to the proportion of her career spent in each occupational category and to the control variables I used to analyze roll call voting in chapter 2: the legislator's other personal characteristics (her party, age, race, gender, and religion), the characteristics of her constituents (percent urban, percent white, occupational composition, median household income, union membership rate, average partisan identification, and average political ideology), the campaign donations the legislator received (total contributions, total corporate contributions, and total labor contributions), and how well the legislator did in her last election (most recent margin of victory).[5] With this approach, I could estimate whether each bill would pass in a Congress made up of the same mix of classes as the country as a whole while holding constant many of the other factors that influence how members of Congress vote.

Figure 5.1 displays the actual proportion of members of Congress who voted in support of each bill, the proportion who would have supported it in a class-balanced Congress according to my simple reweighting analysis, and the proportion who would have supported it according to this more complex regression-based reweighting approach. (Three of the fifteen bills—bankruptcy reform, pension reform, and the 2008 economic stimulus bill—are omitted here because they were decided on strictly party lines in one or both chambers, which made it impossible to carry out the more complex regression-based analysis.)

Figure 5.1 Estimated Vote Margins on Important Economic Bills in Congress, 1999–2008

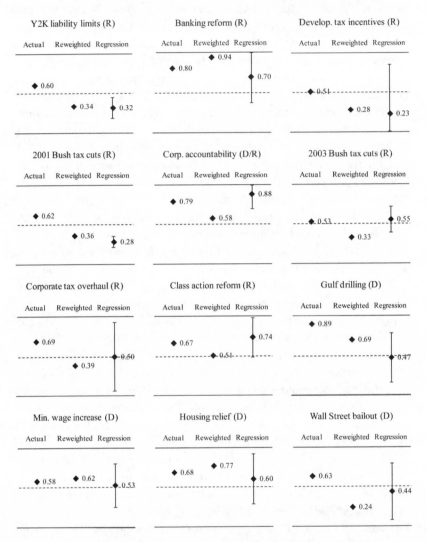

Note: Figures display the actual proportions of members of Congress who voted in favor of each bill, the proportions estimated using a simple reweighting approach, and the estimates from a regression-based approach (with 95 percent confidence intervals represented by vertical lines). The solid line at the top of each panel represents 100 percent support, the dotted line is 50 percent, and the bottom line is 0 percent. The party or parties of each bill's sponsors are noted in parentheses.

Many of the regression-based vote predictions were difficult to estimate precisely—the error bars in many of the panels in figure 5.1 were very large. Across the twelve statistical models these estimates were based on (which are presented in the online appendix), former workers and former business owners were found to vote differently on eight policies, but those differences were only statistically significant for four bills: Y2K liability limits, the 2001 Bush tax cuts, the gulf drilling legislation, and the Wall Street bailout. This was by no means surprising: there were very few working-class legislators in the sample, voting patterns were highly partisan, and the models included many control variables. Extrapolating how a class-balanced Congress would make collective decisions using data on the legislators in a class-*im*balanced Congress is an inherently uncertain exercise.

Despite this uncertainty, the results of my regression-based approach were nearly identical to the results of the simpler reweighting analysis. Of the twelve bills considered here, five of the six that received majority support in the simple reweighting analysis also did so in the more complex approach. Likewise, four of the six policies that did not pass in the simple analysis also did not have majority support in the regression-based estimates: Y2K liability limits, development tax incentives, the 2001 Bush tax cuts, and the Wall Street bailout. And the two bills that failed in the simple reweighting analysis but passed in the regression-based approach—the 2003 Bush tax cuts and the corporate tax overhaul—passed by razor-thin margins. Whether we use a simple weighting scheme or a complex statistical model, a simulated class-balanced Congress would not have enacted many of the conservative economic policies that our actual, class-imbalanced Congress recently passed.

Of course, these findings are only suggestive. What they suggest, however, is striking. Even when high-stakes economic legislation is on the line, lawmakers from different classes think and vote differently. Although we cannot know for certain what would happen if Congress had the same social class makeup as the nation as a whole, the class-based difference in how today's members behave is more than large enough to tip the scales, to change the outcomes of major economic policies. Taken at face value, this analysis suggests that in a class-balanced Congress, businesses probably would have enjoyed fewer tax breaks and would have had to shoulder more of the economic fallout from unforeseeable events. The bailout of the financial sector in 2008 would have looked very different. Perhaps most strikingly, the 2001 Bush tax cuts probably would not have passed. Although these findings are only illustrative, they illustrate how important the individual-level results documented in the previous chapters are. Many economic policies that have had painful consequences for working-class Americans probably exist because white-collar Americans are the ones calling the shots.

When the Working Class Holds Office

Although these findings illustrate that social class gaps in office holding and legislative decision making are large enough to influence policy outcomes, they rest on some big assumptions—they are only projections of how policy *might* have differed in a more class-balanced legislature. They are illuminating, but they are no substitute for data on how economic policy *actually* differs when working-class people play more of a role in government.

One place we can find this kind of data is at the state level. As chapter 1 noted, state legislatures are considerably more diverse than Congress. In some states, lawmakers from the working class make up as much as one-seventh of the membership. State legislatures are by no means identical to Congress, but they have a lot in common with their cousin in DC. States have wide latitude when crafting economic policy, and collectively their choices have enormous consequences. In 2008, state government expenditures totaled more than $1.2 trillion (more than 8 percent of GDP).[6] If the social class makeup of a legislature influences its collective decisions, we should be able to see meaningful differences in economic policy across states governed by different classes of Americans.

Perhaps the most straightforward way to test this idea is to compare how states spend their money.[7] Each year, the Census Bureau's Census of Governments tracks state budgets, disaggregating expenditures into approximately a dozen standardized categories like education, transportation, public safety, utilities, and government administration. With these data, it is easy to see which states have more progressive economic policies and which states' policies are more conservative.

One type of expenditure that clearly distinguishes more and less economically conservative states is social welfare spending. Welfare is a hotly contested issue that engenders direct trade-offs between the material well-being of more and less privileged Americans. It elicits substantial social class divisions in public opinion (Hout 2008). If class matters, it should matter on this issue.

And it does. Figure 5.2 plots the percentage of each state's expenditures that were devoted to social welfare programs against the best available data on the occupational makeup of state legislatures, which were compiled in 1993 and 1995 (Hirsch 1996) by the National Conference of State Legislatures (NCSL).[8] Plotted this way, it is easy to see that state-level spending

Figure 5.2 Welfare as a Percentage of State Expenditures, by the Social Class Makeup of the State Legislature

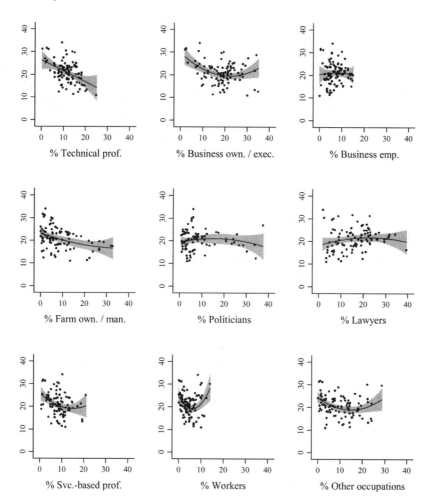

Note: Lines represent quadratic best-fit estimates (with 95 percent confidence intervals shaded gray). For aesthetic reasons, the politicians and other occupations panels each omit a handful of cases in which the state legislature was made up of more than 40 percent lawmakers from the occupational category in question. Excluding these cases did not substantively alter the observed relationship between class and welfare spending.

on social programs in 1994 and 1996 (when budgets enacted in 1993 and 1995 took effect) was strongly correlated with the social class backgrounds of state legislators. States where profit-oriented white-collar professionals— technical professionals, farm owners and managers, and business owners and executives—made up larger shares of the legislature tended to devote less of their resources to social welfare programs. States where working-class people made up greater shares of the legislatures, on the other hand, spent more on the social safety net (despite a modest dip in social spending between states led by legislatures with no workers and those with 5 percent workers). The state with the largest share of legislators from the working class—Maine, which had a 14 percent blue-collar legislature in 1993—de-voted more than 30 percent of its resources to social programs. In contrast, the state where technical professionals made up the largest percentage of any legislature—25 percent in Alaska in 1993—devoted the least to welfare programs, just 11 percent of its budget. In states led by more lawmakers from the classes that tend to favor progressive economic policy, economic policy tends to be more progressive; in states led by lawmakers from more conservative classes, policy is more conservative.

This was true even when I took into account several other factors that influence welfare spending at the state level. States with more fiscal re-sources—measured as per capita personal income or as transfers from other governments—tend to invest more in social spending (Dye 1969; Jennings 1980; Mogull 1978; Orr 1976; Plotnick and Winters 1985). Poverty rates also predict differences in social spending (Fry and Winters 1970; Hicks and Swank 1983; Jennings 1980; Mogull 1993). The party composition of the legislature seems to matter, too (Kousser 2002). And several studies find that states with more racial minorities tend to invest less in welfare (Brown 1995; Kousser 2002).[9]

None of these factors, however, appeared to be responsible for the pat-terns in figure 5.2. Table 5.2 lists the results of two statistical models (or-dinary least squares regressions). The first relates welfare spending rates to data on the occupational makeup of the state legislature, as in figure 5.2.[10] The second also controls for each state's fiscal resources (per capita personal income and total revenues from intergovernmental transfers), the level of demand for social services in the state (the poverty rate), the partisan bal-ance in the state legislature (percent Democrats), the state's racial composi-tion (percent black), and several other control variables (the year, the state's legislative professionalism score, citizens' average partisanship and ideol-ogy, union density, and region).[11] To account for the possibility that states with lower social spending rates could simply be delegating social programs

Table 5.2 Welfare Spending and the Social Class Makeup of State Legislatures, 1993 and 1995

	1	2
Controls?	No	Yes
Profit-oriented professions		
Percent technical professionals	−0.396**	−0.144
	(0.103)	(0.118)
Percent business owners/executives	−0.051	0.047
	(0.122)	(0.130)
Percent business employees	0.107	0.059
	(0.173)	(0.187)
Percent farm owners/managers	−0.199**	−0.109
	(0.067)	(0.097)
Not-for-profit professions		
Percent politicians	0.026	0.158*
	(0.067)	(0.075)
Percent lawyers (omitted category)	—	—
Percent service-based professionals	−0.283+	−0.129
	(0.151)	(0.144)
Working-class jobs		
Percent workers	0.361+	0.532*
	(0.195)	(0.198)
Intercept	26.570**	9.472
	(5.624)	(18.672)
N	100	98
R^2	0.407	0.764

Note: $^+ p < 0.10$, $^* p < 0.05$, $^{**} p < 0.01$, two tailed. The dependent variable is the percentage of state expenditures devoted to social welfare programs. Standard errors are clustered by state. The omitted reference category is lawyer. Coefficients for the control variables and for the other occupations category are not reported.

to counties and cities through intergovernmental transfers, I also controlled for the percentage of local expenditures within each state that were devoted to welfare programs. Like figure 5.2, these models pooled data from 1993 and 1995 (although models estimated separately for each year produced nearly identical results).[12]

Both models in table 5.2 found that states with more working-class legislators and fewer white-collar legislators—especially those from the private sector—tend to invest more in social safety net programs. Because these models relate the percentage of social welfare spending in a state to the percentage of lawmakers from each class, each number in table 5.2 can be thought of as an estimate of how much higher or lower social welfare spending is, on average, in a state with 1 percent more of its legislators from the class in question.[13] The −0.396 next to "Percent technical professionals" in the first column, for instance, suggests that states with 10 percentage points more technical professionals on their legislatures tend to devote 3.96 percentage points *less* of their budgets to social programs.

Technical professionals aren't alone. The estimates in the first model suggested that social spending was significantly lower in states with more legislators from three profit-oriented white-collar professions—farm owners and managers, business owners and executives, and technical professionals—and significantly higher in states with more lawmakers from the working class. Adding controls accounted for some of these differences; the second model found less of a gap between states governed by more profit-oriented white-collar professionals and states led by more not-for-profit white-collar professionals like service-based professionals and lawyers. However, the differences between states with few working-class legislators and states with more were still large and statistically significant. Put differently, even after taking the control variables into account, states with greater shares of working-class legislators still devoted more of their resources to social welfare programs than states led by any other occupational group.[14]

These resource differences were staggering. A 10-point increase in the percentage of working-class people in a state legislature was associated with a 4- to 5-point increase in the percentage of the state budget devoted to welfare programs. A 10-point increase in the percentage of farm owners and managers was associated with a 1- to 2-point decrease in social spending, and a 10-point increase in legislators from technical professions was associated with a 1- to 4-point decrease. Whereas the average state in this sample devoted 21.9 percent of its budget to social welfare, the second model in table 5.2 suggested that if every state legislature in the country had roughly the same occupational makeup as the population as a whole (holding the control variables constant), social spending would be approximately 43 percent of the average state budget, more than twice its current level.[15] California, which devoted 25 percent of its expenditures to social welfare programs in 1996, would have had to allocate an additional $20 billion to reach 43 percent. New Jersey, which spent roughly the national average on social programs, 21 percent, would have had to increase welfare spending by $7 billion. Across all fifty states, the increases necessary to achieve 43 percent social welfare spending would have totaled approximately $152 billion in 1993 and $177 billion in 1995. Taken at face value, the models in table 5.2 suggested that the policy consequences of social class inequalities

Figure 5.3 Economic Policy and the Social Class Makeup of State Legislatures

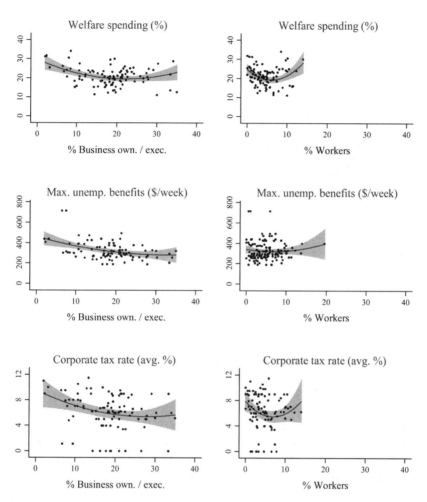

Note: Lines represent quadratic best-fit estimates (with 95 percent confidence intervals shaded gray). Welfare spending and corporate tax rate data are from 1994 and 1996; maximum weekly unemployment benefits data are from 2001.

in state legislatures—and, by extension, the consequences for the material well-being of less fortunate Americans—were enormous.

These patterns, moreover, were not limited to social spending. Figure 5.3 illustrates how two other common economic policies—unemployment benefits and corporate taxation—varied with the social class makeup of

Figure 5.4 Actual and Predicted Welfare Spending in the States, 1993 and 1995

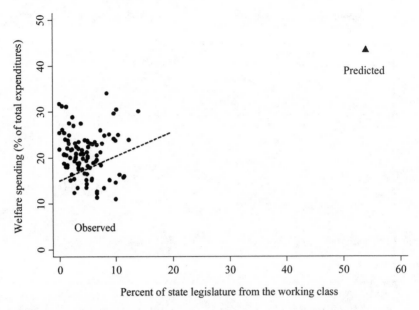

Note: Points labeled "observed" are based on data from the Census of Governments and Hirsch (1996). The dashed line is the best-fit line from a linear regression model estimated with controls for the occupational composition of the state legislature and other determinants of welfare spending (model 2 in table 5.2). The point labeled "predicted" is based on this model and represents the expected spending level for an average state in which legislators' class backgrounds mirror those of ordinary Americans.

state legislatures. The top two panels in the figure simply reproduce the panels from figure 5.2 showing that social welfare spending is lower in states with more legislators from business backgrounds and higher in states with more lawmakers from the working class. The next two panels plot data from 2001 (the earliest year that data were available) on the maximum weekly unemployment benefit level in each state.[16] And the bottom pair of panels plot the average corporate tax rate in each state in 1994 or 1996.[17]

The relationship between class and economic policy was remarkably similar across these three issues. In states where business owners made up more of the legislature, social welfare provisions were more meager, supports for unemployed workers were less generous, and corporations paid less in taxes. In states with more working-class people on their legislatures, social spending was higher, corporations paid higher taxes, and unemployment benefits were slightly more generous. Across the board, white-collar government is good for white-collar Americans and bad for the less fortunate.

Of course, when interpreting results like these, we should bear in mind that one of the central caveats from the previous section still applies to this analysis. Although state legislatures allow us to observe how policy outcomes vary in places governed by different classes of people, we must still extrapolate aggressively when estimating how a class-balanced legislature might behave. No state legislature examined here drew more than 14 percent of its members from the working class. Figure 5.4 replots welfare expenditure percentages in 1994 and 1996 against the percentages of working-class state legislators in 1993 and 1995, this time adding a point representing the predicted level of welfare spending in a class-balanced state legislature (according to the second model in table 5.2). The prediction seems plausible given the trajectory of the observed data. However, the distance between the last actual observation and the predicted data point should give us pause. Even at the state level, we cannot observe a legislature where workers hold office in proportion to their numbers in the population as a whole. The aggregate class compositions of state legislatures matter a great deal—the individual-level differences documented in the previous chapters do, in fact, seem to affect collective decisions in our legislatures. But if we wish to observe legislatures made up of the same mix of classes as the people they represent, we must look elsewhere in the American political process.

Blue-Collar Government

Political scientists pay less attention to local politics than the subject deserves (Sapotichne, Jones, and Wolfe, 2007; Trounstine 2009). Research on political institutions focuses overwhelmingly on Congress, the president, and the Supreme Court. Research on public opinion and elections focuses overwhelmingly on national politics (Arnold and Carnes 2012). Although there are many excellent studies of cities (for a few recent examples, see Arceneaux and Stein 2006; Gerber and Hopkins 2011; Hajnal 2007; Howell 2007; Kaufmann 2004; Oliver and Ha 2007; Stein, Ulbig, and Post 2005; Trounstine 2008, 2010), for the most part, research on local politics is still separated from mainstream American politics research by a "nearly impermeable boundary" (Judd 2005, 123).

There is no good reason not to study towns and cities. Local governments provide most of the public services that citizens encounter in their day-to-day lives. And their decisions collectively constitute major policy action: in 2008, municipal expenditures totaled more than $1.5 trillion, about $300 billion more than total direct expenditures by state governments.[18]

In many instances, moreover, the scientific value of studying towns and cities is enormous. Local governments are far more diverse than Congresses or state legislatures, and this diversity provides opportunities to study political factors that do not vary much in larger jurisdictions. Trounstine (2009, 614) notes, for instance, that "whereas all members of Congress and most members of state legislatures are elected in single-member districts, most cities elect some or all of their members in multi-member (at large) elections." The same could be said of class: whereas only a handful of members of Congress and very few members of state legislatures come from the working class, many cities elect at least some working-class people, and some cities are led by majorities of policy makers from the working class, something that never occurs in national or state legislatures.

Unfortunately for my purposes, cities are more limited in their choices on economic policies than state or national governments. Because of their subordinate place in America's federal system, cities are "distinctly junior partners in [the] complex, intergovernmental system of redistribution programming" (Sharp and Maynard-Moody 1991, 934). Cities also face competitive pressures that further reduce their economic discretion. Because it is relatively easy for citizens and businesses to flee cities (compared to relocating across state or national boundaries), municipal governments constantly compete for labor and capital in ways that state and national governments do not. Attracting and retaining businesses and tax-paying citizens—without which cities would have little tax base—forces many local governments to keep social spending, redistribution, and taxation low (Minkoff 2009; Peterson 1981; Tiebout 1956).

Many cities have at least a little leeway, however. Many choose to invest in social welfare programs, for instance, despite incentives not to. In 2001, 768 (21 percent) of the 3,636 cities surveyed by the International City/County Management Association (ICMA) and the Census of Governments devoted at least some funds to social programs. In most cities, welfare spending as a percentage of revenues is miniscule compared to welfare spending at the state level; in 2001, the average local government devoted just 0.3 percent of its expenditures to social programs. Even so, spending on social programs has varied enough from city to city to inspire a handful of urban politics scholars to investigate the factors that drive welfare provision at the local level (e.g., Craw 2006, 2010).

If cities are the only jurisdictions in the country where we can observe government by the working class, we cannot pass up the opportunity to study them, even if their discretion over economic policy is relatively limited. Do cities with more class-balanced local legislatures—city councils and their equivalents—enact different economic policies?

Figure 5.5 Welfare as a Percentage of City Spending, by the Social Class Makeup of the City Council

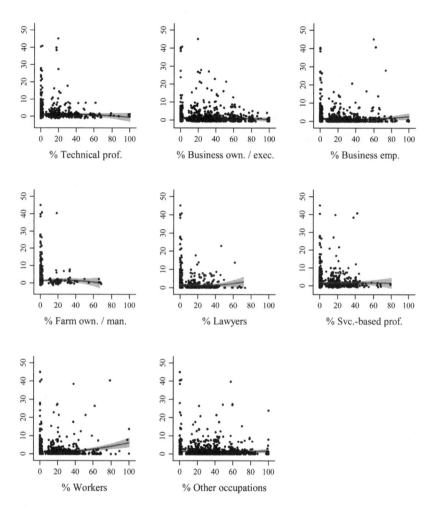

Note: Lines represent quadratic best-fit estimates (with 95 percent confidence intervals shaded gray). Each observation is randomly jittered by 1 percent of the possible scale on each axis to better illustrate areas where the data are heavily concentrated.

Like states, the economic policies that are easiest to compare across cities are spending decisions, and the spending decisions that are most illuminating are welfare spending rates. Figure 5.5 plots welfare spending at the city level (again from the Census of Governments) against measures of the social class makeup of city councils. As with state legislatures, this analysis is limited to two years when other scholars collected data on the occupational backgrounds of city council members. In 1996 and 2001, the ICMA surveyed a nationally representative sample of city clerks about the occupational makeup of the city council (and a variety of other topics).[19] Like the analyses in the previous section, figure 5.5 plots these data against the percentage of city expenditures devoted to social welfare programs in the following years, 1997 and 2002. (Since many municipalities are prohibited by state or local statutes from funding social welfare programs—and because it was impossible to identify those cities on the basis of the data in the Census of Governments or the ICMA survey—figure 5.5 includes only towns and cities that devoted at least some funds to welfare.)[20]

It is obvious from the figure how little cities spend on social programs compared to states—but also how much more socially diverse city councils are than state legislatures. Most cities in this sample spent less than 5 percent of their budgets on social welfare. However, the social class makeup of city councils varied considerably: every occupational group examined here made up a majority of at least one city council in this sample, something we have never seen at the state or national levels.

Two trends stand out clearly in figure 5.5. First, towns and cities led by councils with greater shares of farm owners or managers, business owners or executives, and technical professionals—the same three profit-oriented, white-collar professions that predicted reduced welfare spending at the state level—devoted little or nothing to social programs. The best-fit lines for each of these groups were essentially flat (in fact, they sloped slightly downward for cities led by majorities of council members from these occupations). The second group of cities that stood out in figure 5.5 were those led by greater shares of council members from the working class, which devoted larger percentages of their budgets to social programs. On average, the three cities in which working-class people made up 100 percent of the city council (Crowley, TX; Provincetown, MA; and Wells, ME) spent 5 percent of their budgets on social programs. By comparison, the nineteen cities led entirely by business owners or executives (Allenstown, NH; Candia, NH; Crowley, TX;[21] Derry, NH; Fairview, OK; Farmington, MI; Federal Way, WA; Fort Collins, CO; Friendswood, TX; Granby, MA; Londonberry, NH; North Brookfield, MA; Northumberland, NH; Norwell, MA; Palmer, MA; Sheldon, IA; Skagway, AK; Southwick, MA; and Woodstock, CT) spent one-ninth as much—just 0.54 percent of their budgets—on social programs, the seven cities led entirely by business employees (Bogota, NJ; Charlestown, RI; High Bridge, NJ; Millbury, MA; Waveland, MS; West Paterson, NJ; and Westminster, MA) spent an average of 0.22 percent of their budgets on welfare, and the five cities led entirely by technical professionals (Duxbury, Freetown, Hopedale, and Norfolk, MA; and Marlborough, CT) spent an average of 0.11 percent. Even at the city level, where policy makers have little discretion on economic matters, economic policy appears to depend in part on the social class makeup of the legislature.

There are, as always, many possible non-class-related explanations for the patterns in figure 5.5. Compared to the entire subset of cities that devoted funds to social programs, the forty-four cities in which working-class people made up majorities of the city council tended to be smaller (by about 18,000 residents), less central (almost half were independent townships, compared to 37 percent of all welfare-spending cities), less educated (college graduation rates were 14 percent, compared to 22 percent), and farther east (Thermopolis, WY, was the most western city).

However, these differences—and variations in other attributes that influence social spending at the local level—did not seem to account for the trends in figure 5.5. Table 5.3 reports the results of regression models that related the percentage of the city budget spent on welfare to measures that indicated whether each city's council had a majority of each of the occupational groups (cities where no occupational group made up a majority of the council were the omitted category).[22] In the second model, I also controlled for each city's population size, centrality (center city, suburb, or independent township), racial and ethnic makeup (percent Latino, percent black, percent Asian, and percent other nonwhite races), education level (percent with a college degree), and the year.[23] To account for the potential effects of differences in each city's political institutions (which have been found to be consequential in shaping other local outcomes; Sharp 1991; Sharp and Maynard-Moody 1991), I also included controls for whether city council members were elected by district or in at-large races, the reelection rate among council members, the frequency of city council meetings, the form of government (mayor-council, council-manager, commission, or town meeting), and the state (since some states give cities more authority than others). To account for differences in the need for social spending, I controlled for the percent of the city in poverty. To account for the city's fiscal constraints, I controlled for total revenue and total revenue from intergovernmental transfers.[24] And to account for other differences in the composition of the municipal government, I controlled for the percentage of women and racial minorities on each city council.[25] To keep the analysis simple, the models used indicator variables to represent cities led by majorities of each class—so the estimates in table 5.3 simply illustrate how much

Table 5.3 Welfare Spending and the Social Class Makeup of City Councils, 1996 and 2001

	3	4
Controls?	No	Yes
Profit-oriented professions		
Majority technical professionals	−0.654**	−1.328[+]
	(0.247)	(0.700)
Majority business owners/executives	−0.323*	−0.226
	(0.146)	(0.275)
Majority other business employees	0.880	1.467
	(0.789)	(1.143)
Not-for-profit professions		
Majority lawyers	0.575	5.601
	(1.654)	(4.231)
Majority service-based professionals	−0.922**	−1.971
	(0.227)	(1.359)
Working-class jobs		
Majority workers	1.534	1.273
	(1.173)	(1.879)
Intercept	1.285**	6.168
	(0.099)	(4.750)
N	1,616	812
R^2	0.012	0.200

Note: [+]$p < 0.10$, * $p < 0.05$, ** $p < 0.01$, two tailed. The dependent variable is the percentage of city expenditures devoted to social welfare programs. Standard errors are clustered by city. The omitted reference category is cities in which no occupational group made up a majority of the city council. Coefficients for the control variables are not reported.

more or less cities led by a majority of the class in question (e.g., "Majority technical professionals") devoted to social welfare programs (e.g., 0.654 percent less) than cities not led by a majority of any one class.

The first model in table 5.3 confirmed that cities led by majorities of business owners or technical professionals devoted significantly smaller percentages of their budgets to social welfare programs. It also found—as in the state-level analyses in the previous section—that cities led by majorities of service-based professionals devoted less to social welfare.[26] Cities led by majorities of workers, on the other hand, typically allocated approximately 1.5 percentage points more of their budgets to social programs. This figure was not statistically significant, although this may have been the result of the fact that there were so few instances of majority-working-class city councils, even in a nationwide sample.[27] Moreover, in the first model, cities led by the working class were statistically distinct from cities led by majorities of business owners, technical professionals, and service-based professionals (this was confirmed with simple *F*-tests). The model with controls had fewer cases (since many of the control variables were not available for many of the cities in this sample) and larger standard errors, but it pointed to the same basic conclusions. Cities led by majorities of lawmakers from different classes differ in exactly the ways we would expect based on the individual-level results in chapters 2 through 4.[28]

In absolute terms, the differences between cities led by majorities of working-class people and majorities of white-collar professionals were not striking. The estimates in the models in table 5.3 suggested that towns and cities led by majority-working-class city councils devoted 1.0 to 1.5 percentage points more of their budgets to social programs, hardly a stunning figure (especially compared to the estimate for states, which predicted that those led by majorities of working-class people would give approximately 20 percentage points more of their budgets to social programs). Given the enormous fiscal constraints facing city leaders, however, the finding that their class backgrounds predict *any* differences in welfare spending is somewhat surprising. The differences between cities led by workers and others, moreover, may not be large relative to the differences observed at the state level, but they are nonetheless substantively important. Across municipal governments nationwide, a 1.5 percent increase in welfare funds in 2008 would have been equal to approximately $22.5 billion in additional social spending.

Perhaps most important for my purposes, this analysis suggested that legislatures made up of larger numbers of working-class people do, in fact, differ in the ways we might expect on the basis of what we observe in legislatures with very few blue-collar workers. At the state and national level, we can only guess whether policy outcomes differ in legislatures made up of more than 15 percent working-class people—whether economic policy would really be all that different if working people made up their fair share of the seats in our political institutions. The data plotted in figure 5.5 and summarized in table 5.3 suggest that they would, that we can safely extrapolate how blue-collar legislatures would function on the basis of what we observe in white-collar governments. Nothing in this analysis would lead us to think that class-based differences in how lawmakers act are smaller in more class-balanced legislatures.

If anything, they might be larger. Figure 5.6 summarizes the results of two statistical models. In one, I estimated the relationship between the social class makeup of a city council and social welfare spending, assuming that the relationship was linear, that the difference between a 10 percent

Figure 5.6 Class and Welfare Spending in US Cities, Linear and Quadratic Regression Models

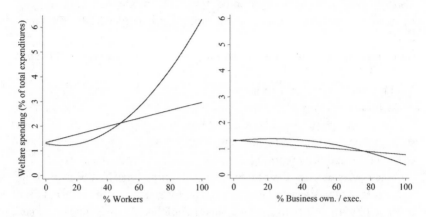

working-class city council and a 20 percent working-class city council was the same as the difference between 80 percent and 90 percent. I then estimated a second model that relaxed this assumption (a linear regression model with squared terms) by allowing for the possibility that the social class gap in policy outcomes might shrink or grow as a given class becomes more numerous in a city council. Figure 5.6 plots the results for two groups: city council members from the working class and those who were business owners or executives. For business owners, the two models were essentially identical: an increase in the proportion of the city council from business backgrounds is associated with roughly the same decrease in social spending regardless of how big of a share of the city council business owners make up. For workers, the policy differences actually appeared to be greater—not smaller—as they made up more and more of the city council. Although we can only guess how congressional or state policy might look if the working class were well represented, if anything, our simple extrapolations may actually *understate* how much more proworker and less probusiness public policy would be in a class-balanced statehouse or a class-balanced Congress. In cities—the one political jurisdiction in the United States where blue-collar government sometimes exists—legislatures led by the working class are even more economically progressive than we would expect.

Welfare policy is a tough sell at the city level, but many cities invest in it all the same. And how much they spend depends in part on the class composition of the city council. When the working class makes up a larger share and when profit-oriented professionals make up a smaller share, redistributive programs that are generally opposed by the upper class and generally supported by working-class Americans receive more funding. Just as the individual-level analyses in chapters 2 through 4 suggested, blue-collar governments enact policies that are more in line with the needs of workers, and white-collar governments enact policies that benefit white-collar Americans.

The Economic Consequences of White-Collar Government

In some sense, the choices that individual legislators make are important in their own right. However, to most scholars, citizens, and political observers, these individual decisions are important because they are a means to a more consequential end: public policy.

Understanding whether legislators from different classes behave differently is important in its own right, but by themselves, differences in individual legislative conduct have no real bearing on the material well-being of ordinary Americans. The unequal representation of social classes in our legislatures does not matter because of class-based differences in individual legislative behavior by themselves—it matters because those differences ultimately affect the kinds of economic policies our legislatures enact, which in turn have enormous consequences for the distribution of resources and power in the United States.

As this chapter has shown, many of the major probusiness and pro-upper-class federal economic reforms of the last decade probably would not have passed if Congress had been made up of the same mix of classes as the people it represents. Spending on social programs designed to help the less fortunate probably would have been billions of dollars higher if state and local policy makers were drawn from the same class backgrounds as ordinary Americans. And other economic policies that are harder to measure at the state and local levels probably would have followed suit. The stakes are truly enormous: our white-collar government makes life easier for white-collar Americans and makes life harder for the working class.

Indeed, economic inequality—a signal marker of unhealthy societies—is substantially higher in places governed by more white-collar lawmakers. Figure 5.7 plots the proportion of all income in each US state that goes to the top 10 percent of earners (a common measure of economic inequality; Frank 2009)—against the percentage of state legislators who were business owners (left panel) and blue-collar workers (right panel). The stakes are indeed high. Where business owners govern in greater numbers, wealthier people take home a bigger piece of the pie. Where workers govern in greater numbers, income inequality is less severe. Part of the explanation may have

Figure 5.7 Economic Inequality and White-Collar Government

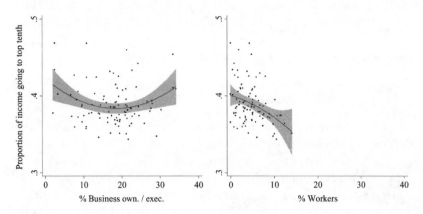

Note: Each panel reports the relationship between the top decile income share in each state in 1994 and 1996 and the percentage of the state legislature that was made up of business owners (left panel) or working-class Americans (right panel) in 1993 and 1995.

to do with other features of the political, economic, and social environments in the states, of course. But part of the explanation lies in the fact that economic policy varies from state to state (Kelly and Witko 2012). And that economic policy depends crucially on who governs. Lawmakers from different classes think, vote, and advocate differently—and ultimately enact different kinds of economic policies. The social class makeup of the people who make decisions for us powerfully affects who wins and who loses in the United States. Government *by* the upper class promotes government *for* the upper class.

Why, then, are working-class Americans so sharply underrepresented in our legislatures? If the unequal social class makeup of our political institutions is so bad for the working class, why don't more working-class people hold office?

SIX

Fixing the Broken Mirror

You [political scientists] have this congressional reform business all wrong. What's wrong with Congress is not the rules, seniority, and all those things. What's wrong with Congress is the *people* in it. You're not going to change anything until you change that.

—Former presidential press secretary, quoted in David Price, *Who Makes the Laws?*, 1972

Well, we're doin' mighty fine, I do suppose,
In our streak-of-lightnin' cars and fancy clothes.
But just so we're reminded of the ones who are held back,
Up front there ought'a be a man in black.

—Johnny Cash, "Man in Black," 1971

Writing about the US Congress of the 1940s, Burns (1949, 1–2) noted that although "men and women of many types, reflecting the diversity of American life, make up the mid-Twentieth Century Congress," a congressional "*type genus*—the member of Congress who best typifies his family—can be singled out for study." This typical legislator was strikingly different from the typical American of the 1940s. Unlike most of his fellow citizens, he had not been raised by manual laborers or tenant farmers, but by a successful father who "had moved to town for a business career." The legislator had a college degree, a distinction conferred on just 5 percent of Americans over the age of twenty-five. And his career had been spent in law and business; his experiences in the kinds of blue-collar jobs most people had at the time was limited to "one summer in a brickyard . . . although he undertook this stint at manual labor mainly as part of training for the school football team."

More than sixty years have passed since Burns wrote, but his concern that Congress had become "as Gambetta once branded the French Chamber of Deputies, a 'broken mirror in which the nation cannot recognize its own image'" (Burns 1949, xi) is just as relevant today. Members of Congress—and, for that matter, officeholders in every level and branch of American government—tend to be drawn overwhelmingly from the most privileged social classes. These inequalities in the makeup of our political institutions raise the troubling prospect that our political process is biased against the needs and interests of the working class, that our white-collar government primarily serves the interests of white-collar Americans.

There has always been a school of American political thought that has regarded the unequal class composition of our political institutions as harmless or even as a desirable feature of our democratic system. In the *Federalist #35*, Alexander Hamilton argued that government by professionals and business-people was "natural" and that they could be trusted to promote the interests of the working class, that blue-collar workers "know that the merchant is their . . . patron and friend; and they are aware that however great the confidence they may justly feel in their own good sense, their interests can be more effectually promoted by the merchants than by themselves." In contemporary political discourse, slogans like "the business of the nation is business," "a rising tide lifts all boats," and "what is good for the country is good for General Motors and vice versa" continue to echo this old idea. We all want prosperity, so what's the harm in letting the upper class call the shots?

The evidence presented in this book suggests that this view is deeply misguided. Lawmakers from different classes bring different perspectives to public office, and they routinely act on them—how they vote and the kinds of bills they introduce often depend on the classes they came from. In the aggregate, legislatures made up of different classes of people tend to enact different kinds of economic policies. My analysis, of course, is far from exhaustive.[1] But across different data sets from different time periods and different levels of government—across every source of data I could find and one that I created from scratch—the basic conclusions are remarkably similar. The rosy notion that lawmakers from business and professional backgrounds want what is best for everyone is seriously out of line with the realities of legislative decision making in the United States. The economic issues at stake in American politics often involve stark trade-offs between the material well-being of different classes of citizens. And the scarcity of

lawmakers from the working class tilts decisions about the distribution of economic resources, protections, and burdens in favor of what white-collar Americans want.

America's class-imbalanced political institutions really are broken: they fail to deliver what most Americans expect from our political process. In a democracy, everyone's voice should count. Everyone's views should be represented—no one should be excluded from decisions that affect everyone. In our class-imbalanced legislatures, however, citizens from different classes are not represented equally, either numerically or in terms of what legislators actually do. Our elected representatives are not a cross-section of our country; people from humble walks of life are all but absent from most of our political institutions. Our lawmakers do not serve the common good regardless of their personal stakes in the issues of the day; how a politician thinks and behaves often depends on the class she came from. At bottom, white-collar government is fundamentally at odds with one of our most cherished political values: the ideal that every citizen's needs and interests should count the same in our governing process.

And the price we pay for our white-collar government isn't just symbolic. The shortage of people from the working class in our political institutions promotes policies that have real consequences, policies that make life worse for the classes of Americans who can least afford it: business regulations that favor businesses at the expense of workers, tax policies that favor the wealthy at the expense of everyone else, social spending policies that favor people who probably won't ever need the social safety net themselves. Many Americans believe that government should promote economic equality, and the vast majority believe that at the very least government shouldn't make economic inequality *worse*, that government shouldn't make the playing field more uneven than it already is. Yet government by white-collar professionals does just that: it promotes policies that help white-collar professionals at the expense of the well-being of the working class.

Even now—in the wake of a financial crisis that propelled economic issues onto center stage in Washington—white-collar government discourages policies that help the less fortunate. Many observers were baffled at the slow pace of the federal response to the late 2000s recession—as Paul Krugman (2010) put it,

Now that the nightmare has become reality . . . —and yes, it is a nightmare for millions of Americans—Washington seems to feel absolutely no sense of urgency. Are hopes being destroyed, small businesses being driven into bankruptcy, lives being blighted? Never mind, let's talk about the evils of budget deficits.

In light of what we know about government by the upper class, a slow federal reaction to economic hard times should hardly come as a surprise. America's class-imbalanced legislative branch tends to favor economic policies more in line with the interests of the haves than with the needs of the have-nots. Why would we expect people from the classes that are most insulated from economic downturns to feel a sense of urgency about an economic crisis that hit the most vulnerable Americans the hardest? Government by the upper class promotes government for the upper class, in good times and in bad.

Our white-collar government is truly an imperfect reflection of who we are, of ideals that go to the very heart of what we stand for as a country. It is a broken mirror.

But it can be fixed. Encouraging greater numbers of working-class Americans to hold public office is easier than many political observers think (especially those who wrongly believe that workers are underrepresented because there's something the matter with the working class). Successful state and local programs to recruit and train working-class candidates have existed for decades. Scholars still have a lot to learn about the factors that are keeping working-class Americans out of office and activists still have a lot to learn about how to expand programs that help get workers in, but the preliminary evidence is extremely encouraging. White-collar government isn't an unavoidable feature of our political process. It isn't a necessary evil. And it isn't invincible.

What's Keeping the Working Class Out of Office?

Just as there have always been people who have questioned whether the social class makeup of government matters, there have always been people who have questioned whether we can do anything about it. Some have argued that government by the upper class is what Americans want. Others have argued that government by the upper class is what Americans need, that working-class people don't have the skills to govern. Both arguments are flat wrong.

Both, however, have deep intellectual roots. Alexander Hamilton embraced both when he argued that workers "know that the merchant is their natural patron and friend; and . . . their interests can be more effectually promoted by the merchants than by themselves." So did the Pulitzer-prize-winning journalist William A. Henry III (1995, 21), who wrote that "voters repeatedly reject insurrectionist candidates who parallel their own ordinariness . . . in favor of candidates of proven character and competence." We seem to hear claims like these all the time in American political discourse. We hear from scholars of *elite theory* that "all social order is necessarily hierarchical, and . . . leadership is a specialization necessitated by the division of labor in all societies" (Cohen 1981, 5). We hear from journalists that "the voters tend to elect wealthy politicos" because they "want a mix of personality and power, but only if they come with a pedigree and bank account to match" (Abdullah 2012). We hear from wealthy campaign donors that "the baby sitters, the nails ladies . . . they don't understand what's going on," that "if you're lower income—one, you're not as educated, two, they don't understand how it works, they don't understand how the systems work" (quoted in Reston 2012).

What we don't hear is hard evidence to support these views. And that's because it doesn't exist. There has never been a single empirical study that has shown that American voters prefer white-collar candidates. And there has never been a single study—not one—that has concluded that working-class people are underrepresented in public office because they aren't qualified for the job.

In elections, candidates from the working class do just as well as candidates from other backgrounds. Figure 6.1 uses my original data on members of the 106th through 110th Congresses to plot each legislator's most recent margin of victory at the polls against the proportion of her career spent in working-class jobs (top panel) or as a business owner or executive (bottom panel). Working in a white-collar job doesn't seem to endear a politician to the electorate, and working in a blue-collar job doesn't seem to cost her votes—time spent in the working class and time spent in business are both uncorrelated with how a legislator performs at the polls.[2] Experiments comparing hypothetical candidates from different classes reach identical conclusions. In a groundbreaking series of studies, Meredith Sadin (2011) finds, for instance, that people randomly assigned to evaluate a hypothetical candidate from the working class are just as likely to report that they would vote for him as people randomly assigned to evaluate an otherwise identical hypothetical candidate from an elite professional background. Far from "reject[ing] . . . candidate[s] who parallel their own ordinariness," voters seem to like working-class candidates just fine.

They just don't get the chance to vote for them very often. Working-class people are not underrepresented in public office because the voters send them packing when they run—they're underrepresented because they aren't

Figure 6.1 Congressional Occupations and General Election Returns, 1999–2008

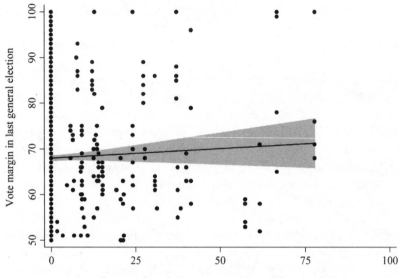

Percent of member's career spent in working-class jobs

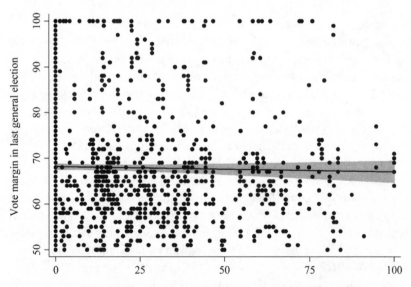

Percent of member's career spent as a business owner / executive

Note: Lines represent best-fit estimates from simple linear regressions, with 95 percent confidence intervals shaded gray.

on the ballot in the first place. When Miller and Stokes surveyed US House members in the 1950s, they also surveyed the candidates who ran against them. When Congress was called to order in 1959, only 2 percent of House members were from the working class—because in 1958, only 2 percent of House *candidates* were workers. The underrepresentation of the working class had nothing to do with the will of the people. By the time voters got to the polls, most had no choice but to elect a white-collar Congress.

Voters seldom have a choice today, either. In the 2008 presidential election, for instance, the three leading contenders in the Republican primary—John McCain, Mike Huckabee, and Mitt Romney—were, respectively, a former naval officer, a former pastor and television executive, and a former corporate executive. In the general election, McCain was joined by Sarah Palin, a former sports telecaster who later helped run a family-owned commercial fishing business. The Democratic primary produced an even more homogenous group: the three frontrunners were a former law professor (Barack Obama), a lawyer (Hillary Clinton), and a lawyer (John Edwards). Obama was joined on the general election ticket by Joe Biden, a lawyer.[3] By the time voters got to the polls, they only had one option: vote for the white-collar candidate. Like most elections in the United States, something screened out candidates from the working class long before November.

Scholars don't yet know exactly what that something is. There are many potential suspects. Perhaps the cost of campaigning deters citizens who aren't as wealthy (or who don't have many wealthy friends). Perhaps the party gatekeepers who recruit candidates to run for office don't know many blue-collar workers, or don't see them as viable candidates (these factors often powerfully disadvantage female candidates; Crowder-Meyer 2010; Sanbonmatsu 2006). Perhaps workers themselves underestimate their own chances of winning an election (a factor that also appears to discourage women; Lawless and Fox 2005). Perhaps workers perceive a mismatch between the two major parties' public images or "brands" and their own views (see Lupu 2011, chap. 2). Perhaps they are deterred by the possibility of losing their jobs—perhaps they have fewer incentives than white-collar professionals, whose careers might actually be advanced by stints in government.

As it stands, there simply isn't much research on this topic; political scientists cannot say for certain what's keeping the working class out of office. Workers themselves, however, don't seem to be the problem. The available data sharply contrast the old idea that "ordinar[y]" people lack the "character and competence" necessary to govern. It is true that *on average* working-class Americans are less likely to have many of the personal qualities that promote success in politics or that we might want in our leaders: knowledge about public affairs, confidence that the political process can be used to achieve real change, "toleran[ce] of unpopular voices" (Verba 2003, 669), and so on. However, there are many more working-class people than there are white-collar professionals—so many more, in fact, that *there are actually more blue-collar workers with many of these desirable characteristics than there are white-collar professionals.*

Figure 6.2 illustrates this point using data from the American National Election Study (ANES), a nationwide political opinion survey conducted every two years. The top panel of the figure plots the *percentages* of people who responded to the survey who indicated that they followed public affairs regularly, who responded "no" when asked whether they sometimes felt that politics and government were too complicated for people like themselves, and who said that they thought that gay and lesbian couples should be allowed to adopt children (a crude and somewhat partisan measure of political tolerance, but one that is a strong predictor of tolerance on a wide range of other issues—and one that speaks to the stereotype that workers are intolerant on social issues; e.g., Frank 2004).[4] In both panels, I have singled out two occupational groups: white-collar professionals and blue-collar workers (semiskilled, clerical, and laborers).[5] As the top panel illustrates, compared to the *average professional*, the *average worker* was 15 percentage points less likely to report that he follows public affairs most of the time (and scored lower on the survey's other measures of political knowledge), 19 percentage points less like to report feeling confident about his ability to understand US politics, and 12 percentage points less likely to say that gay and lesbian couples should be allowed to adopt (see also Verba 2003). However, in these surveys, workers outnumber professionals by almost two to one. Although *any given worker* is less likely to have the traits summarized in figure 6.2, *in total*, there are more workers who have those traits than there are professionals, as the bottom panel of figure 6.2 illustrates.[6] The idea that white-collar professionals are the only ones qualified to govern is sorely mistaken. In the pool of people who follow public affairs regularly, who feel that politics is within their grasp, and who are tolerant on a cardinal social issue, there are actually more blue-collar workers than there are white-collar professionals.

Of course, this set of survey measures is a crude way to gauge how qualified someone is to hold public office. And although more sophisticated analyses using a larger set of survey items reach the same conclusions (Carnes 2012), on some level, no survey can measure everything we might

Figure 6.2 The Percentages (top panel) and Numbers (bottom panel) of Survey Respondents from Different Classes Who Are Politically Engaged, Confident, and Tolerant

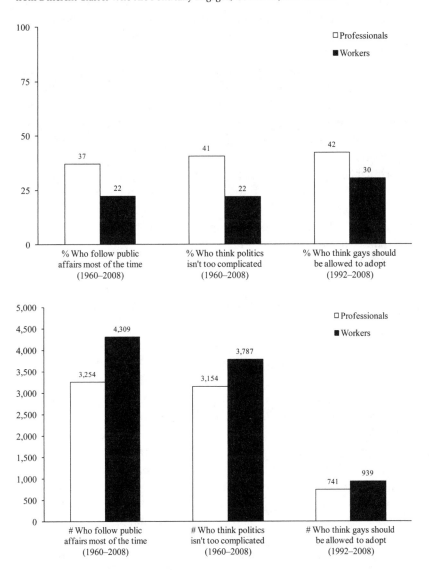

Source: American National Election Study.

want in a political leader: honesty, integrity, creativity, backbone, and so on. The things we can measure, however, lend no empirical support to the idea that working-class people are unqualified to hold office, that the working class is underrepresented in public office because people who are "lower income [or] not as educated . . . don't understand how the systems work." If even just *half a percent* of working-class Americans had what it takes to govern, there would be enough qualified blue-collar workers to fill every seat in Congress and every seat on every state legislature *more than forty times over*—with enough savvy workers left over to run a few thousand city councils.[7] The idea that the working class doesn't govern because it can't govern just doesn't add up.

Scholars don't yet know what's keeping working-class Americans out of office. What's clear, however, is that the underrepresentation of the working class is not a necessary evil. It is not an expression of the popular will. It is not an unavoidable result of inequalities in political qualifications. If we put our minds to it, we can do something about it.

Some reformers have already started.

Thinking Bigger about Inequality

In February 2012, the *New York Times* editorial page blasted the oversized influence of multimillionaires and corporations in American politics. In a piece titled "Donors with Agendas," the *Times* documented how "just two dozen or so individuals, couples and companies have given more than 80 percent of the money collected by super PACs" and how those PACs in turn spent lavishly to support candidates on both sides of the aisle. The article's conclusion was bleak: "all but the most privileged Americans will pay the price if the nation's wealthiest can buy elections."

The *Times* is by no means alone in sounding the alarm about the disproportionate political influence of the wealthy. In the last decade, journalists and pundits have increasingly warned that US politics is beholden to the interests of the privileged few. Political scientists have, too. Scholars have analyzed how politicians make choices and found that their decisions are strongly associated with the opinions of their richest constituents and essentially uncorrelated with the views of the less affluent (Bartels 2008, chap. 9; Jacobs and Druckman 2011). Scholars have analyzed how public policy changes over time and found that it tends to move toward outcomes that the wealthiest Americans favor, regardless of what less affluent Americans want (Gilens 2005; 2012).

Like the *Times,* many of the people who care about the upper class's oversized influence in US politics have been quick to point out that money is a big part of the problem, in particular, organized money—well-funded PACs and interest groups. Hacker and Pierson (2010) have vividly illustrated how affluent Americans and big businesses organized in the 1970s to quietly loosen business regulations and shift more of the federal tax burden onto poor and middle-class Americans. Winters (2011) has shown how an entire "wealth defense industry" has sprung to life in the last half century to help the superrich find loopholes in federal laws and bend public policy to their ends. Others have highlighted the dwindling organizational resources of unions and other working-class groups (Western and Rosenfeld 2011). As Massey (2007, 185) bluntly put it, "How have policies that so obviously benefit the few been implemented and ratified in an electoral system ostensibly controlled by the many? An obvious answer is that money talks and politicians listen."

A second answer that has been a focal point in conversations about the disproportionate influence of the wealthy is that the wealthy are more engaged in public affairs. For every commentator who ponders how we can get the money out of politics, there seems to be another who ponders how we can get more working-class people to the polls. The evidence on this point is actually somewhat mixed: Bartels (2008, chap. 9) finds that senators are more responsive to the wealthy, even when we take into account the differences between the rich and poor in terms of political knowledge, voter turnout, and contact with politicians. Gilens (2012, chap. 3) reaches the same basic conclusions. The case is hardly closed, however—unequal political engagement may yet turn out to be a crucial part of the explanation for inequalities in political influence. And for the time being, many observers remain convinced that "the wealthy are more highly engaged across the whole range of activities and so the political process is heavily tilted in favor of their preferences," that the real problem is that "90 percent of life is just showing up, and . . . the top one percent . . . show up" (Yglesias 2011).

If we want to understand why the privileged have more of a voice in US politics, we cannot ignore the facts that "the privileged participate more than others and are increasingly well organized to press their demands on government" (Jacobs and Skocpol 2005, 1). However, there is more to the story than just participation and organization. Whether our political process listens to one voice or another depends not just on who's doing the talking or how loud they are; it also depends on who's doing the listening. To fully understand why the upper class gets its way so often in US politics, we cannot only focus on the inputs of the political process, on who pressures government through routine forms of political participation or through larger organizational efforts. We must also pay close attention to the people who decide what to do with those inputs. Lawmakers are drawn overwhelmingly from the top social strata, and they bring their classes' perspectives with them to office in ways that shape what they do, both individually and as a group. In his classic work on interest groups, E. E. Schattschneider ([1960] 1975, 35) famously warned that "the flaw in the pluralist heaven is that the heavenly chorus sings with a strong upper-class accent." There is another flaw, however—the *gods* of the pluralist heaven have a strong upper-class accent, too.

Those of us who care about political inequality have to start thinking bigger about its causes. For too long, scholars and political observers have been fixated on the same handful of familiar policy proposals. If we could reform lobbying and campaign finance—if we could get a handle on the flow of money in politics—the rich wouldn't have as much of a say in government. If we could promote broader political participation, the poor would have more of a say. These proposals would almost certainly help to reduce the gaping influence gap in our political process. But as long as policy makers have some discretion and as long as they are drawn overwhelmingly from white-collar America, white-collar Americans will continue to have a disproportionate say in the legislative process, which will in turn tilt economic policy in favor of the interests of white-collar Americans. Even if we somehow equalized routine forms of political participation, even if we somehow stopped organized interests from buying influence, millionaires would still get to set the tax rate for millionaires. White-collar professionals would still get to set the minimum wage for blue-collar workers. People who have always had health insurance would still get to decide whether to help people without it. If we want government *for* the people, we've got to start working toward government *by* the people. Those of us who care about the oversized political influence of the upper class should press on toward the goals of reducing the influence of well-heeled interest groups and promoting routine forms of political participation. But we need to bring a third goal to the table, too: we need to start thinking about the social class makeup of government as seriously as we think about political participation and money in politics.

Of the three, the social class makeup of government may actually be the easiest to reform. Regulating lobbying and campaign finance has been fraught with technical hurdles. Some compare it "to squeezing a balloon—if you squeeze in one place the balloon simply pops out in another" (Gilens

2012, 248). Getting the money out of politics (or equalizing the money in politics), moreover, requires not just an airtight plan but also the political muscle to make it happen—something that is nearly impossible to marshal when most lawmakers depend on big money to finance tomorrow's campaigns. The same is true of efforts to equalize political participation. As Hacker and Pierson (2010, 303) note, "We actually know how to increase voter turnout with relatively straightforward reforms" like same-day registration and early voting, but those reforms "have, not surprisingly, failed to gain traction within elite Washington."

We also know how to increase the number of working-class people in public office—or, at least some organizations do. But they don't need any traction within elite Washington to do it. Or much money, either.

In the 1990s, the president of the New Jersey AFL-CIO, Charlie Wowkanech, realized that the traditional methods of grassroots influence weren't working in Trenton, and his organization's financial resources were no match for the well-funded business groups lobbying against the AFL-CIO. So Wowkanech thought bigger. He started instructing local union officers to identify and recruit politically adept workers. He applied the apprenticeship model from the building trades to running for office—he recruited successful politicians from the working class to train his novice working-class candidates. His program eventually grew into the New Jersey Labor Candidates School described in chapter 5. Using only the organizational resources that the New Jersey AFL-CIO already had—people, newsletters, word-of-mouth, endorsements, and so on—and an annual operating budget of roughly $500,000 (less than 1 percent of what Jon Corzine spent on his Senate campaign in 2000), the New Jersey AFL-CIO has helped working-class citizens win approximately seven hundred state and local elections. The program boasts a 76 percent win rate, and its graduates currently serve on fire commissions, school boards, city councils, county boards of freeholders, and in both chambers of the state legislature.[8]

And New Jersey isn't alone. In 2011, the New Haven, Connecticut, union UNITE HERE recruited and trained new candidates to run for 17 of the seats up for election in the city's Board of Alderman race. Of the 17 candidates they fielded, 16 won. Overnight, the institution at the center of Dahl's ([1961] 2005, 25) classic study of political influence—an institution where once "businessmen [had] virtually crowded [out] all other occupations"— was made up of a majority of prounion politicians, many who had been recruited and trained to run for office just a few months earlier.

In both cases, reform didn't happen in a political vacuum: the organizations supporting working-class candidates also sponsored get-out-the-vote efforts and other routine forms of political participation and helped candidates from the working class raise money to fund their campaigns. Efforts to encourage workers to run for office have not typically been *alternatives* to programs that seek to counter big money or promote broader political participation. Just the opposite—the three goals seem to be quite complementary. Recruiting and training working-class candidates seems to work best when it is a part of a larger effort to empower middle- and working-class Americans.

Of course, New Jersey and New Haven are both places where labor unions are strong. However, the basic principles underlying these candidate recruitment programs should work just as well in places where unions are weak. The model at the heart of both programs rests on a few simple principles: that there are many politically capable working-class citizens and that simply identifying, recruiting, and training talented workers is usually enough to launch them on successful careers in politics. There are no obvious reasons to expect anything different in places where unions are weak. The available evidence suggests that, indeed, there are many politically capable working-class citizens (see figure 6.2). And the idea that reformers simply need to find and recruit talented workers is consistent with a broad consensus in the literature on candidate recruitment; it is well established, for instance, that women are more likely to run for office when they are actively recruited by political gatekeepers. In places where there aren't as many unions, other organizations will have to fill in, but there are many organizations that fit the bill: churches, civic groups, community action projects. There are progressive grassroots organizations in all fifty states: any of them could use its membership network to identify and train the next generation of working-class candidates. The leaders of the two major parties—at the national, state, and local levels—could start doing this kind of work today.

Expanding existing working-class candidate recruitment programs will be difficult, but the efforts in New Jersey and New Haven illustrate that reform is possible—and that the prospects for success are remarkably bright. Scholars still need to learn a lot about the factors that are discouraging blue-collar workers from holding public office, but reformers who don't want to wait can simply take a page from existing reform efforts: use existing organizational networks to identify politically interested and capable working-class people, encourage them to run for public office, provide them with any training that they need, and support them with grassroots mobilization and campaign money.

These are big jobs, but they're well within the reach of politicians, activists, and reform-minded citizens. We know how to do this. In 1945, the

House and the Senate were each 98 percent men. In the decades since, party leaders and interest groups actively recruited women to run for office, and today women make up 18 percent of Congress. We still have a long way to go before we achieve gender equality in Congress, of course. But if the old boys' club isn't invincible, white-collar government isn't, either.

Changes like these aren't rocket science. They just take a little hard work.

Up Front There Ought'a Be a Man in Black

In the 1954 book *The Social Background of Political Decisionmakers*, the congressional scholar Donald Matthews showed that working-class citizens were sharply underrepresented in American political institutions. Matthews urged scholars of American politics to investigate the consequences of this phenomenon and to explore its causes. For the next sixty years, however, political scientists ignored Matthews's calls for work on "the relationship between [legislators' class] backgrounds and the conduct of government" (Matthews 1954a, 38). Even as research on representation, legislatures, and inequality flourished, scholars of American politics never bothered to ask whether it mattered that working-class Americans were all but absent from our political institutions.

Those of us who care about political equality cannot afford to continue turning a blind eye to this defining feature of our political process, to the reality that decisions that affect everyone are made by a white-collar government. The near absence of people from the working class in our legislatures strikes at our most cherished political ideals. It makes life worse for the most vulnerable Americans.

But we can do something about it. Scholars of US politics have all the tools we need to illuminate the factors that are keeping working-class Americans out of office. Reformers and political stakeholders have heaps of real-world experience with programs that recruit and train working-class candidates. It's time for the rest of us to start paying attention, to start using those tools. It's time we start asking why there are so few working-class people in public office—and what we can do about it.

Our broken mirror can be fixed, but it isn't going to fix itself.

1. These are Truman (raised by a small farmer), Eisenhower (raised by an unemployed engineer), Nixon (raised by an unsuccessful small business owner), Reagan (raised by a shoe salesman), and Clinton (raised by a salesman who battled gambling and alcohol addictions). According to the criteria that I use to identify this group—whether the president was raised by people who suffered chronic economic hardships or by people who worked in manual labor or service industry jobs—Obama does not qualify as coming from a poor or working-class family. Although his upbringing was likely challenging, his parents and maternal grandparents were financially stable and were not employed in manual labor or service work during his childhood.

2. The estimates in this figure were drawn from several sources. For twentieth-century presidents, I relied on *Congressional Quarterly* biographical entries (CQ Press 2008) for education, occupation, and family background data and on a recent article in the *Atlantic Online* for wealth estimates (McIntyre, Sauter, and Allen 2010). For the Supreme Court, I drew education, occupation, and family background information from CQ biographies (CQ Press 2004) and wealth data from a newspaper article (*New York Times* 2010). For Congress, I used data from OpenSecrets.org to estimate the percentage of current members who are millionaires, and I used my own data on the 106th through 110th Congresses to generate education, occupation, and family background estimates (see the online appendix). For state legislators, occupation data came from the National Conference of State Legislators (2011) and the *Chronicle of Higher Education* (2011). For city council members, I used education data from the 1991 ICMA Form of Government survey (ICMA 1991) and occupation data from the 2001 survey (ICMA 2001). Finally, for the public, education and occupation data came from the 2000 census (Ruggles et al. 2009), data on the percentage of Americans who are millionaires came from an international survey by the Deloitte (2011) financial firm, and I assumed that the percentage of citizens raised by blue-collar workers was equal to the average number of Americans who worked in manual and service-based occupations during the twentieth century (Ruggles et al. 2009).

3. The makeup of the working class has changed in important ways during that period, of course. In 1900, manual labor jobs made up close to 60 percent of the labor market, while service-industry work made up less than 10 percent. A century later, manual labor jobs made up only about 35 percent of the labor market, whereas

more than a quarter of all jobs were service-industry positions. Despite these seismic changes in the makeup of the American workforce, the occupational composition of Congress has been remarkably stable. In 1900, fewer than 2 percent of members came from manual labor or service industry jobs. Today, fewer than 2 percent of members come from manual labor or service industry jobs.

4. The success of women and racial or ethnic minorities does not appear to have occurred *at the expense* of working-class representation, however. Since 1961, 4 percent of the nonwhite legislators in the data set summarized in figure 1.2 were from the working class, while just 1 percent of white legislators were. None of the female legislators in that data set came directly from working-class jobs, but according to my more detailed biographical data on members of Congress (described later in this chapter), the average woman in Congress between 1999 and 2008 spent about 3 percent of her precongressional career in working-class jobs while the average man spent just 1 percent. The political fortunes of women and minorities do not appear to be tied to the political *misfortunes* of the working class (or vice versa). To the contrary, the success of women and minorities is weakly associated with *increases* in the numerical representation of the working class in Congress.

5. These occupation and race/ethnicity estimates are from the National Conference of State Legislatures (2011) and the gender estimates are from Equal Representation in Government and Democracy, http://www.ergd.org/StateLegislatures.htm (accessed January 5, 2011).

6. Aristotle ([350 BC] 1953, 17) asserted that "the best legislators have been of a middle condition." Adam Smith ([1776] 1953, 19) described the owners of a society's productive technologies as "an order of men, whose interest is never exactly the same with that of the public, who have generally an interest to deceive and even to oppress the public, and who accordingly have, upon many occasions, both deceived and oppressed it." John Stuart Mill ([1861] 2001, 133) advocated government that would "bring together the best members of both classes, under such a tenure as shall induce them to lay aside their class preferences, and pursue jointly the path traced by the common interest." Marx and Engels ([1848] 1972, 475, 487) argued that "the bourgeoisie has at last, since the establishment of Modern Industry and of the world-market, conquered for itself, in the modern representative State, exclusive political sway. The executive of the modern State is but a committee for managing the common affairs of the whole bourgeoisie" and that "[bourgeoisie] jurisprudence is but the will of your class made into a law for all, a will, whose essential character and direction are determined by the economical conditions of existence of your class."

7. A handful of studies have examined whether lawmakers from specific occupations such as business (Witko and Friedman 2008) or law (Eulau and Sprauge 1964; Miller 1995) stand out from other legislators, but this work has been sporadic and inconclusive.

8. There are many possible explanations. Perhaps we have paid too much attention to political institutions and not enough attention to the social processes at work in elite decision making. Perhaps the scarcity of reliable data on legislators' class backgrounds has encouraged scholars to pursue other topics where the barriers to research are lower. Perhaps our concerns shifted to postmaterialist questions (Berry 1999). Perhaps we are guilty of "selectively focus[ing] on the American character, war, party politics, ideas, and great men to the virtual exclusion of the 'faceless,' 'inarticulate' working people" (Graham 1990, ix). Perhaps there just aren't enough political scientists from the working class.

9. During the first half of the twentieth century, many scholars actively studied how politicians' own experiences and backgrounds affected their decisions in office. Charles Beard's (1913, 17) famous study of the drafting and ratification of the US Constitution emphasized "the economic advantages which the beneficiaries expected would accrue to themselves." Harold Lasswell's ([1930] 1986, 124) influential model of officeholder conduct "stressed three terms, [lawmakers'] private motives, their displacement onto public objects, and their rationalization in terms of public interests." Donald Matthews's (1954a, 2) pioneering congressional scholarship argued that "the social and psychological characteristics of the individual officials acting within a political institutional framework must be considered before an adequate understanding of politics and government is possible." By the 1960s, however, many leading scholars began to notice—and to embrace—what Mayhew (1974, 3) described as a "disciplinary drift toward the purposive, a drift, so to speak, from the sociological toward the economic."

10. As one of its early proponents complained, power elite theory "fail[ed] to tell us clearly what the [social] elite does with its [political] power" (Wrong 1968, 90–91).

11. Although it is true that working-class people are less likely to have many measurable characteristics that we might want in an officeholder (e.g., experience in civic organizations), there are many more working-class people than there are white-collar professionals—so many more, in fact, that the total number of blue-collar workers with many desirable characteristics is actually higher than the total number of, say, lawyers or business owners (Carnes 2012; see also chapter 6).

12. The years when the questions were asked vary, and not every question was asked during every election cycle within the range of years when it appeared on the survey. The ways the questions were phrased also sometimes changed slightly over time. The complete wordings of the first three questions were as follows: (1) "Should federal spending on [poor people/aid to the poor/aid to poor people] be increased, decreased or kept about the same?" (2) "Next, I am going to ask you to choose which of two statements I read comes closer to your own opinion. You might agree to some extent with both, but we want to know which one is closer to [your/your own] views: ONE, we need a strong government to handle today's complex economic problems; or TWO, the free market can handle these problems without government being involved." (3) "'The government in Washington ought to see to it that everybody who wants to work can find a job.' Do you have an opinion on this or not? Do you agree that the government should do this or do you think the government should not do it?" or "[In general, some/Some] people feel that the government in Washington should see to it that every person has a job and a good standard of living. Others think the government should just let each person get ahead on [his/their] own. [Have you been interested enough in this to favor one side over the other?/Which is closer to the way you feel or haven't you thought much about this?]" The fourth question was the standard ANES feeling thermometer item, which asks respondents to rate the group in question on a 0 to 100 "warmth" scale, where groups they feel warmest or most favorably toward receive higher values and groups they dislike receive lower values.

13. Even after controlling for the respondents' party, race, gender, age, religion, and region, the differences between working-class respondents and professionals/managers were statistically significant and comparable in magnitude to those in figure 1.3 (except on the question about the government's ability to handle economic problems relative to the free market, for which the difference was just shy of conventional statistical significance levels).

14. Scholars still debate these competing explanations, and each probably contains an element of truth. For a useful review, see Manza, Hout, and Brooks (1995).

15. This is not to say that lawmakers from the professional or upper class are in some sense corrupt or engaged in a conspiracy to exploit the working class. Lawmakers, like the rest of us, bring different perspectives to what they do depending on what they did before. This fact of political life has serious consequences, but those consequences do not flow from any sort of wrongdoing on the part of our lawmakers. By design, our political process entrusts our elected decision makers with a great deal of discretion. As a result, people from different backgrounds behave differently in office. It makes little sense to blame legislators from different classes for voting differently when they have different views about the issues before them. But it is just as nonsensical to ignore how those differences affect the policies our government enacts.

16. Simple dichotomous schemes such as owners vs. workers or manual vs. nonmanual jobs, which were widely used in earlier waves of research on the American class structure, are too blunt for most empirical applications (Hamilton 1972; Hout, Manza, and Brooks 1995). Measurement approaches that use education and income data to place occupations on continuous socioeconomic status scales—which came into fashion in the 1960s and 1970s—are now widely regarded as methodologically flawed (Grusky and Sørensen 1998; Weeden and Grusky 2005). Many scholars still use continuous data on income and education to study political issues that divide workers with different skill levels (e.g., Scheve and Slaughter 2001), but leading class analysts generally recommend grouping occupations into a small number of discrete classes (e.g., professionals, business owners, unskilled workers) that capture both differences in skills and other distinctions, like authority over others or orientation to the free market (e.g., Wright 1997).

17. This coding scheme is similar to the six-category occupational coding system that Hout, Manza, and Brooks (1995) use to study voting in the United States: professionals; managers, administrators, and nonretail sales workers; owners and proprietors; nonmanagerial white-collar workers; skilled workers and foremen; and semiskilled and unskilled blue-collar workers. There are essentially three differences between these occupational categories and those that I use. First, I split Hout, Manza, and Brooks's professionals category into four groups: private-sector professionals like doctors and architects (whom I expect to behave more like businesspeople), service-based professionals like teachers and social workers (whom I expect to have more progressive economic preferences), lawyers, and politicians (whom I regard as not-for-profit professionals). Second, I distinguish between farm owners and other businesspeople to allow for the possibility that they might differ, although my sense is that farm owners occupy a place in the class structure similar to that of business owners (in that they own the means of the production, profit is a paramount motive in their work, and their interests are often at odds with the interests of lower-level employees). And, third, my coding scheme has one occupational category—workers—that combines the skilled and semiskilled workers categories in Hout, Manza, and Brooks's coding scheme. This is out of necessity; there are simply too few politicians from these occupations to analyze them separately with any real precision.

18. In this book, I categorize lawyers as not-for-profit professionals, as white-collar workers whose jobs are not centrally oriented toward maximizing profits in the private sector. Obviously, many lawyers resemble profit-oriented professionals; those who represent corporations, for instance, may often have more in common with

businesspeople than with public defenders. Many others like public defenders and prosecutors probably more closely resemble public servants. It was impossible to determine what kind of law many members of Congress practiced, however, so I have treated lawyers as a single group and placed them where the literature on legal socialization (see Miller 1995, chap. 2) suggests they belong, namely, among professionals who are not oriented toward profit maximization per se (lawyers who represent private-sector clients actually have incentives to *favor* government regulations that tie businesses' hands—more regulation means more work for lawyers). Because I have not collapsed the individual occupational categories within each of the three broad class groups, if lawyers in fact belong among business owners and other profit-oriented professionals, the data will say so.

19. I have included technical details in the online appendix for readers interested in my collection procedure or in how I categorized specific occupations.

CHAPTER TWO

1. For more detailed discussions of the Federalists' and Anti-Federalists' positions on this point, see Lewis (1961) and Manin (1997).

2. Of course, the ease of studying legislative voting should not discourage us from also studying other equally important stages of the legislative process (Hall 1996). I take up questions about bill introductions and legislative entrepreneurship in chapter 3.

3. There are other factors that could mediate the relationship between lawmakers' backgrounds and their choices in office, of course. Chapter 4 examines the role of preferences more closely.

4. Some recent examples include Representative Rush Holt (2010), who often discusses the importance of his background in engineering ("As a scientist . . . I appreciate the challenges we face in trying to prevent terrorists from boarding American airliners. That same background also gives me an understanding of why TSA's current obsession with fielding body imaging technology is misguided, counterproductive, and potentially dangerous.") and Representative Michael Michaud (quoted in *National Journal* 2010), who often discusses his working-class past ("I know what it's like to work the day shift, the midnight shift. I've been on strike. I know what it's like to worry about whether you will have a job or not.").

5. Studying both the AFL-CIO's and the Chamber of Commerce's voting scores, moreover, helps ensure that we have not privileged the economic perspective of either labor or business.

6. Lincoln Chafee is a somewhat unusual case. Unlike most lawmakers from the working class, Chafee was born to privilege. His father, John Chafee, was a governor, a senator, and the Secretary of the Navy, and Lincoln Chafee attended an Ivy League university. After that, however, he worked for seven years as a blacksmith—a textbook manual labor occupation—before getting involved in politics. The procedure I use to classify legislators focuses only on how they earn a living, not on their education or their parents' occupations (see chapter 1). As such, my analysis treats Lincoln Chafee as a legislator from the working class. My view is that he was one: although he had wealthy parents and a fancy degree to fall back on, he worked with his hands, he answered to his bosses, he punched his time card, and he spent all day interacting with other people who did the same things. To be on the safe side, I have replicated the analysis in this chapter without Chafee. Excluding him did not change my findings in any meaningful way.

7. Of the 783 members of Congress who held office between 1999 and 2008, 547 (approximately 70 percent) spent the majority of their precongressional careers in just one of these nine occupational categories.

8. Legislators who worked primarily in blue-collar occupations exhibited an astounding uniformity on this third measure. Their average rescaled AFL-CIO score of 2 was equivalent to siding with unions on important economic legislation 98 percent of the time.

9. Age, race, and gender data are from Congress's online *Biographical Directory*; campaign receipts are from the Federal Elections Commission; constituency characteristics are from the 2000 decennial census and the 2000, 2004, and 2008 National Annenberg Election Studies; and legislators' past vote margins are from legislators' biographies in *Congressional Quarterly*'s online *Politics in America* almanac.

10. In the model for Chamber of Commerce scores, the coefficient for technical professions was statistically indistinguishable from the coefficient for working-class jobs.

11. *F*-tests (results available on request) confirmed that the coefficients for workers were statistically distinct from the coefficients for business owners, business employees, farm owners, and technical professionals.

12. In light of the many other influences members of Congress face, the existence of a 10 to 18 percentage point difference in composite measures of members' voting behaviors on economic questions is a striking finding in itself. Moreover, the legislator class variables were fairly good predictors of legislative voting *by themselves*: regression models estimated using only class had R^2 values of 0.20 when DW-NOMINATE scores were the dependent variable, 0.17 for Chamber of Commerce scores, and 0.18 for AFL-CIO scores.

13. Of course, if I have omitted a variable that drives legislative conduct and that is correlated with the legislator's class, these models might overstate the importance of class. I see little reason to be concerned about this possibility, however. The models account for nearly all of the variance in the outcome variable—two of the three R^2 estimates in table 2.1 are above 0.90—and I have included a wide range of controls for the strongest predictors of legislative voting: party and constituency.

14. I also estimated models that used different class measures such as education, income, wealth, and family background. In general, these measures did not predict differences in roll call voting: occupational differences divide members of Congress in ways that we would miss if we relied on other measures of class. The online appendix outlines these analyses in greater detail.

15. Data on legislators' vote margins are from Lublin (1997) and Swift et al. (2009). Data on district characteristics are from Lublin (1997) and were only available starting in 1963. Data on presidential voting are from Brady and D'Onofrio (2009) and were only available starting in 1953. The averages reported in each panel in figure 2.3 were based on data pooled across as many twentieth-century Congresses as possible, subject to these availability restrictions. In the panels divided by median family income and median age, I divided the districts in the pooled data set into terciles based on the variable in question. In the presidential vote panel, districts were divided into election-specific terciles based on the Republican vote share, although results were similar when districts were divided into those where the Republican share of the two-party vote was less than 40 percent, 40 to 60 percent, and greater than 60 percent.

16. Data on presidential voting are from Brady and D'Onofrio (2009) and were available beginning in 1953. Data on legislators' vote margins and district characteristics are from Lublin (1997) and were available starting in 1963.

17. Moreover, as before, if legislators' class backgrounds drove any of the control variables, these models may understate the true association between class and roll call voting.

18. I focused here on DW-NOMINATE scores, which are available for every Congress, in order to maximize the number of cases in my matching analysis.

19. As a result, the estimated differences reported in the middle and bottom panels of figure 2.4 are less statistically precise than the estimates in the regression analysis—in the bottom panel, they fall shy of conventional levels of statistical significance.

20. Of course, attrition complicates the analyses in the top panel of figure 2.5; not all members of Congress last ten terms. Further disaggregating the data by both how long a member has been in Congress and how long the member will ultimately be in Congress produces similar results.

21. In theory, of course, the process of getting into office in the first place could reduce legislators' ties to their classes. Because every legislator has run for and won office at least once, I cannot rule out this possibility. We cannot know how a working-class legislator behaves in Congress before he is elected to Congress. Once lawmakers get into office, however, political experience hardly makes a dent in the social class divisions in their choices.

22. Available online from http://library.cqpress.com/pia/document.php?id=CQs_Politics _in_America _2008_OE/california39.pdf (accessed March 5, 2012).

23. These estimates were generated by setting the occupational proportion variables at their averages among ordinary Americans (and, when control variables were used, setting the controls at their observed values). Using the 2000 census, I estimated that approximately 1 percent of Americans are farm owners or managers, 1 percent are business owners or executives, 20 percent are business employees, 14 percent are technical professionals, 9 percent are service-based professionals, 54 percent are manual laborers and service industry workers, and 2 percent are in the military or in law-enforcement jobs. For politicians (who are not a census occupation category), I simply assumed that they constitute half a percent of the population. (Percentages do not sum to 100 due to rounding.)

24. Chapter 5 returns to this point.

CHAPTER THREE

1. Burden's (2007) analysis of the personal roots of proactive legislative activity, for instance, focuses only on legislative goals and effort, not on legislative effectiveness.

2. Available online from http://www.webb.senate.gov/aboutjim/index.cfm (accessed January 20, 2011).

3. Available online from http://myrick.house.gov/index.cfm?sectionid=17&sectiontree =13,17 (accessed January 30, 2011).

4. Available online from http://capps.house.gov/about-me/full-biography (accessed December 20, 2011).

5. Available online from http://brady.house.gov/about-me/full-biography (accessed December 20, 2011).

6. By comparison, just 4 percent of respondents reported that racial conflicts or the environment were the most important issues facing the nation; a 7 percentage point increase in concern about these problems would have almost tripled the number of Americans who viewed them as important. The differences between working-class respondents and professionals/managers were statistically significant, moreover, even after controlling for the respondent's party, race, gender, age, religion, and region.

The gaps were even more pronounced, moreover, when I limited my analysis to citizens who vote.

7. Caplan (2007, 21) is right that "if you classify 'social welfare' issues like welfare, the environment, and health care as economic, then economic issues were 'the most important problem' in *every* election year from 1972 to 2000." However, he overlooks the fact that within this large category of economic issues, Americans tend to focus on the specific concerns that are most relevant to people like themselves, a fact that casts voters' knowledge of economic affairs in a slightly more positive light than Caplan does.

8. Available online from http://www.nationaljournal.com/almanac/person/phil-hare -il/ (accessed December 22, 2011).

9. Legislative scholars have recently started attempting to compute ideal point scores based on bill cosponsorship data (Alemán et al. 2009), but the statistical methods used in these efforts are still the subject of considerable debate (Desposato, Kerney, and Crisp 2011).

10. Slightly expanding this list to include issues somewhat related to economic problems (e.g., health policy) did not affect the findings reported here.

11. Because legislators from different occupational backgrounds tend to propose roughly the same number of bills on average, the findings in this chapter were substantively identical when I used a measure of the *percentage* of members' economic bills that passed at each stage (which was more common in the first wave of research on legislative effectiveness, e.g., Matthews 1960) instead of a measure of the *number* of bills passed.

12. It seems likely that the patterns evident in the limited data on the bills that reach a final passage vote are representative of larger class-based differences in the economic goals legislative entrepreneurs pursue, especially given the magnitude of the differences in economic roll call voting documented in chapter 2, the differences in legislators' economic preferences documented in chapter 4, and the consistency between those findings and the class-based differences in legislative goals documented in this chapter.

13. As others have noted (e.g., Takeda 2000, 249–50), Poisson regression—the most common alternative way to model count variables—requires a number of assumptions that are not reasonable in the context of studying the legislative process, most notably the independence assumption, which implies that the occurrence of an event in one period (i.e., a member passing a bill early in Congress) does not influence the occurrence of an event at a later period (i.e., the same member passing another bill). If this assumption is violated, the standard errors in a Poisson model can be biased. The negative binomial model allows for this and many other violations of the assumptions of Poisson regression.

14. In the *Roster* data set, each occupational measure is an indicator variable identifying members who last worked in that occupation before holding elected office. To generate the estimates in figure 3.5, I simply computed the predicted number of cosponsors for members who last worked in business and working-class jobs (holding the other variables at their observed values). In my original data set, the occupational measures record the proportion of the member's career spent in that occupation. To generate the estimates in figure 3.5, I computed the predicted number of cosponsors for a member who worked her entire career as a business owner or manager and for a member who worked exclusively in working-class jobs before serving in Congress (again, setting other controls at their actual values).

15. Of course, H.R. 123 will sometimes pass and S. 4 will not (or vice versa), or both will pass in their chambers but die in conference committee, or both will pass only to be vetoed by the president.

16. Results were similar in models that used indicators instead of continuous measures of bill proposals and cosponsorship counts to allow for the possibility that the relationship between effort and effectiveness was nonlinear.

17. I set the other variables in the model at their observed values (see Hanmer and Kalkan 2012).

18. The fact that lawyers fare so well on the effectiveness measures in figure 3.6 could be interpreted in those terms as well. People who "talk the talk"—whose occupational backgrounds prepare them to interact confidently and persuasively with white-collar professionals—undoubtedly have an advantage in Washington.

CHAPTER FOUR

1. Of course, that is an interesting exercise in itself (e.g., Butler 2012).

2. Of course, even in this information environment, lawmakers may still be uninformed about what working-class Americans want or need (see, for instance, Miler 2010). Lawmakers seldom have face-to-face contact with working-class Americans—they live and work around other white-collar professionals. Moreover, well-heeled interest groups have a natural advantage in shaping the kinds of information lawmakers receive. It may be difficult for news about the working class to make it through Gucci Gulch. However, these biases affect everyone in our legislatures, not just lawmakers from white-collar backgrounds. If we want to explain why legislators from different classes behave differently in office, what they know may not take us very far.

3. Burden's model allows for the possibility that lawmakers from different backgrounds know different things, but in Burden's view, this difference in knowledge is only politically consequential insofar as it influences lawmakers' policy preferences.

4. Past research on this point is by no means bulletproof, however. Few studies have attempted to directly demonstrate that variations in legislators' attitudes account for variations in their behaviors. Most have simply pointed out that the two coexist, for instance, that female legislators have more liberal policy preferences and that they vote more liberally in office, but not that their distinct preferences can account for their distinct voting. Moreover, research on race- and gender-based differences in legislative conduct has focused primarily on legislators' attitudes and has never actually tested the possibility that these behavioral differences stem from differences in what they know. The bulk of the available evidence suggests that preferences are more important than information, but that evidence isn't perfect.

5. Project Vote Smart also collects data on candidates for other kinds of offices, ranging from local to national. However, its most comprehensive data are on state lawmakers.

6. Miller and Stokes took great pains to ensure the anonymity of their respondents; in doing so, they essentially sealed the data set. Adding data on legislative entrepreneurship—or any kind of data, for that matter—is therefore impossible.

7. Moreover, the *American Representation Study* seemed to elicit the most honest answers of any of the three surveys considered here. Of the 176 representatives Miller and Stokes contacted for the study, 141 (80 percent) agreed to participate, a figure that exceeded the response rate for ordinary citizens in the 1958 American National Election Study (78 percent) and the response rates for the 1995 *State Legislative Survey* (47 percent) and the Project Vote Smart *Political Courage Test,* the one survey of the

three that was not anonymous (18 percent among the legislators in each state's upper chamber in 2012, the group I focus on here). Moreover, many *American Representation Study* respondents seemed comfortable admitting to holding politically sensitive views: 8 percent reported that they did not consider the preferences of individuals, groups, or their larger constituency when casting roll call votes, 9 percent expressed dissatisfaction with their experiences in the House and revealed that they had not accomplished what they had wanted, and 34 percent said that they had recently faced a conflict between their own views and the views of their constituents and ultimately voted the way they preferred. Many *American Representation Study* respondents also reported holding personal opinions that were at odds with their choices in office: of the twenty-four members whose own views about economic issues fell into the most conservative response category, eight (33 percent) voted for the liberal positions on at least half of the economic roll call votes that Miller and Stokes recorded. Some legislators may have answered the survey with an eye to the electoral implications of their responses, but many seemed happy to take off their halos and discuss how they really made tough choices.

8. The *American Representation Study* classified legislators into nine occupational categories based on their responses to a question about their "main occupation[s] immediately preceding House membership": big businessmen, doctors/dentists, lawyers, service-based workers (educators, clergy, and social workers), medium-level businessmen (insurance salesmen, mid-level managers, and small business owners), technical professionals (accountants, architects, and engineers), government administrators, farmers, and laborers. For the sake of consistency, I have relabeled several of these categories (big businessmen are labeled here as business owners or executives, medium-level businessmen are labeled business employees, service-based workers are labeled service-based professionals, and farmers are labeled farm owners or managers). I have also merged doctors/dentists into the technical professionals category.

9. In figures 4.1 and 4.2, I have combined the military/law enforcement and politician/staffer categories in my own data set to match the *American Representation Study*'s coding scheme, which does not differentiate between the two.

10. See also figure 1.2 in chapter 1.

11. The social welfare scales were created using data on legislators' votes on seven important, nonunanimous economic bills in the Eighty-Fifth Congress and eight in the Eighty-Sixth Congress. These bills covered issues like public housing, federal funding for education, public works programs, labor-management relations, and funding for the Department of Labor and Health and the Department of Education and Welfare. To make the Eighty-Fifth and Eighty-Sixth Congresses comparable, I grouped members who supported all eight bills in the Eighty-Sixth Congress with those who supported only seven. This produced similar distributions of scores within each Congress. I also reverse-coded the variable so that lower values signified more liberal voting.

12. Of course, the two panels in figure 4.2 use two different measures of roll call voting. Figure 4.2 accounts for their different scales by graphing each measure's entire range in the same horizontal space. Figure 2.2 in chapter 2 shows, moreover, that class-based gaps in a single measure of roll call voting—DW-NOMINATE scores—have been stable since the 1950s.

13. Results were similar when I used a more fine-grained measure of legislators' spending preferences and when I included several other programs legislators were asked about, such as infrastructure and policing, or just welfare by itself.

14. The occupational data in the *American Representation Study* and the *Political Courage Test* were sufficiently detailed that I could code them according to the coding scheme I used in chapters 2 and 3. (The one exception is that the *Political Courage Test* did not have a military category.) However, some of the *State Legislative Survey*'s occupational categories could not be perfectly matched to my own coding system. To make them as comparable as possible, I merged the politics/government and officials/administrators categories in the *State Legislative Survey* into a single politics category, I combined the media and other professionals categories into a single technical professionals category, and I treated the farm category as equivalent to farm owners or managers. The occupations in the *State Legislative Survey* were still not a perfect match; in particular, the only business employees who could be singled out were sales professionals, the only service-based professionals who could be identified were educators, and the study did not identify legislators from working-class jobs. These differences are noted on the vertical axis of the middle panel in figure 4.3.

15. The *State Legislative Survey*'s occupational data did not allow me to single out working-class legislators. And the *Political Courage Test* sample was so small that there were only a few cases for former workers and former farmers. To be consistent with the standard I used in chapter 2—excluding categories with fewer than ten cases—I omitted those groups in the bottom panel of figure 4.3. Although the 1995 and 2012 surveys' occupational measures do not permit us to single out certain groups, the trajectories of opinions across the other occupational categories in these studies were comparable to what we observed in the *American Representation Study*.

16. With the *American Representation Study* data, I could control for several of the legislator's personal characteristics (party, race, gender, and age), his constituent's characteristics (region, average economic attitudes, Republican vote share in the last presidential election), his vote margin in the last election, and his perceptions of several characteristics of his district (its racial and partisan makeup). Similarly, in the *State Legislative Survey*, I controlled for several legislator characteristics (party, age, race, religion, gender), one constituency characteristics (partisan composition), several state-level characteristics (population, professionalism of the state legislature), and the legislator's most recent margin of victory. In the *Political Courage Test*, I could control for only the three legislator characteristics: party, gender, and education level.

17. Ordinary least squares models were used to generate these estimates. The results were substantively similar when I used ordered logit models instead.

18. Although this section has not used the terminology from Baron and Kenny's (1986) well-known work on mediation analysis, its findings can be understood in terms of their four-step framework for studying causal mediation: figure 4.2 measures the relationship between class and roll call voting (step one), figure 4.3 measures the relationship between class and the possible mediating variables (step two), and figure 4.4 measures the extent to which the mediating variable accounts for the association between class and roll call voting (step four). For the sake of space, this section does not present data on the relationship between the hypothesized mediators and roll call voting (step three), although legislators' policy preferences are strongly and significantly associated with roll call voting in the *American Representation Study*.

19. The question asked, "I'm not interested in getting names but, in connection with voting on bills (as a member of Congress), are there any individuals and groups from your district whose opinions you would say are (were/would be) particularly important?"

20. The questions asked, "Is there much union political activity?" and "Is there much political interest on the part of business or industry?"

21. Of course, lawmakers' responses might also reflect real differences in union and business political activity. Unfortunately, Miller and Stokes's data set did not include objective information about the actual political strength of unions and businesses.

22. Specifically, the question asked, "How about legislation concerning the role of the federal government in domestic affairs? How do the people of your district feel about things like public power and public housing?"

23. To avoid confusing legislators who return home often with legislators whose home districts are close to the statehouse, the bottom panel of figure 4.8 focuses only on legislators who lived more than one hundred miles from the capital.

24. It is worth repeating that the analysis in this chapter has left a number of questions unanswered. The available data allow us to study the attitudinal processes behind legislative voting, but not legislative entrepreneurship. They allow us to study how economic attitudes mediate the relationship between class and voting, but they do not allow us to explore the social and psychological processes behind the link between class and attitudes. These topics are beyond the scope of what we can accomplish with the data that exist and what I can accomplish in the space of a single chapter. They deserve more careful attention in future work.

CHAPTER FIVE

1. Available online from http://www.njaflcio.org/pages/labor_candidates/ (accessed March 7, 2012).

2. I used the list of bills in the second edition of Mayhew's (2005) text for the 106th and 107th Congresses. For the 108th through 110th Congresses, I relied on Mayhew's online supplements, which are available at http://pantheon.yale.edu/~dmayhew/data3.html (accessed August 3, 2010). For the Congresses considered here, Mayhew has only identified important bills using his Sweep I methodology, which is based on newspaper accounts, and has not yet been able to rate bills using the Sweep II approach, which is based on experts' retrospective judgments long after passage.

3. Because there were too few senators from the working class to examine the Senate separately, this section groups senators and representatives together. Auxiliary analyses using only data from the House reach similar conclusions.

4. More formally, I estimated the proportion who would have voted for each bill as $(1/n) \times \Sigma \, (v_{ij}(p_j/c_j))$, where n was the number of members who voted on the bill who spent the majority of their careers in a single occupational category, v_{ij} was an indicator for whether member i from occupation group j voted for the bill, p_j was the percentage of individuals from occupational group j in the population, and c_j was the percentage of individuals from occupational group j in Congress. Using the 2000 census, I estimated that approximately 1 percent of Americans were farm owners or managers, 1 percent were business owners or executives, 20 percent were business employees, 14 percent were technical professionals, 9 percent were service-based professionals, 54 percent were manual labor and service industry workers, and 2 percent were in the military or in law-enforcement jobs. For politicians (who are not a census occupational category), I simply assumed that they constituted half a percent of the population.

5. For each bill, after estimating the model, I computed the predicted probability that each member would have supported the bill, holding constant all of the characteristics of the member besides class, and assuming that the member had worked

exclusively as a farm owner or manager. I then repeated the exercise assuming that the member had worked exclusively as a business owner or executive, and so on for the other occupational categories. At each iteration, I generated an estimate of the total proportion of the chamber that would have supported each bill. After all of the iterations, I simply reweighted these vote margin estimates using the population percentages for each occupational category in the general public.

6. Available online from http://www.census.gov/govs/estimate/ (accessed August 16, 2010). This estimate reflects direct expenditures excluding intergovernmental transfers to local governments.

7. Composite policy outcome measures like Erikson, Wright, and McIver's (1994, chap. 4) state policy liberalism scores typically incorporate data on both economic issues and noneconomic policies such as criminal justice and gambling. These measures are useful for studying the broader ideological orientation of state policy but are too general for an analysis of the links between the class composition of legislatures and economic policy.

8. The NCSL's website also lists data for the year 2007, but the marginals for many states do not sum to 100 percent (even taking into account rounding errors), the methodology used to collect them is opaque, and including them with the 1993 and 1995 data does not substantively change the findings presented here.

9. For a useful review of the literature on state welfare expenditures, see US Department of Health and Human Services (2004).

10. Models that added squared terms for each occupational variable in order to approximate the quadratic relationships sometimes observed in figure 5.2 produced results (available on request) that were qualitatively similar to the linear model results presented in table 5.2. Once the concentration of working-class people exceeded a few percentage points, both models predicted increases in social welfare spending. Given that the social welfare variable could not possibly continue increasing quadratically in response to increases in the proportion of workers on the state legislature and given that no other group exhibited the quadratic pattern observed for workers in figure 5.2, table 5.2 simply reports linear regression results.

11. Results (available on request) were substantively similar when I omitted these additional control variables. I used data on per capita personal income for 1993 and 1995 from the US Department of Commerce; intergovernmental transfers data for 1994 and 1996 from the US Census Bureau's Census of Governments; poverty and racial composition estimates from the 1990 decennial census; data on the partisan composition of state legislatures that I computed by averaging estimates from 1992 and 1994 and from 1994 and 1996 from the US Census Bureau; legislative professionalism data estimated using Squire's (1992) method; and average partisanship, political ideology, and union density estimates generated using the 1988–92 *Senate Election Study* (Miller et al. 1999).

12. Because each state is observed more than once, the standard error estimates in table 5.2 are clustered by state. Nebraska's state legislators are elected in nonpartisan races, so the second model in table 5.2—which controls for the partisan composition of the state legislature—omits the two observations from the Cornhusker State.

13. Of course, where that 1 percent comes from is important, too. To estimate the total difference in social spending associated with a 1 percent increase in the share of one class in a state legislature, we must sum the change associated with the increase *and* the changes associated with a corresponding decrease in the shares of lawmakers from one or more of the other classes.

14. Coefficients for the control variables in the models in table 5.2 predicted sensible but often nonsignificant differences in social spending. Intergovernmental revenues were associated with significant increases in welfare provision, while legislative professionalism predicted significant decreases. Poverty predicted substantial but nonsignificant increases in social spending, and the partisan and ideological composition of the state predicted nonsignificant changes in expected directions. The only coefficient with the wrong sign was the point estimate for a measure of the percentage of households in the state in which one or more residents belonged to a union, which predicted modest and nonsignificant reductions in welfare spending.

15. A similar exercise using the results of the first model in table 5.2 predicted an average social spending rate of 40.1 percent. Both estimates were statistically distinct from the actual mean social spending rate, 20.9 percent.

16. Available online from http://www.ows.doleta.gov/unemploy/statelaws.asp (accessed August 7, 2012).

17. Available online from http://taxfoundation.org/article/state-tax-rates-and-1994 -collections and http://taxfoundation.org/article/state-tax-rates-and-1996-collections (accessed August 7, 2012). For the fifteen states with multiple corporate tax brackets, I simply averaged the maximum and minimum corporate tax rate.

18. Available online from http://www.census.gov/govs/estimate/ (accessed August 16, 2010). This estimate reflects direct expenditures excluding intergovernmental transfers.

19. The analyses that follow draw on Trounstine's data on government and finances in American cities (see, for instance, Trounstine and Valdini 2008), which combine information from several of the ICMA's *Municipal Form of Government* surveys (the only available source of systematic data on the occupational backgrounds of policy makers in local government), city finance data from the US Census Bureau's Census of Governments, and data on other city characteristics from the decennial census. I focus here on data from 1996 and 2001, the years when the ICMA study included detailed occupational measures. The survey asked respondents (city clerks) to record the number of city council members who fell into each of eleven occupational categories, which I grouped according to the same occupational coding scheme that I have used to study Congress and state legislatures. As with the NCSL's state-level data, there was no way to distinguish military or law enforcement workers in these city data. The ICMA survey also did not have a category for career politicians. When respondents indicated that some council members had "other occupations," they were given the option to list those jobs in an open-ended survey question. I independently coded these open-ended responses.

20. This reduced the pooled sample of cases from the 1996 and 2001 waves of the survey from 8,789 to just 1,616. The subset of cities that devoted funds to social spending were not dramatically different from the larger sample in most respects: they had an average population of 28,958 (compared to 22,863 in the entire sample); they were made up of 12 percent central cities, 50 percent suburbs, and 38 percent independent townships (compared to 7 percent, 56 percent, and 37 percent in the larger sample); they were 8 percent Latino, 10 percent black, and 2 percent Asian (compared to 8 percent, 8 percent, and 2 percent); and they had poverty and college graduation rates of 12 percent and 22 percent (compared to 13 percent and 22 percent). The one notable difference was regional; cities in northeastern states made up approximately a quarter of the larger sample and roughly half of the subset of cities that devoted funds to social programs.

21. Crowley, Texas, appears twice in this paragraph because its city council consisted of 100 percent workers in 1996 and 100 percent business executives in 2001. This change coincided with a sharp drop in the city's social spending rate, which fell from roughly average in 1997, 0.44 percent, to roughly nothing, 0.07 percent, in 2002.

22. Only thirteen cities were led by majorities of farmers, too few to reliably estimate average social spending rates. As such, I simply included these cities with those that did not have a majority of any occupational group.

23. Because some cities are observed more than once, the standard error estimates in table 5.3 are clustered by city.

24. Data on the racial and gender compositions of city councils and on cities' political institutions came from the ICMA surveys. Data on total revenues and intergovernmental transfers came from the Census of Governments. Data on the racial and gender compositions of cities and on local poverty rates came from the decennial census; for observations from 2001, I used data from the 2000 census, and for observations from 1995, the data were interpolated between the 1990 and 2000 censuses.

25. Data on the partisan backgrounds of citizens and policy makers—which have been included in most other regression analyses in this book—are not available at the city level. Parties play far less of a role in urban politics than in other levels of government (Wright 2008), however, and many of the other control variables should be sufficiently correlated with party to capture at least some (if not all) of its effects.

26. In individual-level analyses at the national level, this group has typically been among the most economically liberal. The differences we observe here may be an artifact of sampling variability or may reflect a genuine difference in the priorities of this group at the local and national levels. Perhaps in city politics, where funding is more scarce, some service-based professionals (e.g., teachers) might see welfare spending as a potential drain on resources that could otherwise be devoted to government programs related to their occupations (e.g., schools).

27. There were just forty-four cases in the first model and, after adding controls, just fifteen cases in the second model.

28. Coefficients for the control variables (not reported but available on request) were imprecise but generally sensible as well. As research on black mayors finds (e.g., Keller 1978), cities led by greater shares of black city council members devoted (nonsignificantly) greater percentages of their budgets to social programs. Larger cities and cities with higher poverty rates devoted less to social programs (consistent with literature emphasizing the negative effects of need on social provision), although coefficients for these variables were again shy of statistical significance at conventional levels. And cities with higher revenues and higher levels of incoming intergovernmental funds devoted (again, nonsignificantly) more to social programs.

CHAPTER SIX

1. I have done my best to illuminate how our class-imbalanced legislatures tilt economic policy, but my findings have raised at least as many questions as they have answered. I have focused on legislatures, but in doing so I have left out the other important institutional players in the policy-making process: executives, judges, and bureaucrats. I have focused most of my attention on federal politics, but in doing so I have devoted less attention to state and city governments and no attention to other jurisdictions like counties and special districts. And I have focused on the role that opinions play in mediating the relationship between legislators' class backgrounds

and their choices in office, but in doing so I have sidestepped questions about the social and psychological processes underlying the relationship between class and opinions.

2. Regression models that relate vote margins to my complete set of occupational measures reach the same conclusion.

3. Of course, many candidates selectively played up the humbler aspects of their biographies (as presidents have always done; Pessen 1984). Obama's campaign messages routinely focused on his three years as a community organizer in Chicago and downplayed the year he spent working for Business International Corporation, a firm that advised American companies on their overseas operations, and the dozen years he spent as a lecturer at an elite private university. Palin's exploits as a hunter and wildlife enthusiast were more often the subject of media coverage than her time running a family-owned commercial enterprise.

4. The question about respondents' interest in politics asked, "Some people seem to follow what's going on in government and public affairs most of the time, whether there's an election going on or not. Others aren't that interested. Would you say you follow what's going on in government and public affairs most of the time, some of the time, only now and then, or hardly at all?" The question about the complexity of government affairs asked respondents whether they agreed with the statement, "Sometimes politics and government seem so complicated that a person like me can't really understand what's going on." And the question about adoption asked, "Do you think gay or lesbian couples, in other words, homosexual couples, should be legally permitted to adopt children?"

5. This measure excludes people who work in agriculture. The ANES did not distinguish between farm owners and farm laborers, so I focus here on the occupational categories that can be divided more clearly.

6. When I limited this analysis to citizens who voted in the last presidential election, there were still comparable or greater numbers of blue-collar workers.

7. According to the Bureau of Labor Statistics, there were 140,863,000 people in the labor force in 2000. By my count, approximately 54 percent of those people—roughly 76,066,000 Americans—worked in manual labor and service industry jobs. Half a percent of 76,066,000 is 380,330. Congress has 535 members, and there are 7,382 state legislators—together, there are 7,917 state and federal legislators. 380,330 divided by 7,917 rounds to 48.04.

8. Available online from http://www.njaflcio.org/pages/labor_candidates/ (accessed December 19, 2012).

REFERENCES

Abdullah, Halimah. 2012. "Romney, Obama: Why They Have Trouble Connecting." *CNN Online*, June 12. Available online from http://www.cnn.com/2012/06/12/politics /obama-romney-connecting/index.html?hpt=hp_c2 (August 14, 2012).

Achen, Christopher H. 1977. "Measuring Representation: Perils of the Correlation Coefficient." *American Journal of Political Science* 21:805–15.

———. 1978. "Measuring Representation." *American Journal of Political Science* 22:475–510.

———. 2005. "Let's Put Garbage-Can Regressions and Garbage-Can Probits Where They Belong." *Conflict Management and Peace Science* 22:327–39.

"The Address and Reasons of Dissent of the Minority of the Convention of the State of Pennsylvania to their Constituents." 1787. Available online from http://memory.loc .gov/cgi-bin/query/h?ammem/bdsbib:@field%28NUMBER+@od1%28bdsdcc+c0401 %29%29 (June 27, 2011).

Adler, E. Scott, and John Wilkerson. 2005. "The Scope and Urgency of Legislation: Reconsidering Bill Success in the House of Representatives." Paper presented at the Annual Meeting of the American Political Science Association, Washington, DC.

———. 2011. *Congressional Bills Project: 1947–2008*. Available online from http://www .congressionalbills.org/download.html (February 23, 2011).

Aldrich, John H. 1995. *Why Parties?* Chicago: University of Chicago Press.

Alemán, Eduardo, Ernesto Calvo, Mark P. Jones, and Noah Kaplan. 2009. "Comparing Cosponsorship and Roll-Call Ideal Points." *Legislative Studies Quarterly* 32:449–74.

Alpert, Eugene J. 1979. "A Reconceptualization of Representational Role Theory." *Legislative Studies Quarterly* 4:587–603.

American National Election Studies. 2010. *Time Series Cumulative Data File* [data set]. Stanford, CA: Stanford University; and Ann Arbor, MI: University of Michigan [producers and distributors].

Anderson, William D., Janet M. Box-Steffensmeier, and Valeria Sinclair-Chapman. 2003. "The Keys to Legislative Success in the U.S. House of Representatives." *Legislative Studies Quarterly* 28:357–86.

Anyon, Jean. 1996. "Social Class and the Hidden Curriculum of Work." In *Transforming Curriculum for a Culturally Diverse Society*, ed. Etta R. Hollins. Philadelphia: Lawrence Erlbaum Associates.

Arceneaux, Kevin, and Robert M. Stein. 2006. "Who Is Held Responsible When Disaster Strikes?" *Journal of Urban Affairs* 28:43–53.

Aristotle. [350 BC.] 1953. "Social Classes: A Classical View." In *Class, Status, and Power: A Reader in Social Stratification,* ed. Reinhard Bendix and Seymour Martin Lipset. Glencoe, IL: Free Press.

Arnold, R. Douglas. 1990. *The Logic of Congressional Action.* New Haven, CT: Yale University Press.

———. 2004. Foreword to *Congress: The Electoral Connection.* 2nd ed. New Haven, CT: Yale University Press.

Arnold, R. Douglas, and Nicholas Carnes. 2012. "Holding Mayors Accountable: New York's Executives from Koch to Bloomberg." *American Journal of Political Science* 56:949–63.

Associated Press. 1980. "Legislators Like a Homey Touch." *Los Angeles Times,* July 2.

Austin-Smith, David, and John R. Wright. 1994. "Counteractive Lobbying." *American Journal of Political Science* 38:25–44.

Barber, James Alden, Jr. 1970. *Social Mobility and Voting Behavior.* Chicago: Rand McNally and Company.

Baron, Reuben M., and David A. Kenny. 1986. "The Moderator-Mediator Variable Distinction in Social Psychological Research: Conceptual, Strategic, and Statistical Considerations." *Journal of Personality and Social Psychology* 51:1173–82.

Barrett, Edith J. 1995. "The Policy Priorities of African American Women in State Legislatures." *Legislative Studies Quarterly* 20:223–47.

Bartels, Larry M. 2008. *Unequal Democracy: The Political Economy of the New Gilded Age.* New York: Russell Sage Foundation; and Princeton, NJ: Princeton University Press.

Beard, Charles A. 1913. *An Economic Interpretation of the Constitution of the United States.* New York: Macmillan Company.

Beck, Elizabeth L., Deborah M. Whitley, and James L. Wolk. 1999. "Legislators' Perceptions about Poverty: Views from the Georgia General Assembly." *Journal of Sociology and Social Welfare* 26:87–104.

Beckett, Paul, and Celeste Sunderland. 1957. "Washington State's Lawmakers: Some Personnel Factors in the Washington Legislature." *Western Political Quarterly* 10:180–202.

Berelson, Bernard R., Paul F. Lazarsfeld, and William N. McPhee. 1954. *Voting: A Study of Opinion Formation in a Presidential Campaign.* Chicago: University of Chicago Press.

Berkman, Michael B., and Robert E. O'Connor. 1993. "Do Women Legislators Matter? Female Legislators and State Abortion Policy." *American Politics Quarterly* 21:102–24.

Berry, Jeffrey M. 1999. *The New Liberalism: The Rising Power of Citizen Groups.* Washington, DC: Brookings Institution Press.

Besley, Timothy J., and Marta Reynal-Querol. 2012. "Do Democracies Select More Educated Leaders?" *American Political Science Review* 105:552–66.

Black, Gordon. 1972. "A Theory of Political Ambition: Career Choices and the Role of Structural Incentives." *American Political Science Review* 66:144–59.

Boehner, John. 2010. "Boehner 'Knows What It Takes to Create Jobs.'" http://www.john boehner.com/blog/boehner-knows-what-it-takes-create-jobs (October 25, 2011).

Brady, David, and Rob D'Onofrio. 2009. "Presidential Vote by Congressional District, 1952–1998." http://www.princeton.edu/~clinton/datacode.html (October 20, 2009).

Bratton, Kathleen A., and Kerry L. Haynie. 1999. "Agenda Setting and Legislative Success in State Legislatures: The Effects of Gender and Race." *Journal of Politics* 61:658–79.

Bricker, Jessee, Arthur B. Kennickell, Kevin B. Moore, and John Sabelhaus. 2012. "Changes in U.S. Family Finances from 2007 to 2010: Evidence from the Survey of Consumer Finances." *Federal Reserve Bulletin*, June, 1–80.

Brown, Robert D. 1995. "Party Cleavages and Welfare Effort in American States." *American Political Science Review* 89:23–32.

Burden, Barry C. 2007. *The Personal Roots of Representation*. Princeton, NJ: Princeton University Press.

Burns, James MacGregor. 1949. *Congress on Trial: The Legislative Process and the Administrative State*. New York: Harper and Brothers.

Burrell, Barbara C. 1994. *A Woman's Place Is in the House: Campaigning for Congress in the Feminist Era*. Ann Arbor: University of Michigan Press.

Butler, Daniel M. 2012. "Why Does Descriptive Representation Work? An Experimental Investigation of the Potential Mechanisms." Unpublished manuscript.

Button, James, and David Hedge. 1996. "Legislative Life in the 1990s: A Comparison of Black and White State Legislators." *Legislative Studies Quarterly* 21:199–218.

Campbell, Angus, Philip E. Converse, Warren E. Miller, and Donald E. Stokes. 1960. *The American Voter*. Chicago: University of Chicago Press.

Campbell, James E. 1982. "Cosponsoring Legislation in the U.S. Congress." *Legislative Studies Quarterly* 7:415–22.

Canes-Wrone, Brandice, David W. Brady, and John F. Cogan. 2002. "Out of Step, Out of Office: Electoral Accountability and House Members' Voting." *American Political Science Review* 96:127–40.

Canon, David T. 1999. *Race, Redistricting and Representation: The Unintended Consequences of Black Majority Districts*. Chicago: University of Chicago Press.

Caplan, Bryan. 2007. *The Myth of the Rational Voter: Why Democracies Choose Bad Policies*. Princeton, NJ: Princeton University Press.

Carey, John M., Richard G. Niemi, and Lynda W. Powell. 1995. *State Legislative Survey and Contextual Data, 1995* [computer file]. Columbus: Kathleen Carr, Ohio State University, Polimetrics Lab [producer]; and Ann Arbor, MI: Inter-university Consortium for Political and Social Research [distributor].

Carnes, Nicholas. 2012. "Why Are There So Few Working-Class People in Political Office? Evidence from State Legislatures." Working paper.

Carnes, Nicholas, and Noam Lupu. 2012. "Rethinking the Comparative Perspective on Class and Representation: Evidence from Latin America." Working paper.

Carpenter, Daniel. 2010. "Institutional Strangulation: Bureaucratic Politics and Financial Reform in the Obama Administration." *Perspectives on Politics* 8:825–46.

Carpiano, Richard M., Bruce G. Link, and Jo C. Phelan. 2008. "Social Inequality and Health: Future Directions for the Fundamental Cause Explanation." In *Social Class: How Does It Work?*, ed. Annette Lareau and Dalton Conley. New York: Russell Sage Foundation.

Cash, Johnny. 1971. "Man in Black." *Man in Black* [album]. Columbia Records [producer and distributor].

Center for Responsive Politics. 2012. "Personal Finances: Overview." http://www.open secrets.org/pfds/index.php (October 9, 2012).

Centers, Richard. 1953. "Children of the New Deal: Social Stratification and Adolescent Attitudes." In *Class, Status, and Power: A Reader in Social Stratification*, ed. Reinhard Bendix and Seymour Martin Lipset. Glencoe, IL: Free Press.

Childs, Sarah, and Mona Lena Krook. 2008. "Critical Mass Theory and Women's Representation." *Political Studies* 56:725–36.

Chronicle of Higher Education. 2011. "How Educated Are State Legislators?" http://chronicle
.com/article/Degrees-of-Leadership-/127797/ (October 17, 2011).

Clark, Terry Nichols, Seymour Martin Lipset, and Michael Rempel. 1993. "The Declining
Political Significance of Social Class." *International Sociology* 8:293–316.

Clinton, Joshua D., and John Lapinski. 2008. "Laws and Roll Calls in the U.S. Congress,
1889–1994." *Legislative Studies Quarterly* 33:511–41.

Cnudde, Charles F., and Donald J. McCrone. 1966. "The Linkage between Constituency
Attitudes and Congressional Voting Behavior: A Causal Model." *American Political Science Review* 60:66–72.

Cohen, Abner. 1981. *The Politics of Elite Culture: Explorations in the Dramaturgy of Power in
a Modern African Society.* Berkeley: University of California Press.

Cox, Gary W., and Mathew D. McCubbins. 1993. *Legislative Leviathan: Party Government in
the House.* Berkeley: University of California Press.

Cox, Gary W., and William Terry. 2008. "Legislative Productivity in the 93rd–105th Congresses." *Legislative Studies Quarterly* 33:603–18.

CQ Press. 2008. "Biographies of the Presidents: Introduction." In *CQ Press Electronic Library,
Guide to the Presidency Online Edition.* Originally published in *Guide to the Presidency,*
4th ed., edited by Michael Nelson, vol. 2. Washington, DC: CQ Press. http://library
.cqpress.com/presidencyguide/g2p4e2–906-36753-1850497 (July 3, 2010).

Craw, Michael. 2006. "Overcoming City Limits: Vertical and Horizontal Models of Local
Redistributive Policy Making." *Social Science Quarterly* 87:361–79.

———. 2010. "Deciding to Provide: Local Decisions on Providing Social Welfare." *American Journal of Political Science* 54:906–20.

Crowder-Meyer, Melody Ara. 2010. "Local Parties, Local Candidates, and Women's Representation: How County Parties Affect Who Runs for and Wins Political Office." Dissertation. Princeton University, Princeton, NJ.

Dahl, Robert A. [1961] 2005. *Who Governs? Democracy and Power in an American City.* 2nd
ed. New Haven, CT: Yale University Press.

Delli Carpini, Michael X., and Scott Keeter. 1996. *What Americans Know about Politics and
Why It Matters.* New Haven, CT: Yale University Press.

Deloitte, LLP. 2011. "The Next Decade in Global Wealth among Millionaire Households."
http://www.deloitte.com/us/globalwealth (October 17, 2011).

Desposato, Scott W., Matthew C. Kearney, and Brian F. Crisp. 2011. "Using Cosponsorship to Estimate Ideal Points." *Legislatives Studies Quarterly* 36:531–65.

Domhoff, G. William. 1967. *Who Rules America?* Englewood Cliffs, NJ: Prentice-Hall, Inc.

Downs, Anthony. 1957. *An Economic Theory of Democracy.* New York: Harper and Row.

Dye, Thomas R. 1969. *Politics in States and Communities.* Englewood Cliffs, NJ: Prentice-Hall.

Erikson, Robert S. 1978. "Constituency Opinion and Congressional Behavior: A Reexamination of the Miller-Stokes Representation Data." *American Journal of Political Science*
22:511–35.

Erikson, Robert S., Gerald C. Wright, and John P. McIver. 1994. *Statehouse Democracy: Public Opinion and Policy in the American States.* New York: Cambridge University Press.

Eulau, Heinz, and Paul D. Karps. 1977. "The Puzzle of Representation: Specifying Com-
ponents of Responsiveness." *Legislative Studies Quarterly* 2:233–54.

Eulau, Heinz, and John D. Sprague. 1964. *Lawyers in Politics: A Study in Professional Conver-
gence.* Indianapolis, IN: Bobbs-Merrill.

Fenno, Richard F., Jr. 1973. *Congressmen in Committees.* New York: Little, Brown, and Co.

Frank, Mark W. 2009. "Inequality and Growth in the United States: Evidence from a New
State-Level Panel of Income Inequality Measures." *Economic Inquiry* 47:55–68.

Frank, Thomass. 2004. *What's the Matter with Kansas: How Conservatives Won the Heart of America.* New York: Henry Holt and Company.

Frantzich, Stephen. 1979. "Who Makes Our Laws? The Legislative Effectiveness of Members of the U.S. Congress." *Legislative Studies Quarterly* 4:409–28.

Fry, Brian R., and Richard F. Winters. 1970. "The Politics of Redistribution." *American Political Science Review* 64:508–22.

Gelman, Andrew, and Gary King. 1990. "Estimating Incumbency Advantage without Bias." *American Journal of Political Science* 34:1142–64.

Gelpi, Christopher, and Peter D. Feaver. 2002. "Speak Softly and Carry a Big Stick? Veterans in the Political Elite and the American Use of Force." *American Political Science Review* 96:779–93.

Gerber, Elisabeth R., and Daniel J. Hopkins. 2011. "When Mayors Matter." *American Journal of Political Science* 55:326–39.

Gilens, Martin. 2005. "Inequality and Democratic Responsiveness." *Public Opinion Quarterly* 69:778–96.

———. 2009. "Preference Gaps and Inequality in Representation." *PS: Political Science and Politics* 42:335–41.

———. 2012. *Affluence and Influence: Economic Inequality and Political Power in America.* New York: Russell Sage Foundation; and Princeton, NJ: Princeton University Press.

Graham, John, ed. 1990. *"Yours for the Revolution": The Appeal to Reason, 1895–1922.* Lincoln: University of Nebraska Press.

Griffin, John D., and Brian Newman. 2008. *Minority Report: Evaluating Political Equality in America.* Chicago: University of Chicago Press.

Gross, Bertram M. 1953. *The Legislative Struggle: A Study in Social Combat.* New York: McGraw-Hill.

Gross, Donald A. 1978. "Representative Styles and Legislative Behavior." *Western Political Quarterly* 31:359–71.

Grusky, David B., and Jesper B. Sørensen. 1998. "Can Class Analysis Be Salvaged?" *American Journal of Sociology* 103:1187–234.

Hacker, Jacob S., and Paul Pierson. 2010. *Winner-Take-All Politics: How Washington Made the Rich Richer—and Turned Its Back on the Middle Class.* New York: Simon & Schuster.

———. 2011. "The Case for Policy-Focused Political Analysis." Working paper.

Hall, Richard L. 1992. "Measuring Legislative Influence." *Legislative Studies Quarterly* 17:205–31.

———. 1996. *Participation in Congress.* New Haven, CT: Yale University Press.

Hall, Richard L., and Alan V. Deardorff. 2006. "Lobbying as Legislative Subsidy." *American Political Science Review* 100:69–84.

Hall, Richard L., and Frank W. Wayman. 1990. "Buying Time: Moneyed Interests and the Mobilization of Bias in Congressional Committees." *American Political Science Review* 84:797–820.

Hamilton, Alexander. 1788. "Federalist 35." In *The Federalist.* Available online from http://thomas.loc.gov/home/histdox/fedpapers.html (June 27, 2011).

Hamilton, Richard F. 1972. *Class and Politics in the United States.* New York: John Wiley and Sons, Inc.

Hanmer, Michael J., and Keren Ozan Kalkan. 2012. "Behind the Curve: Clarifying the Best Approach to Calculating Predicted Probabilities and Marginal Effects from Limited Dependent Variable Models." *American Journal of Political Science* 57:263–77.

Hansen, John Mark. 1991. *Gaining Access: Congress and the Farm Lobby, 1919–1981.* Chicago: University of Chicago Press.

Hajnal, Zoltan L. 2007. *Changing White Attitudes toward Black Political Leadership.* New York: Cambridge University Press.

Hawkesworth, Mary. 2003. "Congressional Enactments of Race-Gender: Toward a Theory of Raced-Gendered Institutions." *American Political Science Review* 97:529–50.

Henry, William A., III. 1995. *In Defense of Elitism.* New York: Doubleday.

Hibbing, John. 1991. *Congressional Careers: Contours of Life in the U.S. House of Representatives.* Chapel Hill: University of North Carolina Press.

Hicks, Alexander, and Duane H. Swank. 1983. "Civil Disorder, Relief Mobilization, and AFDC Caseloads: A Reexamination of the Piven and Cloward Thesis." *American Journal of Political Science* 27:695–716.

Hirsch, Eric. 1996. *State Legislators' Occupations, 1993 and 1995.* Washington, DC: National Conference on State Legislatures.

Holt, Douglas B. 1998. "Does Cultural Capital Structure American Consumption?" *Journal of Consumer Research* 25:1–25.

Holt, Rush. 2010. "Holt Continues to Question Science, Effectiveness of TSA Full Body Scanners." http://holt.house.gov/index.php?Itemid=18&id=651&option=com_content&task=view (October 25, 2010).

Hout, Michael. 2008. "How Class Works: Objective and Subjective Aspects of Class since the 1970s." In *Social Class: How Does it Work?*, ed. Annette Lareau and Dalton Conley. New York: Russell Sage Foundation.

Hout, Michael, Jeff Manza, and Clem Brooks. 1995. "The Democratic Class Struggle in the United States, 1948–1992." *American Sociological Review* 60:805–28.

Howell, Susan E. 2007. *Race, Performance, and Approval of Mayors.* New York: Palgrave Macmillan.

International City/County Management Association (ICMA). 1991. *Municipal Form of Government Survey* [computer file]. Washington, DC: International City/County Management Association [producer and distributor].

———. 1997. *Municipal Form of Government Survey* [computer file]. Washington, DC: International City/County Management Association [producer and distributor].

———. 2001. *Municipal Form of Government Survey* [computer file]. Washington, DC: International City/County Management Association [producer and distributor].

Inter-university Consortium for Political and Social Research (ICPSR) and Carroll McKibbin. 1997. *Roster of United States Congressional Officeholders and Biographical Characteristics of Members of the United States Congress, 1789–1996: Merged Data* [computer file] (Study #7803). 10th ICPSR ed. Ann Arbor, MI: Inter-university Consortium for Political and Social Research [producer and distributor].

Jacobs, Lawrence R., and James N. Druckman. 2011. "Segmented Representation: The Reagan White House and Disproportionate Responsiveness." In *Who Gets Represented?*, ed. Peter Enns and Christopher Wlezien. New York: Russell Sage Foundation.

Jacobs, Lawrence R., and Robert Y. Shapiro. 2000. *Politicians Don't Pander: Political Manipulation and the Loss of Democratic Responsiveness.* Chicago: University of Chicago Press.

Jacobs, Lawrence R., and Theda Skocpol. 2005. "American Democracy in an Era of Rising Inequality." In *Inequality and American Democracy: What We Know and What We Need to Learn*, ed. Lawrence R. Jacobs and Theda Skocpol. New York: Russell Sage Foundation.

Jennings, E. T., Jr. 1980. "Urban Riots and the Growth of State Welfare Expenditures." *Policy Studies Journal* 9:33–40.

Jewell, Malcolm E. 1982. *Representation in State Legislatures.* Lexington: University Press of Kentucky.

Judd, Dennis R. 2005. "Everything Is Always Going to Hell: Urban Scholars as End-Times Prophets." *Urban Affairs Review* 41:119–31.

Kam, Dara, and Jane Smith. 2008. "Legislators' Worth." *Palm Beach News Post Online.* http://www.palmbeachpost.com/news/databases/searchable-database-of-state -legislators-net-worth-2008–11933.html (July 13, 2010).

Katz, Michael B. 1972. "Occupational Classification in History." *Journal of Interdisciplinary History* 3:63–88.

Kaufmann, Karen M. 2002. "Culture Wars, Secular Realignment, and the Gender Gap in Party Identification." *Political Behavior* 24:283–307.

———. 2004. *The Urban Voter.* Ann Arbor: University of Michigan Press.

Keely, Louise C., and Chih Ming Tan. 2008. "Understanding Preferences for Income Redistribution." *Journal of Public Economics* 92:944–61.

Keller, Edmond J. 1978. "The Impact of Black Mayors on Urban Policy." *Annals of the American Academy of Political and Social Science* 439:40–52.

Kelly, Nathan J., and Christopher Witko. 2012. "Federalism and American Inequality." *Journal of Politics* 74:414–26.

Keysers, Christian. 2011. *The Empathic Brain: How the Discovery of Mirror Neurons Changes Our Understanding of Human Nature.* CreateSpace.

Kingdon, John W. 1981. *Congressmen's Voting Decisions.* 2nd ed. New York: Harper and Row.

———. [1984] 2011. *Agendas, Alternatives, and Public Policies.* Boston: Little and Brown.

Koger, Gregory. 2003. "Position Taking and Cosponsorship in the U.S. House." *Legislative Studies Quarterly* 28:225–46.

Kondracke, Morton. 1977. "Can a Congressman Wear a Blue Collar?" *Chicago Tribune,* June 4.

Kousser, Thad. 2002. "The Politics of Discretionary Medicaid Spending, 1980–1993." *Journal of Health Politics, Policy and Law* 27:639–71.

Krehbiel, Keith. 1991. *Information and Legislative Organization.* Ann Arbor: University of Michigan Press.

———. 1998. *Pivotal Politics: A Theory of U.S. Lawmaking.* Chicago: University of Chicago Press.

Krugman, Paul. 2010. "The Feckless Fed." *New York Times,* July 11. http://www.nytimes .com/2010/07/12/opinion/12krugman.html (June 27, 2011).

———. 2011. "The Forgotten Millions." *New York Times,* March 18. http://www.nytimes .com/2011/03/18/opinion/18krugman.html?emc=eta1 (March 18, 2011).

Krutz, Glenn. 2005. "Issues and Institutions: Winnowing in the U.S. Congress." *American Journal of Political Science* 49:313–26.

Lamont, Michèle. 1992. *Money, Morals, and Manners.* Chicago: University of Chicago Press.

Langton, Kenneth P. 1969. *Political Socialization.* New York: Oxford University Press.

Lareau, Annette. 2008. "Introduction: Taking Stock of Class." *In Social Class: How Does It Work?*, ed. Annette Lareau and Dalton Conley. New York: Russell Sage Foundation.

Lasswell, Harold D. [1930] 1986. *Psychopathology and Politics.* Chicago: University Of Chicago Press.

Lawless, Jennifer L., and Richard L. Fox. 2005. *It Takes a Candidate: Why Women Don't Run for Office.* New York: Cambridge University Press.

Lee, David S., Enrico Moretti, and Matthew J. Butler. 2004. "Do Voters Affect or Elect Policies? Evidence from the U.S. House." *Quarterly Journal of Economics* 119:807–59.

Lewis, John D., ed. 1961. *Anti-Federalists versus Federalists: Selected Documents.* Scranton, PA: Chandler Publishing Company.

Little, Thomas H., Dana Dunn, and Rebecca E. Deen. 2001. "A View from the Top: Gender Differences in Legislative Priorities among State Legislative Leaders." *Women and Politics* 22:29–50.

Lott, Bernice. 2002. "Cognitive and Behavioral Distancing from the Poor." *American Psychologist* 57:100–110.

Lublin, David. 1997. "Congressional District Demographic and Political Data." Washington, DC: American University.

Lupu, Noam. 2011. "Party Brands in Crisis: Partisanship, Brand Dilution, and the Breakdown of Political Parties in Latin America." Dissertation. Princeton University, Princeton, NJ.

Manin, Bernard. 1997. *The Principles of Representative Government.* New York: Cambridge University Press.

Manza, Jeff, and Clem Brooks. 2008. "Class and Politics." In *Social Class: How Does It Work?*, ed. Annette Lareau and Dalton Conley. New York: Russell Sage Foundation.

Manza, Jeff, Michael Hout, and Clem Brooks. 1995. "Class Voting in Democratic Capitalist Societies since World War II: Dealignment, Realignment, or Trendless Fluctuation?" *Annual Review of Sociology* 21:137–63.

Mariani, Mack D., and Gordon J. Hewitt. 2008. "Indoctrination U.? Faculty Ideology and Changes in Student Political Orientation." *PS: Political Science and Politics* 41: 773–83.

Marx, Karl, and Friedrich Engels. [1848] 1972. "The Communist Manifesto." In *The Marx-Engels Reader*, 2nd ed., ed. Robert C. Tucker. New York: W. W. Norton and Company.

Massey, Douglas S. 2007. *Categorically Unequal: The American Stratification System.* New York: Russell Sage Foundation.

Matthews, Donald R. 1954a. *The Social Background of Political Decision-Makers.* New York: Random House.

———. 1954b. "United States Senators and the Class Structure." *Public Opinion Quarterly* 18:5–22.

———. 1960. *U.S. Senators and Their World.* New York: W. W. Norton and Company.

———. 1985. "Legislative Recruitment and Legislative Careers." In *Handbook of Legislative Research*, ed. Gerhard Loewenberg, Samuel C. Patterson, and Malcolm E. Jewell. Cambridge, MA: Harvard University Press.

Mayhew, David R. 1974a. *Congress: The Electoral Connection.* New Haven, CT: Yale University Press.

———. 1974b. "Congressional Elections: The Case of the Vanishing Marginals." *Polity* 6:295–317.

———. 2000. *America's Congress: Actions in the Public Sphere.* New Haven, CT: Yale University Press.

———. 2005. *Divided We Govern: Party Control, Lawmaking, and Investigations, 1946–2002.* 2nd ed. New Haven, CT: Yale University Press.

———. 2008. "Congress as Problem Solver." In *Promoting the General Welfare: New Perspectives on Government Performance*, ed. Alan S. Gerber and Eric M. Patashnik. Washington, DC: Brookings Institution Press.

McCarty, Nolan, Keith T. Poole, and Howard Rosenthal. 2006. *Polarized America: The Dance of Ideology and Unequal Riches.* Cambridge, MA: MIT Press.

McIntyre, Douglas A., Michael B. Sauter, and Ashley C. Allen. 2010. "The Net Worth of the U.S. Presidents." *Atlantic Online*, May 20. http://www.theatlantic.com/business

/archive/2010/05/net-worth-of-the-us-presidents-from-washington-to-obama/57020/ (January 11, 2011).

McPherson, Miller, Lynn Smith-Lovin, and James M. Cook. 2001. "Birds of a Feather: Homophily in Social Networks." *Annual Review of Sociology* 27:415–44.

Melzer, Allan, and Scott Richard. 1981. "A Rational Theory of the Size of Government." *Journal of Political Economy* 89:914–27.

Mettler, Suzanne. 2011. *The Submerged State: How Invisible Government Policies Undermine American Democracy.* Chicago: University of Chicago Press.

Mezey, Susan Gluck. 1978. "Women and Representation: The Case of Hawaii." *Journal of Politics* 40:369–85.

Miler, Kristina C. 2010. *Constituency Representation in Congress: The View from Capitol Hill.* New York: Cambridge University Press.

Mill, John Stuart. [1861] 2001. *Representative Government.* Kitchener, Ontario: Batoche Books.

Miller, Mark C. 1995. *The High Priests of American Politics: The Role of Lawyers in American Political Institutions.* Knoxville: University of Tennessee Press.

Miller, Warren E., Donald R. Kinder, Steven J. Rosenstone, and the National Election Studies. 1999. *National Election Studies, 1988, 1990, 1992: Pooled Senate Election Study* [data set]. Ann Arbor, MI: University of Michigan, Center for Political Studies [producer and distributor].

Miller, Warren E., and Donald E. Stokes. [1958] 1984. *American Representation Study, 1958: Candidate and Constituent, Incumbency* [computer file]. Conducted by University of Michigan, Survey Research Center. ICPSR ed. Ann Arbor, MI: Inter-university Consortium for Political and Social Research [producer and distributor].

———. 1963. "Constituency Influence in Congress." *American Political Science Review* 57:45–56.

———. 1969. *Representation in the American Congress.* Unpublished manuscript.

Mills, C. Wright. 1956. *The Power Elite.* New York: Oxford University Press.

Minkoff, Scott L. 2009. "Minding Your Neighborhood: The Spatial Context of Local Redistribution." *Social Science Quarterly* 90:516–37.

Mogull, Robert G. 1978. "State and Local Antipoverty Expenditures." *Public Finance Quarterly* 6:287–303.

———. 1993. "Determinants of States' Welfare Expenditures." *Journal of Socio-Economics* 22:259–76.

Moore, Michael K., and Sue Thomas. 1991. "Explaining Legislative Success in the U.S. Senate: The Role of the Majority and Minority Parties." *Western Political Quarterly* 44: 959–70.

Naples, Nancy A. 1997. "The 'New Consensus' on the Gendered 'Social Contract': The 1987–1988 U.S. Congressional Hearings on Welfare Reform." *Signs* 22:907–45.

National Conference of State Legislatures. 2011. http://www.ncsl.org (January 5, 2011).

National Journal. 2010. "Rep. Michael Michaud." http://www.nationaljournal.com/almanac /person/michael-michaud-me/ (January 25, 2011).

New York Times. 2010. "Supreme Court Runs Financial Gamut." *New York Times,* June 12. Available online from http://www.nytimes.com/2010/06/12/us/12scotus.html (July 3, 2010).

Newcomb, Theodore M. 1958. "Attitude Development as a Function of Reference Groups: The Bennington Study." In *Readings in Social Psychology,* 3rd edition, ed. Theodore M. Newcomb, Eleanor E. Maccoby, and Eugene Hartley. New York: Holt.

Norpoth, Helmut. 1976. "Explaining Party Cohesion in Congress: The Case of Shared Party Attitudes." *American Political Science Review* 70:1156–71.

Norris, Pippa, and Joni Lovenduski. 1995. *Political Recruitment: Gender, Race, and Class in the British Parliament.* New York: Cambridge University Press.

Oliver, J. Eric, and Shang E. Ha. 2007. "Vote Choice in Suburban Elections." *American Political Science Review* 101:393–408.

Orr, Larry L. 1976. "Income Transfers as a Public Good: An Application to AFDC." *American Economic Review* 66:359–71.

Pessen, Edward. 1984. *The Log Cabin Myth: The Social Backgrounds of the Presidents.* New Haven, CT: Yale University Press.

Peterson, Paul. 1981. *City Limits.* Chicago: University of Chicago Press.

Philpott, Ben. 2011. "Republican Hispanics Gain Seats in State House." *Texas Public Radio Online* http://www.tpr.org/news/2010/11/news1011052.html (October 24, 2011).

Piketty, Thomas. 1995. "Social Mobility and Redistributive Politics." *Quarterly Journal of Economics* 110:551–84.

Pitkin, Hannah Fenichel. 1967. *The Concept of Representation.* Berkeley: University of California Press.

Plotnick, Robert D., and Richard F. Winters. 1985. "A Politico-Economic Theory of Income Redistribution." *American Political Science Review* 79:458–73.

Poole, Keith T. 2007. "Changing Minds? Not in Congress!" *Public Choice* 131:435–51.

Poole, Keith T., and Howard Rosenthal. 1997. *Congress: A Political Economic History of Roll Call Voting.* New York: Oxford University Press.

Price, David. 1972. *Who Makes the Laws? Creativity and Power in Senate Committees.* Cambridge, MA: Schenkman Publishing Company

Putnam, Robert D. 1976. *The Comparative Study of Political Elites.* Englewood Cliffs, NJ: Prentice Hall.

Reeher, Grant. 1996. *Narratives of Justice: Legislators' Beliefs about Distributive Fairness.* Ann Arbor: University of Michigan Press.

Rehm, Philipp. 2010. "Risk Inequality and the Polarized American Electorate." *British Journal of Political Science* 41:363–87.

Reston, Maeve. 2012. "Protesters Raise Cloud of Sand as Romney Raises $3 Million in N.Y." *Los Angeles Times,* June 8. Available online from http://www.latimes.com/news/nationworld/nation/la-na-romney-protests-20120709,0,5308609.story (August 8, 2012).

Rohde, David W. 1991. *Parties and Leaders in the Postreform House.* Chicago: University of Chicago Press.

Ruggles, Steven, Matthew Sobek, Trent Alexander, Catherine A. Fitch, Ronald Goeken, Patricia Kelly Hall, Miriam King, and Chad Ronnander. 2009. *Integrated Public Use Microdata Series: Version 4.0* [machine-readable database]. Minneapolis: Minnesota Population Center [producer and distributor].

Ryan, Jake, and Charles Sackrey. 1984. *Strangers in Paradise: Academics from the Working Class.* Cambridge, MA: South End Press.

Sadin, Meredith. 2011. "Campaigning with Class: The Effect of Candidate Social Class on Voter Evaluations." Unpublished manuscript.

Sanbonmatsu, Kira. 2006. *Where Women Run: Gender and Party in the American States.* Ann Arbor: University of Michigan Press.

Sapotichne, Joshua, Bryan D. Jones, and Michelle Wolfe. 2007. "Is Urban Politics a Black Hole?" *Urban Affairs Review* 43:76–106.

Schattschneider, E. E. [1960] 1975. *The Semisovereign People: A Realist's View of Democracy in America.* Wadsworth Publishing.

Scheve, Kenneth F., and Matthew J. Slaughter. 2001. "What Determines Individual Trade-Policy Preferences?" *Journal of International Economics* 54:267–92.

Schiller, Wendy J. 1995. "Senators as Political Entrepreneurs: Using Bill Sponsorship to Shape Legislative Agendas." *American Journal of Political Science* 39:186–203.

Schlozman, Kay Lehman, Benjamin I. Page, Sidney Verba, and Morris P. Fiorina. 2005. "Inequalities of Political Voice." In *Inequality and American Democracy: What We Know and What We Need to Learn*, ed. Lawrence R. Jacobs and Theda Skocpol. New York: Russell Sage Foundation.

Sennett, Richard, and Jonathan Cobb. 1972. *The Hidden Injuries of Class*. New York: Vintage Books.

Sharp, Elaine B. 1991. "Institutional Manifestations of Accessibility and Urban Economic Development Policy." *Western Political Quarterly* 44:129–47.

Sharp, Elaine B., and Steven Maynard-Moody. 1991. "Theories of the Local Welfare Role." *American Journal of Political Science* 35:934–50.

Shor, Boris, and Nolan McCarty. 2011. "The Ideological Mapping of American Legislatures." *American Political Science Review* 104:530–51.

Siddon, Arthur. 1977. "11 Members of House Spawn a New Caucus—Blue Collar." *Chicago Tribune*, April 6.

Smith, Adam. [1776] 1953. "Class Interest and Public Interest." In *Class, Status, and Power: A Reader in Social Stratification*, ed. Reinhard Bendix and Seymour Martin Lipset. Glencoe, IL: Free Press.

Squire, Peverill. 1992. "Legislative Professionalization and Membership Diversity in State Legislatures." *Legislative Studies Quarterly* 17:69–79.

Stein, Robert, Stacy Ulbig, and Stephanie Shirley Post. 2005. "Voting for Minority Candidates in Multiracial/Multiethnic Communities." *Urban Affairs Review* 41:157–81.

Stevens, Arthur G., Jr., Arthur H. Miller, and Thomas E. Mann. 1974. "Mobilization of Liberal Strength in the House, 1955–1970: The Democratic Study Group." *American Political Science Review* 68:667–81.

Stokes, Donald E. 1970. "Compound Paths in Political Analysis." In *Mathematical Applications in Political Science*, ed. James F. Herndon and Joseph L. Bernd. Charlottesville: University Press of Virginia.

Stuart, Peter C. 1977. "Blue-Collar Congressmen—a Few More Settle In." *Christian Science Monitor*, March 9.

Swers, Michele. 2002. *The Difference Women Make*. Chicago: University of Chicago Press.

Swift, Elaine K., Robert G. Brookshire, David T. Canon, Evelyn C. Fink, John R. Hibbing, Brian D. Humes, Michael J. Malbin, and Kenneth C. Martis. 2009. *Database of [United States] Congressional Historical Statistics, 1789–1989* [computer file]. (Study #3371) 2nd ICPSR ed. Ann Arbor, MI: Inter-university Consortium for Political and Social Research [distributor].

Takeda, Okiyoshi. 2000. "Bill Passage in the United States House of Representatives." Dissertation. Princeton University, Princeton, NJ.

Thomas, Sue. 1991. "The Impact of Women on State Legislative Policies." *Journal of Politics* 53:958–76.

Thomas, Sue, and Susan Welch. 1991. "The Impact of Gender on Activities and Priorities of State Legislators." *Western Political Quarterly* 44:445–56.

Tiebout, Charles M. 1956. "A Pure Theory of Local Expenditures." *Journal of Political Economy* 64:416–24.

Tolchin, Martin. 1977. "Pipefitters, Painters Join Forces in Blue Collar Caucus." *Lakeland*

Ledger, June 18. http://news.google.com/newspapers?id=buMdAAAAIBAJ&sjid= 2_oD AAAAIBAJ&pg=7052%2C4876974 (June 3, 2010).

Trounstine, Jessica. 2008. *Political Monopolies in American Cities.* Chicago: University of Chicago Press.

———. 2009. "All Politics Is Local: The Reemergence of the Study of City Politics." *Perspectives on Politics* 7:611–18.

———. 2010. "Representation and Accountability in Cities." *Annual Review of Political Science* 13:407–23.

Trounstine, Jessica, and Melody E. Valdini. 2008. "The Context Matters: The Effects of Single-Member versus At-Large Districts on City Council Diversity." *American Journal of Political Science* 52:554–69.

Turley, Jonathan. 2010. "Evidence of a Supreme Court Bias." *Los Angeles Times,* May 12. http://articles.latimes.com/2010/may/12/opinion/la-oe-turley-supreme-court-2010 0512 (May 19, 2010).

US Department of Education, National Center for Education Statistics. 1998. Integrated Postsecondary Education Data System (IPEDS): Higher Education Finance Data, 1995–1996 [computer file]. ICPSR version. Washington, DC: US Department of Education, National Center for Education Statistics [producer]; Ann Arbor, MI: Interuniversity Consortium for Political and Social Research [distributor], 1999.

US Department of Health and Human Services. 2004. "Spending on Social Welfare Programs in Rich and Poor States." http://aspe.hhs.gov/hsp/social-welfare-spending04 (August 16, 2010).

Verba, Sidney. 2003. "Would the Dream of Political Equality Turn Out to Be a Nightmare?" *Perspectives on Politics* 1:663–77.

Verba, Sidney, Kay Lehman Schlozman, and Henry E. Brady. 1995. *Voice and Equality: Civic Voluntarism in American Politics.* Cambridge, MA: Harvard University Press.

Volden, Craig, and Alan E. Wiseman. 2008. "Measuring Legislative Effectiveness in Congress." Unpublished manuscript. Available online from http://harrisschool.uchicago .edu/Programs/beyond/workshops/pol_econ_papers/fa1108-wiseman.pdf (March 10, 2011).

Wawro, Gregory J. 2000. *Legislative Entrepreneurship in the U.S. House of Representatives.* Ann Arbor: University of Michigan Press.

Weeden, Kim A., and David B. Grusky. 2005. "The Case for a New Class Map." *American Journal of Sociology* 111:141–212.

Weingast, Barry R., and William J. Marshall. 1988. "The Industrial Organization of Congress; or, Why Legislatures, Like Firms, Are Not Organized as Markets." *Journal of Political Economy* 96:132–63.

Weissberg, Robert. 1978. "Collective vs. Dyadic Representation in Congress." *American Political Science Review* 72:535–47.

Western, Bruce, and Becky Pettit. 2010. "Incarceration and Social Inequality." *Dædalus:* 8–19.

Western, Bruce, and Jake Rosenfeld. 2011. "Unions, Norms, and the Rise in US Wage Inequality." *American Sociological Review* 76:513–37.

Whitby, Kenny J. 1997. *The Color of Representation: Congressional Behavior and Black Interests.* Ann Arbor: University of Michigan Press.

———. 2002. "Bill Sponsorship and Intraracial Voting among African American Representatives." *American Politics Research* 30:93–109.

Winters, Jeffrey A. 2011. *Oligarchy.* New York: Cambridge University Press.

Witko, Christopher, and Sally Friedman. 2008. "Business Backgrounds and Congressional Behavior." *Congress & the Presidency* 35:71–86.

Woon, Jonathan. 2008. "Bill Sponsorship in Congress: The Moderating Effect of Agenda Positions on Legislative Proposals." *Journal of Politics* 70:201–16.

Wright, Erik Olin. 1997. "Rethinking, Once Again, the Concept of Class Structure." In *Reworking Class*, ed. John Hall. Ithaca, NY: Cornell University Press.

———. 2008. "Logics of Class Analysis." In *Social Class: How Does It Work?*, ed. Annette Lareau and Dalton Conley. New York: Russell Sage Foundation.

Wright, John R. 1995. *Interest Groups and Congress: Lobbying, Contributions, and Influence.* New York: Longman.

Wrong, Dennis H. 1968. "Power in America." In *C. Wright Mills and* The Power Elite, ed. G. William Domhoff and Hoyt B. Ballard. Boston: Beacon Press.

Yglesias, Matthew. 2011. "90% of Life Is Just Showing Up, and the 99% Don't." *Slate. com*, December 18. Available online from http://www.slate.com/blogs/moneybox /2011/12/18/rich_people_are_politically_active.html?fb_ref=sm_fb_like_blogpost&fb _source=home_multiline (August 16, 2012).

Zeller, Belle, ed. 1954. *American State Legislatures.* New York: Thomas Y. Crowell Company.

INDEX

Achen, Christopher H., 48, 92
Adler, Scott E., 60, 70, 80
affordable housing, 65, 70, 95, 162n11,
    164n22
AFL-CIO: candidate schools, 109–10,
    149; legislative voting scores, 1, 31, 32,
    33–34, 37–38, 42–43, 45–46, 53, 55,
    56, 96. *See also* unions
agenda setting, 60, 63, 64, 73, 77, 82–84.
    See also legislative entrepreneurship
agriculture policy, 34, 67, 70, 73–74
Alaska, 122
Aldrich, John, 13
Aliseda, Jose, 28
American Civil Liberties Union (ACLU),
    39–41
American National Election Study (ANES),
    14–15, 65–66, 144–45, 155nn12–13,
    168n5
American Political Science Association
    (APSA) Task Force on Inequality and
    American Democracy, 9
American Representation Study, 87, 92–104,
    143, 161nn7–8, 162n9, 163nn14–16,
    163nn18–19. *See also* Miller, Warren E.;
    Stokes, Donald E.
Anti-Federalists. *See* Federalists
Arnold, R. Douglas, 11, 13, 27, 127
assistance to low-income Americans. *See*
    welfare

banking, 70, 73, 74. *See also* Wall Street
    bailout

bankruptcy reform, 117, 118, 140
Baron, Reuben M., 163n18
Bartels, Larry M., 41, 117, 146, 147
Beard, Edward, 1–2, 49
Biden, Joe, 143
bill proposals. *See* legislative entrepreneur-
    ship: measurement of
Blue Collar Caucus, 1, 2. *See also* Beard,
    Edward
blue-collar workers. *See* working class
Boehner, John, 29, 39, 49, 85, 99
Brady, Henry E., 4, 18
Brady, Robert, 32, 65
Brooks, Clem, 4, 14, 17, 29, 41, 156n14,
    156nn16–17
Burden, Barry C., 13, 63, 90, 159n3, 161n3
Bureau of Labor Statistics, 168n7
Burns, James MacGregor, 137, 138
Bush tax cuts, 23, 114–17, 119
Business International Corporation, 168n3
business regulations, 113, 114; how the
    shortage of workers in office affects, 16,
    110, 139; opposition to, 64–65, 67. *See
    also* Chamber of Commerce, legislative
    voting scores; corporate accountability
    legislation; corporate taxes; workplace
    safety
Butler, Daniel M., 161n1

California: ninth congressional district, 38;
    Representative Johnson of, 71; sister
    legislators from, 54; welfare spending
    in, 128